Whose Criminal Justice?

State or Community?

Editors

Katherine Doolin
John Child
John Raine
Anthony Beech

Whose Criminal Justice?
State or Community?

Editors Katherine Doolin, John Child, John Raine, Anthony Beech

Published 2011 by
Waterside Press Ltd.
Sherfield Gables
Sherfield on Loddon
Hook
Hampshire
United Kingdom RG27 0JG

Telephone +44(0)1256 882250
Low cost UK landline calls
0845 2300 733
E-mail
enquiries@watersidepress.co.uk
Online catalogue
WatersidePress.co.uk

ISBN 9781904380627 (Paperback)
ISBN 9781906534905 (E-book)

UK distributor Gardners Books, 1 Whittle Drive, Eastbourne, East Sussex, BN23 6QH. Tel: +44 (0)1323 521777; sales@gardners.com; www.gardners.com

North American distributor International Specialised Book Services (ISBS), 920 NE 58th Ave, Suite 300, Portland, Oregon, 97213-3786, USA. Tel: 1 800 944 6190 Fax 1 503 280 8832; orders@isbs.com; www.isbs.com

Copyright © 2010 This work is the copyright of Katherine Doolin, John Child, John Raine and Anthony Beech. All intellectual property and associated rights are hereby asserted and reserved by the authors in full compliance with UK, European and international law. No part of this book may be copied, reproduced, stored in any retrieval system or transmitted in any form or by any means, including in hard copy or via the internet, without the prior written permission of the publishers to whom all such rights have been assigned worldwide.

Cover design © 2010 Waterside Press. Design by www.gibgob.com

Cataloguing-In-Publication Data A catalogue record for this book can be obtained on request from the British Library.

e-book *Whose Criminal Justice?* is available as an ebook (ISBN 9781906534905) and also to subscribers of Myilibrary and Dawsonera.

Printed by MPG Books Group, Bodmin and King's Lynn.

Whose Criminal Justice?

State or Community?

Editors

Katherine Doolin
John Child
John Raine
Anthony Beech

WATERSIDE PRESS

> This work represents a timely discussion of one of the key issues facing criminal justice over the next decade: namely how to reconcile the new drive for localism with the need to ensure fairness and efficiency in an increasingly complex criminal justice system.
>
> **Professor Stephen Shute, Head of Sussex University Law School**

> *Whose Criminal Justice?* provides a thoughtful and principled perspective on criminal justice at a time when the country seems ready to move on from the rigid attitudes and misguided assumptions that have dominated policy and practice for almost 20 years. The Coalition government is committed to devolving power and influence to local communities and citizens, in criminal justice as in other matters, with elected Police and Crime Commissioners as its headline policy and the 'Big Society' as its overall vision. Much of the detail is still to emerge, and much will depend on the dynamics and relationships of the new formations and new situations as they develop.
>
> This useful and well written body of work identifies the main issues to be addressed – the proper role and limits of the criminal law and the criminal courts; the culture and practice of the criminal justice services; issues relating to religious and ethnic minorities; the special problems of anti-social young people, sexual offenders and domestic violence; and the implications and practicability of empowering communities to take more control of the criminal justice process and the alternatives to it. The authors examine them dispassionately from a variety of perspectives – their own research, the historical background and the empirical and theoretical studies which have been made of the various subjects.
>
> Policy makers and practitioners would do well to reflect on the wisdom that is contained in this volume.
>
> **David Faulkner, University of Oxford Centre for Criminological Research**

Contents

Contributors — xi
Preface — xiii
Acknowledgements — xiv

1. Introduction: The Changing Politics of Law and Order 15
John Raine and Paul Keasey

A Changing Context 15
The Problem of Public Confidence 18
The New Localism 22
Regulatory State or Empowered Communities? 28

PART 1: THE REGULATORY STATE AND THE MANAGEMENT OF RISK . 31

2. Limiting Criminal Justice and Regulation: The 'Freedom' Perspective 33
Andrew Sanders

The Relationship Between Criminal Justice and Regulation 33
Frameworks of Analysis: Models and Aims of Criminal Justice 35
A New Framework: The 'Freedom' Approach 42
Regulating Criminal Justice 45
Conclusion 47

3. Risk, Pre-Emption, and the Limits of the Criminal Law 51
John Child and Adrian Hunt

Introduction 51
Pre-emptive Offences and Other Criminal Offences Distinguished ... 53
A Search for Coherence 58
Conclusion 67

4. Criminalising the Purchase of Sexual Services: The Use of Strict Liability as a Form of Risk Management? 69
Jessica Elliott

Introduction 69

Criminalising the Prostitute User: Tackling the 'Demand' *71*
Why Target the Purchaser? *73*
Is Criminal Sanction Justified? *76*
Conclusion. *83*

5. The ASBO: Regulating Behaviour and Manipulating Law *87*
Theresa Lynch

Introduction. *87*
The ASBO: Background and Context. *89*
The Civil Classification of the ASBO: Subverting the Right to Fair Trial. 94
A Criminal Classification: Re-asserting the Right to a Fair Trial? *104*
Conclusion. *105*

6. Managing Risk and Changing Priorities for Probation Practice and Youth Justice. *107*
Kathryn Farrow, Gill Kelly and Bernadette Wilkinson

Risk and Community Protection *108*
Impact on Practice *110*
Risk Assessment Tools *114*
Risk-led Approaches. *117*
Managerialism and the Growth of Information Technology *118*
Impact on Offenders *120*
Conclusion. *121*

7. (In)Security, Risk, Muslim Communities, Policing and the 'New Terrorism' 123
Shamila Ahmed and Basia Spalek

Introduction. *123*
'New Terrorism' Discourse and the Pathologisation of Muslim Minorities *125*
'New Terrorism' Discourse and Counter-terrorism Legislation *127*
'New Terrorism', Policing and Community Engagement *130*
Muslim Communities' Perceptions of Risk and (in)Securities. *135*
Conclusion. *138*

PART 2: EMPOWERED COMMUNITIES AS LOCAL STAKEHOLDERS IN CRIMINAL JUSTICE... 141

8. Empowering Communities through Restorative Justice... 143
Katherine Doolin
Introduction... 143
An Understanding of Restorative Justice... 146
Strengthening and Empowering Communities through Restorative Justice... 150
The Challenge of Empowering Communities through Restorative Justice... 153
Conclusion... 156

9. Safer Communities and Community Justice... 159
David Prior
Crime, Disorder and Community Justice... 160
Regulating Safer Communities... 163
Safer Communities in Practice... 167
Conclusion... 170

10. Community Justice and the Courts: A Step Forwards, Backwards or Sideways?... 173
John Raine
Introduction... 173
The Roots of Community Justice... 174
Community Justice in Practice: from Red Hook to North Liverpool... 177
Evaluating the Community Justice Centre Concept... 180
Community Justice and Community Engagement... 182
Conclusion: Community Justice Centres as a Step Forwards, Backwards or Sideways?... 184

11. Intolerant or Intolerable?: Anti-social Youth in Asocial Communities... 187
Nathan Hughes
'The Kids of Today': Images of 'Problem Youth'... 188
A Moral Panic over Youth Misbehaviour?... 192
Empowering the Law-abiding (Adult) Majority... 195

Disempowering 'Problem Youth'?...................................*197*
Tackling Anti-social Behaviour Amongst Young People *198*
Conclusion...*201*

12. Policing Sexual Offenders in the Community: Is it Time to Move from the Invisible to the Visible? *203*
Mark Blandford and Anthony Beech
Introduction...*203*
Background to Current Arrangements *206*
Towards More Dynamically-based Assessment and Management of Risk *212*
Encouraging Community Integration................................*214*
Conclusion..*218*

13. Towards a Community Response to the Perpetration of Domestic Violence..*223*
Zahira Latif
Introduction...*223*
What is Domestic Violence?......................................*224*
Domestic Violence Legislation *227*
Institutionalising Responses to Domestic Violence......................*229*
Alternative Models to Tackle Domestic Violence *232*
Conclusion..*240*

14. Conclusions and the Way Forward for Criminal Justice........*243*
Anthony Beech, John Child, Katherine Doolin and John Raine
Learning from Experience..*246*
Where Next for Criminal Justice?..................................*249*

References   255

Index   277

Contributors

All the editors of and contributors to this book are (or recently have been) academics, teachers, researchers or associates of the University of Birmingham. We are from various disciplinary backgrounds (the Schools of Law, Psychology, Government and Society and Social Policy), but share a common academic interest in criminal law, criminal justice and community justice.

Shamila Ahmed is a Doctoral Researcher in the Institute of Applied Social Studies, School of Social Policy, University of Birmingham.

Anthony Beech is Director of the Centre for Forensic and Criminological Psychology and Professor of Criminal Psychology in the School of Psychology, University of Birmingham.

Mark Blandford is a Detective Constable with the Staffordshire Police Public Protection Unit and Associate of the School of Psychology, University of Birmingham.

John Child is a Lecturer in Law at Oxford Brookes University. He was a Doctoral Researcher and Postgraduate Teaching Assistant in the Law School, University of Birmingham.

Katherine Doolin is Director of the Institute of Judicial Administration and Lecturer in the Law School, University of Birmingham.

Jessica Elliott is a Lecturer in Law at the University of the West of England. She was a Doctoral Researcher and Postgraduate Teaching Assistant at the Law School, University of Birmingham.

Kathryn Farrow is a Lecturer in the Institute of Applied Social Studies, School of Social Policy, University of Birmingham.

Nathan Hughes is a Teaching and Research Fellow in the Institute of Applied Social Studies, School of Social Policy, University of Birmingham.

Adrian Hunt is a Lecturer in the Law School, University of Birmingham.

Paul Keasey is a Chief Inspector with West Midlands Police and Doctoral Researcher in the Institute of Local Government Studies, School of Government and Society, University of Birmingham.

Gill Kelly is an Independent Trainer at KWP and Associate of the Institute of Applied Social Studies, School of Social Policy, University of Birmingham.

Zahira Latif is a Doctoral Researcher in the Institute of Applied Social Studies, School of Social Policy, University of Birmingham.

Theresa Lynch is a Doctoral Researcher and Postgraduate Teaching Assistant in the Law School, University of Birmingham.

David Prior is a Senior Research Fellow in the Institute of Applied Social Studies, School of Social Policy, University of Birmingham.

John Raine is Professor of Management in Criminal Justice and Director of the Institute of Local Government Studies, School of Government and Society, University of Birmingham.

Andrew Sanders is Professor of Criminal Law and Criminology in the Law School, University of Birmingham.

Basia Spalek is a Reader in Communities and Justice in the Institute of Applied Social Studies, School of Social Policy, University of Birmingham.

Bernadette Wilkinson is an Independent Trainer at KWP and Associate of the Institute of Applied Social Studies, School of Social Policy, University of Birmingham.

Preface

This volume represents the first publication from the newly founded Birmingham Criminal and Community Justice Group (BCCJ). The BCCJ comprises scholars from across the University of Birmingham, who represent a range of disciplinary and professional backgrounds (law, socio-legal studies, criminology, forensic psychology, social work and public management) and who share a passion for criminal justice in this country and for its positive development into the future.

That, above all, is what has inspired this volume. It explores the increasingly apparent tension between criminal justice, on the one hand as a key component of the central regulatory state and on the other as the framework through which local communities can have a stake in and respond responsibly to the problems of crime (and anti-social behaviour) in their midst.

Written at a time of significant change in the macro-politics of the UK, the volume both looks back and takes stock of the legacy for criminal justice of more than a decade of the New Labour administration and ahead as interest grows in 'new localism' and the new Prime Minister's notion of 'the Big Society'. From its analysis of all that has happened in criminal justice in this country, the key question the volume sets out to answer is: 'What is the appropriate balance to be struck in criminal justice between the roles of the regulatory state and of empowered communities?'

We would like to thank all of the authors for their valuable contributions. We would also like to acknowledge the inspiration of Lady Foley's Tearoom at Great Malvern Railway Station where the idea for this book was born.

A B
J C
K D
J R

Acknowledgements

The editors and authors would like to express our appreciation to Bryan Gibson (Director of Waterside Press) for the confidence he showed in our proposal for this volume; to Amanda Williams for her diligence in compiling the index and reference list; and to the team at Waterside Press who have worked so efficiently to ensure timely publication.

CHAPTER 1

INTRODUCTION: THE CHANGING POLITICS OF LAW AND ORDER

JOHN RAINE AND PAUL KEASEY

A Changing Context

In May 2010, criminal justice in Britain appeared to be at a pivotal moment. This date marked not only the end of 12 years of a New Labour administration, but also the election of a new Conservative-Liberal Democrat Coalition government. Certainly the early signs were of significant policy shifts being in prospect and, although the full nature of such shifts was not immediately clear, the underlying context and reasons for change were readily apparent.

In the first place, after at least a decade of significant expansion in public spending, including on criminal justice and particularly in relation to policing, the new Coalition government embarked on a substantial programme of cuts in public spending. This was mostly in response to the large national deficit that had accrued in the wake of the global recession and banking crisis in the preceding three years, although for the Conservative elements of the Coalition at least, a high priority, in any case, was the pursuit of a smaller state and a lower tax economy. Initial expectations were of cuts of at least 20% for most areas of public spending, including criminal justice, and suddenly the future prospects for criminal justice services seemed uncertain and much of the progress of the past decade at risk. In Summer 2010, for example, a report from the Ministry of Justice to the Treasury (the overseeing department for the expenditure reduction programme), referred to a total of more than £2 billion of cuts out of an existing criminal justice budget of about £9 billion. Speculation followed about the potential effects of staff reductions on court delays and of the possibility of prison closures.[1] The latter, no doubt, was at least partially fuelled by earlier comments from the Justice Secretary, the Right Honourable Kenneth Clarke MP, who had declared his desire to see a reduction in the size of the prison population, which had been at record levels for several years.[2]

But spending cuts aside, two other issues underlay the mood for a policy shift in criminal justice.

First was a problem of low public confidence in criminal justice which persisted despite at least a decade of effort and relentless initiatives to address the law and order agenda. Indeed, there was a mounting sense of frustration and disappointment within government at the relatively limited impact of such efforts on citizens' perceptions about criminal justice and the progress made on crime reduction. While the trend in the overall level of reported crime had continued to fall from its peak in 1995, certain types of offence, notably violent crime, gun, gang and drug-related crime and youth-centred anti-social behaviour, continued to dominate the newspaper headlines. With these offences shaping public opinions of crime, the result was that too few people felt any sense of improvement in the state of criminality or had greater confidence in the competence of the police and other criminal justice agencies to address the level of crime and anti-social behaviour.

Second was the reality that, after a long period of mainly central government-driven reforms, a resurgence of interest for localism had begun to take root across the public policy arena, including within criminal justice. The genesis of this, somewhat paradoxically, lay in what might be understood as a counter-trend to New Labour's more generally centralist approach to public policy and management (for example in the commitments to 'neighbourhood renewal', neighbourhood policing, the 'stronger communities' agenda and the concern to develop citizen engagement and enhance local public accountability). But as the General Election approached, both the Conservatives and Liberal Democrats (the latter more traditionally associated

---

1. 'Public spending cuts put justice at risk' (2010, August 10th), *Independent* newspaper.
2. The Ministry of Justice has estimated the average cost per prisoner as being in the region of £45,000, and throughout most of the first decade of the 21st-century, the prison population had remained close to maximum capacity of 85,000 — one of the highest rates of imprisonment in the western world.

with localist politics) actively promoted a more radically decentralist alternative to the 'big central state' perspective with which they caricatured New Labour. And the formation of a Coalition government certainly provided new momentum for change in this regard.

In part, the underlay for this new localism was the very different perspective on the role of the state captured in Prime Minister David Cameron's vision of a 'Big Society', canvassed in the general election campaign. Within this Big Society, citizens and communities would become less dependent on the state and its public services and feel more empowered to take on responsibility for themselves, in a spirit of self-help and mutual support. But more than this, it could also be seen as a reaction to the shortcomings of a decade of largely centre-driven initiative—as evident in criminal justice as anywhere. For despite the very considerable amount of research commissioned under New Labour to try to identify 'What Works' to reduce offending and re-offending,[3] and a plethora of initiatives involving changes to the law, criminal justice processes, the institutional structures, sentencing and offender management practices, and much more besides, there was an overarching sense of disappointment at the outcomes achieved, most notably in relation to levels of criminality and re-offending rates. Quite simply, the much vaunted, top-down 'crime reduction programme' of New Labour had not lived up to expectations and now there was a growing sense that more bottom-up, locality-focused, approaches might just perhaps hold better prospect.

In this chapter, then, we consider these two issues—'the problem of public confidence' and 'the new localism'—to provide a back-drop and context for the analysis presented in the following chapters. The aim, then, is to examine in turn the main achievements, shortcomings and potential of criminal justice, on the one hand as predominantly driven by the politicians and officials of the central state and, on the other, under more decentralised and localist principles through more empowered communities.

---

3. See for example, 'The Crime Reduction Programme in England and Wales: reflections on the vision and the reality' (2004), Maguire M, *Criminology and Criminal Justice*, 4, 3, 213-237.

The Problem of Public Confidence

According to the official statistics, the crime rate in England and Wales had been falling in most years since its statistical peak in 1995. As well as the official statistics derived from police records of reported crimes, the British Crime Survey (BCS)[4] also indicates that the incidence of crime fell by some 9% in just one year (2008/09-2009/10)[5] and the overall number had reached its lowest level since 1981, at 9.6 million offences. Moreover, contrary to pessimistic warnings within government that this downward trend might be arrested and reversed in recessionary times of rising unemployment, by the end of 2010 at least, no such effect had been experienced.

Besides the continuing overall reduction in the number of crimes, the narrative told by the official police statistics was of violent crime remaining fairly constant, while the numbers of murders and of gun-related offences had fallen quite markedly. The larger categories of vehicle crime, other theft, burglary and criminal damage, had also reduced and, with these declines, the risk of becoming a victim of crime had similarly fallen — from 40% in 1995 to around 25% in 2010.

However, despite much government effort to disseminate a positive message from such statistics, this was not how public opinion tended to view things.[6] Indeed, as indicated, according to successive surveys, a clear majority of respondents believed that crime nationally had been increasing in the previous two years. In 2009, some three-quarters of respondents in the British Crime Survey were of the opinion that crime was on the increase, compared with a figure of 65% for 2008, with the implication that public confidence in the success of law and order policies was actually falling. The survey also

---

4. A regularly-taken statistical census of people's experience of crime taken from a sample of some 10,000 households.
5. 'Crime in England and Wales, 2008/09, Findings from the British Crime Survey, and Police Recorded Crime' (2009) Walker A, Flately J, Kershaw C, and D Moon (eds) *Home Office Statistical Bulletin 11/09*; London: Home Office; British Crime Survey, 2008-2009, London: HMSO.
6. *Understanding Public Attitudes to Criminal Justice* (2005), Roberts J and Hough M, Maidenhead: McGraw-Hill Education.

revealed that only 39% of respondents had confidence in the effectiveness of the criminal justice system as a whole.[7]

So why might the perceptions about trends of crime in society have been so at odds with the official statistics? Almost certainly it was more than simply a consequence of shortcomings in communication between government, the police or the media and the general public. In addition, other researchers[8] argued that it reflected the prevailing significance of fear about crime, which many commentators had come to recognise as almost more of a problem to be addressed than the level of crime itself. In this respect, much media reporting of law and order issues in general, and of a few individual and especially salacious and horrifying crimes, was undoubtedly playing its part. But so too, almost certainly, was all the rhetoric from politicians at national level who seemed constantly to compete with and trump one another's ideas in trying to convince the electorate that theirs was the party most determined to 'tackle crime', to be tough on offending behaviour and to develop a more victim-centred criminal justice system.

Indeed, the high level of concern at the heart of government about the significance and impact of fear of crime was reflected in the decision taken in 2008 to focus exclusively on 'Trust and Confidence' as the all-important measure of performance in criminal justice. This replaced the plethora of different performance measures and targets that had previously provided the focus of attention for the more managerially-minded in and around government.[9]

The scores for public confidence of course, as with crime statistics, would vary from locality to locality across the country. However, interestingly, this did not necessarily happen in the perhaps to-be-expected manner of 'more crime equalling lower public confidence'. What, in fact, the research on this issue tended to suggest was that levels of confidence correlated more with levels of affluence/disadvantage in neighbourhoods—with lower confi-

---

7. Walker A, Flately J, Kershaw C, and D Moon (eds) (2009) Op cit.
8. For example, 'Explaining Fear of Crime' (1988), Box S, Hale C and Andrews G, *British Journal of Criminology*, 28,3,340-356.
9. Indeed, this was to become one of the new Public Service Agreement targets (PSA 23) to be used to assess the effectiveness of the police and other agencies in tackling crime and anti-social behaviour.

dence associating with higher levels of deprivation.[10] Evidence was also found that showed initiatives in collective security to be likely to increase public confidence[11] and that neighbourhoods with stronger bonds of social cohesion were similarly likely to exhibit higher public confidence in relation to crime. Unsurprisingly perhaps, the research would also suggest that residents' perceptions about their neighbourhood—for example, their sense of identity and pride in the place—were generally more important as correlates of fear of crime than physical or environmental quality or household deprivation.[12]

Direct experiences of policing have also been shown to be important in shaping perceptions and confidence. In this respect research by Skogan[13] suggested a disproportionately negative impact on confidence for those who had had a particularly poor personal interaction with a police officer, although, interestingly, positive interactions were found to be less likely to have an equivalently positive effect on confidence.

The notions of 'public confidence' and of 'trust' (whether in the police or in relation to crime and criminal justice more generally) are, of course, slippery ones which, as Goldsmith has suggested,[14] are more easily discussed in general terms than defined with any precision. In seeking to understand individual differences in regard to policing in particular, Goldsmith also highlighted the problem of distinguishing between beliefs and perceptions relating, on the one hand, to the police as individuals and, on the other, to the police as an institution. His suggestion here was that much would be dependent on the particular perceptual filters that people individually might apply to the set of circumstances and experiences that they happened to encounter. Thus, while different people might in practice receive much the same treatment from the police, the levels of confidence and trust they would individually have in the police could depend on what each happened

---

10. 'Experience, Quality of Life and Neighbourhood Context: A hierarchical analysis of satisfaction with the police' (2000), Reisig M D and Parks R, *Justice Quarterly*, 17, 607-629.
11. 'Race, Community Context and Confidence in the Police', *American Journal of Police* (1996), Cao L, Frank J and Cullen F, XV(1).
12. 'African- American and White Perceptions of Police Services: within and between group variation' (2004), Huebner B, Schafer J, and T Bynum, *Journal of Criminal Justice*, 32, 123-155.
13. 'Asymmetry in the impact of encounters with the police' (2006), Skogan W, *Policing and Society*, 16(2), 99-126.
14. 'Police Reform and the Problem of Trust' (2005), Goldsmith A, *Theoretical Criminology*, 9, 443.

to believe and understand about the police (as an institution) and what they had experienced (from individual encounters).

A further important contribution on this theme has been made by Jackson et al,[15] who have suggested a conflict between two ideologies regarding public perceptions about policing priorities at local level. Under one such ideology (which they termed the 'instrumental model'), a link would be made between, on the one hand, actual crime rates, perceived probability of victimisation and fear of crime and, on the other, levels of public confidence, with media reporting and politicians' rhetoric mostly tending to raise (rather than diminish) any sense of anxiety. Under the other ideology (which they described as the 'expressive model'), however, it could be assumed that confidence would link much more to the strength of community ties and bonds and to the extent to which citizens felt the police were being responsive and held to account in relation to crime and related problems within the locality.

It is important to emphasise the special significance of the activities of the police in shaping public opinions about criminal justice as a whole. For it is policing, of course, which takes place in the most widely visible manner — even those who have hardly conversed with a police officer would at least see officers patrolling the streets and responding to incidents. In contrast, relatively few could be expected to observe first-hand prosecutors, court officials, defence advocates, probation officers or prison officers at work, and would rely instead on TV portrayals for their impressions and perceptions of their contribution and for the confidence they might hold in them. The police are also the largest of the criminal justice agencies in terms of numbers of staff, and indeed the establishments of all police forces had grown significantly under New Labour, particularly with the advent of 'neighbourhood policing' and the recruitment of some 16,000 more personnel — these as police community support officers (PCSOs).[16] For this reason, public confidence in the police would be likely itself to provide the all-important barometer of confidence with criminal justice as a whole.

---

15. 'Does Fear of Crime Erode Public Confidence in Policing?' (2009), Jackson J, Bradford B, Hohl K and Farrell S, *Policing*, 3(1), 100-111.
16. 'Does Plural Suit Rural? Reflections on Quasi Policing in the Countryside' (2010), Merritt J and Dingwall G, *International Journal of Police Science and Management*, 10, 3.

Here, certain findings from a survey of 1,000 residents conducted in 2008 in three local neighbourhoods of the district of Kings Norton, Birmingham offer some helpful illustrations and insights on public perceptions and the confidence problem.[17] This survey was particularly designed to assess the impact of the introduction of neighbourhood policing through a team of PCSOs. In the survey, respondents were asked what they felt about the trend in crime locally over the previous 12 months, and an equal proportion (18%) felt that it had increased as decreased, while 50% felt it about the same (the remaining 14% feeling unable to proffer a view on the situation). A similar picture was identified in relation to anti-social behaviour, with some 26% feeling its incidence had increased, 13% thinking it had reduced and with 47% feeling there had been no change (the remaining 14% being unable to give a view). As to the impact of PCSOs, while 81% of respondents felt that patrols by police officers had made them feel safer, only 71% felt so in relation to PCSOs. Significantly also, less than a quarter of residents said they felt safer now with the PCSO patrols than a year ago (before their introduction), with 65% feeling it had made no difference to them. This survey, then, leaves something of a question mark over the efficacy, at least in its early years, of the major policy (and spending) commitment to 'reassurance policing'[18] through the recruitment and deployment of PCSOs (i.e. officers without the full powers and equipment of a police constable).

The New Localism

The second key issue forming the backcloth to this volume and to the mood for a change of policy direction in criminal justice in this country relates to the growth and form of localism. As indicated, the approach of the New Labour government in office from 1997 to 2010 had been characterised, perhaps above all, by its strongly centre-driven and managerialist ethos in

---

17. 'Do Police Community Support Officers reduce the fear of crime in local communities?' (2010), Keasey P, Unpublished MSc Dissertation, Birmingham: Institute of Local Government Studies, University of Birmingham.
18. 'Reinventing Tradition? Reassurance, Neighbourhood Policing and Security' (2004), Innes M, *Criminal Justice*, 4, 151.

relation to public service development. Indeed, in criminal justice, as across the public service spectrum, the agencies at local level found themselves, for the most part, increasingly driven by the seemingly relentless reform agenda. This agenda could be seen as both a ratcheting-up and a further development of the earlier trend of New Public Management that had begun in the late-1970s and early-1980s.[19]

Greater efficiency, productivity and competition were certainly still important elements in New Labour's strong focus on performance management. This could be seen in the emphasis placed on 'contestability' and 'contracting' in relation, for example, to probation activity, on civilianisation of more functions within police organisations, in promoting the concept of sentencing discounts to incentivise early submission of pleas of guilty in court (to reduce the number of collapsed trials), in empowering the police and other agencies to issue more fixed penalties (for example penalty notices for disorder) to avoid the costs and potential delays of court hearings and so on.

But there were other elements too which marked out the development of criminal justice under New Labour and which distinguished it from previous developments. In particular was the added emphasis on achievement of 'outcomes' and on 'joining-up' (whether by organisational mergers, partnership working, or developing stronger lines of accountability). In both respects, centralisation and standardisation were key features. It was, for example, central departments that took the lead in defining the set of service outcomes for criminal justice and for shaping and approving the framework of Public Service Agreements and key indicators by which local areas and services could be expected to be judged.[20]

Under New Labour, for the first time, the oft-used phrase 'the Criminal Justice System' also began to have much more of a reality about it, with the establishment of a National Criminal Justice Board to oversee performance and a set of Local Criminal Justice Boards (one per police area) formed to co-ordinate and lead performance improvement at local level through closer

---

19. 'A Public Management for all Seasons?' (1991), Hood C, *Public Administration*, 69, 1, 3-19. *Managing Criminal Justice* (1993), Raine J and Willson M, Hemel Hempstead: Harvester Wheatsheaf. *The New Politics of Criminal Justice* (1998), James A and Raine J, London: Addison Wesley Longman.
20. This issue is discussed in *Chapter 9*.

collaboration of the agencies.[21] Responsibility for the administration of courts (magistrates' courts, the Crown Court and the County Court) was centralised into a new single national agency — Her Majesty's Court Service. The prison and probation services were similarly drawn together into a new National Offender Management Service, and a new Youth Justice Board was established at national level to oversee and steer the work of the newly-created youth offending teams at local level, and which brought together a set of professionals from a range of different backgrounds and services to provide a multi-agency and more 'joined up' approach to youth justice.

Alongside the organisational systematisation also came developments in more standard 'processes'. For example, the institution of template forms for probation staff to use in assessing the risk of re-offending (the Offender Assessment System or 'OASys'[22]); and the development of a set of standardised and formally accredited programmes for offenders, of evidence-based practice approaches to be adopted and applied by probation officers in working with offenders, and of course the attempts to link criminal justice agencies electronically for information management and communication purposes.

Although such reforms seemed hardly to affect public perceptions about crime and criminal justice, their impact and legacy within the sphere of criminal justice practice was surely significant and, in many respects, positive. The focus on performance management certainly did much to promote a keener focus on many aspects of criminal justice that had hitherto been sloppily treated or neglected — for example, the interests of victims and witnesses in having to attend court to give evidence, the time taken from arrest of a suspect by the police to case completion in court, the scope for offenders to evade part or all of their sentences, whether by not paying their fines or by failing to report to their probation officers for community service projects as instructed. And while there was certainly some evidence of perverse effects too, of 'gaming', particularly by the police to present their performance in

---

21. At national level itself, the new Ministry of Justice was created and brought together the 'correctional services' functions of prisons and probation previously in the Home Office with courts administration from the former Department for Constitutional Affairs.
22. This issue is discussed in *Chapter 7*.

good light,[23] on the whole, policing performance, like that for criminal justice more generally, improved in most of the ways intended.

The institutional reforms, too, addressed some longstanding problems. On the whole, a more joined-up criminal justice process and the closer collaboration between agencies in addressing issues that required shared attention such as drug-related and alcohol-related crime, the victim's experience of criminal justice, and domestic violence, facilitated progress where previously little had been apparent. However, there were some understandable sensitivities around the involvement of the courts, and particularly the judiciary, in such multi-agency working, because of the risk of compromise to their independence.

Some of the changes were, of course, less easily seen as beneficial. For instance, the pay-back from creating a national unified court administrative organisation (Her Majesty's Court Service) seemed questionable in practice, since, despite the new national, regional and area tiers of management that were introduced here, most courts continued to operate largely as before, with their own local administrative teams of staff and local management. Likewise, the creation of a National Offender Management Service (by seeking to merge prison and probation services) was viewed by many as, on balance, more troublesome than beneficial, not least because of major cultural differences between the two organisations. Further, a major issue in this context was the continuing record size of the prison population—causing, as indicated, the incoming Justice Secretary, The Right Honourable Kenneth Clarke MP, in 2010, to express dismay at what he had inherited in this respect.

To a significant extent, the overstretched prisons were one legacy of New Labour's policy change agenda that ran alongside its more managerially-inspired reform programme. While of course it was never ministers' intention for more offenders to be locked up, the new government's toughening approach in relation to sentences in general, and particularly the stricter regimes for those found in breach of their community sentences, were undoubtedly key contributory factors. Indeed, the whole anti-social behaviour agenda—which was hugely significant in the overall New Labour

---

23. See for example, 'Police force tricks to fiddle crime figures' (2009), Barratt D, *Daily Telegraph*, 5 December.

policy framework—had the effect of drawing many more people into the criminal justice arena, and many of these into the prisons, in response to breaches of the civil orders (for ASB) initially imposed on them.

In an intriguing analysis and critique of the New Labour policy agenda of crime and criminal justice, Garside suggested that the government had developed 'a quaint fixation with policing petty irritations and minor disorder, rather than engaging seriously with the underlying causes (of crime)'.[24] His core argument was that, while the government was right to regard criminal justice as having underperformed and having failed to promote public confidence, its analysis of the causes of such failure was misguided and that, as a result, political energies and extensive resources had been wastefully diverted into a whole range of initiatives that were, in Garside's view, largely irrelevant. Instead, he suggested,

> the real policy challenge involves greater honesty about what criminal justice cannot achieve and a genuine openness to thinking on a much broader policy canvas, beyond the usual suspects of the police, the courts and the prisons.[25]

For Garside, the more pressing priorities would be investment in crime reduction through preventative actions to do more to address the circumstances and inequalities underlying the propensity to offend. And indeed, this was to be a message reiterated a few years later in a House of Commons Select Committee report on 'Justice Reinvestment'[26] and in the report of the Youth Crime Commission.[27] This latter report urged the case for prevention and early intervention being given a much higher profile in tackling crime and anti-social behaviour, and highlighted some of the research demonstrating

---

24. *'Right for the Wrong Reasons: Making sense of criminal justice failure,'* (2006), Garside R, 7; and Crime and Society Foundation, Monograph No. 2.
25. *Ibid*, 5.
26. *The Case for Justice Reinvestment* (2009), House of Commons Justice Committee, First Report, Cutting Crime, London: Home Office
27. *Time for a Fresh Start, Report of the Independent Commission on Youth Crime and Anti-social Behaviour* (2010), Independent Commission on Youth Crime and Anti-social Behaviour, London; The Police Foundation.

how action to raise the quality of upbringing, education and support that children receive can significantly influence outcomes, including less involvement in crime.[28]

To be fair, this argument had always been understood by New Labour, and indeed reflected in the words of Tony Blair, then Leader of the Opposition, in the run-up to the 1997 general election, 'tough on crime and tough on the causes of crime'. Furthermore, his new government did introduce a number of significant and directly responding social programmes, most notably, 'Sure Start' and 'New Deal for Communities'. But it was patently not enough and, in any case, it became increasingly apparent that, on their own, such national programmes could only go so far in addressing the deep-seated social inequalities with which high rates of crime and anti-social behaviour would tend to associate. In addition, what was needed were complementary programmes of tailored action and well-resourced interventions at local level—engaging proactively with children and young people in their communities and investing in community infrastructure, sports provision and other constructive activities. But, unfortunately, for the most part, the funding for such action and interventions was never sufficiently forthcoming.

So to the 'new localism' that, as indicated, was also increasingly apparent in New Labour's criminal justice policy agenda, as it was across the public policy sphere in the latter few years before the 2010 general election. Most obviously, it had been expressed in the very significant commitment to neighbourhood policing, as discussed earlier. But it was subsequently strongly apparent in a set of proposals from the Office for Criminal Justice Reform[29] to promote greater community engagement in criminal justice, for example, by local residents nominating projects in their areas on which offenders might work as 'community payback', by establishing community prosecutors in each local area, by encouraging the submission to the courts of 'community impact statements' on local crimes, and by courts adopting a more proactive 'problem solving approach' in dealing with offenders.

---

28. *Time for a Fresh Start, Report of the Independent Commission on Youth Crime and Anti-social Behaviour* (2010), Independent Commission on Youth Crime and Anti-social Behaviour, London; The Police Foundation.
29. *Engaging Communities in Criminal Justice* (2009), Office for Criminal Justice Reform, Green Paper Cm 7583, London: Home Office.

INTRODUCTION: THE CHANGING POLITICS OF LAW AND ORDER

While such proposals for a more localist approach did not seek to dismantle or replace the national infrastructure and standardising processes, there was certainly a different tone and mood from then on. It was this tone which, as indicated, was picked up with fresh vitality by the incoming Coalition government, keen to make its mark and, no doubt, also content to take any opportunity to be seen to be doing things differently.

Regulatory State or Empowered Communities?

This brings us to the purpose of this volume. We seek to take stock of the shifts and progress in criminal justice made over the past decade and a half under the strong regulatory and risk reducing dynamic of the central state. However, we also explore the potential and prospects for a contrasting and more localist dynamic in which communities are empowered to take more responsibility for addressing the problem of crime in their neighbourhoods.

From this introductory point, the book provides a set of case-study chapters that illustrate and explore these two dynamics in criminal justice—the regulatory state-led approach and the empowered communities approach—in theory and in practice.

All the chapters are authored by criminal justice scholars of the University of Birmingham, whose work reflects and draws on a range of relevant disciplines—criminal law, criminology, forensic psychology, social work and public management—and who together seek to build an insightful analysis of the strengths and limitations of these respective dynamics.

Part I–The Regulatory State begins with reflections by Andrew Sanders on criminal justice as a form of regulation and on the case for limiting its role in this regard—the 'freedom' approach, as it is described. Then three chapters, by John Child and Adrian Hunt, by Jessica Elliott, and by Theresa Lynch in turn provide case-studies of the impacts of the regulatory state through the extending reach of the criminal law, and concerning respectively risk and pre-emption, liability in relation to the purchase of sexual services, and the development of the anti-social behaviour order. To conclude *Part I*, two further chapters consider the way in which the state has approached risk minimisation—first a chapter by Kathryn Farrow, Gill Kelly and Bernadette Wilkinson, on the nationalising, regulating and standardising of probation practice, and second, by Shamila Ahmed and Basia Spalek on security responses to the 'new terrorism'.

In Part II–*Empowered Communities as Stakeholders in Criminal Justice* we turn to community-level responses to crime and disorder, beginning with an examination by Katherine Doolin of the potential for, and challenges to, engaging and empowering communities through restorative justice. This is followed by David Prior's account of the pursuit at the local level of the notion of 'safer communities' and community justice and by John Raine's exploration of the way such ideas have begun to find expression in the concept of 'community justice centres'. Nathan Hughes' chapter complements Theresa Lynch's chapter in *Part I* on anti-social behaviour by considering community-level responses to this challenge, while Mark Blandford and Anthony Beech examine the developing approach to 'policing' sex offenders in local communities and Zahira Latif considers community-based approaches to the largely hidden problem of domestic violence.

Then, in the final chapter, we seek to draw the threads together and proffer suggestions about the way ahead and about how the respective benefits and limits of state and community-led approaches in criminal justice might best be reconciled and balanced.

PART I

THE REGULATORY STATE AND THE MANAGEMENT OF RISK

The evolution of criminal law and practice is never simple or one-dimensional, taking place across a multitude of topics and amidst an equally abundant range of priorities. However, within this complexity, it is possible to identify a number of trends that have developed in a manner that characterise the broader direction of reform. A major trend in this regard, the focus of this Part, has been the tendency of the previous government in particular to employ formal state regulation to combat risk in society. Ever more unwilling to leave such risks to the more informal mechanisms of the community, it is an area that has become the target for a raft of criminal law and procedural legislation.

Within this Part, each chapter has selected an aspect of the more general trend for close examination. *Chapter 2* explores the theoretical foundations of the criminal law, explaining that if the law is designed to promote freedom (as the author contends) then it becomes difficult to justify several areas of criminalisation. For *Chapter 3*, the focus is on offences that target the actions of defendants prior to the completion of future crimes, asking whether such offences have been created on a coherent and principled basis. *Chapter 4*, again focusing on a preparatory offence, goes beyond the coherence of the offence itself to ask how effective such offences are in the context of preventing the abuse of trafficked or controlled women. Completing this particular line of discussion, *Chapter 5* goes on to explore what seems like the state's attempt to overreach the boundaries of criminal law, employing civil law and hybrid mechanisms to target potentially risky behaviour at an ever more remote stage. In *Chapter 6*, the focus switches from the risks associated with those yet to commit offences, to those that pose a risk of re-offending. Again, exposing state measures that have led to a more centralised and standardised method of offender management, the chapter questions whether such reforms have achieved their original aims. Finally, *Chapter 7* explores a further dimension of the trend in state regulation. This time, looking beyond the regulations themselves, this chapter explores the effects that state regulation can have upon communities that feel targeted by such mechanisms.

CHAPTER 2

LIMITING CRIMINAL JUSTICE AND REGULATION: THE 'FREEDOM' PERSPECTIVE[1]

ANDREW SANDERS

The idea for this book originated, in part, from a concern about the continual expansion of criminal law and state regulation. Unless the huge financial and personal cost of this—e.g. stress, disaffection and the erosion of freedom—can be justified, this expansion should be rolled back. This chapter therefore has several aims: to clarify the relationship between 'criminal justice' and 'regulation'; to discuss different frameworks of analysis of the costs and benefits of criminal justice; and to suggest a reasoned basis and strategy for rolling back state power.

The Relationship Between Criminal Justice and Regulation

Is criminal justice a form of regulation, or is regulation a form of criminal justice? The answer, in abstract, is both. At one level, criminal justice is just one way of attempting to regulate our behaviour. For example, anti-social behaviour orders (ASBOs) are, technically, civil orders. They are a form of non-criminal regulation, like injunctions taken out, for example, to restrain perpetrators of domestic violence. Moreover, as Prior (*Chapter 9*) observes,

---

[1]. This chapter draws heavily on two sources: First, *Chapter 1* of my book, *Criminal Justice*, co-written with Richard Young and Mandy Burton (Oxford University Press, Fourth Edition, 2010), in which we set out the 'freedom approach' advocated here. Without Richard this paper, and much of my other work, would not have been possible. Second, my chapter in Quirk H, Seddon T and Smith G (eds), *Regulation and Criminal Justice* (CUP, 2010). I also thank the members of the BCCJ group, whose discussions greatly helped the final product.

they are only the most visible tip of a set of non-criminal justice practices that regulate anti-social behaviour. But if these civil-penal orders are breached, criminal consequences can follow.

At another level, regulation can form part of criminal justice. The police, for example, rarely arrest and prosecute demonstrators who breach public order legislation, but they regulate demonstrations, sometimes leading to the mass temporary detention and control of hundreds or thousands of people. 'Kettling' (a public order policing tactic to contain protestors in a confined area) is therefore a form of regulation. The Health and Safety Executive, Environment Agency, and HM Revenue and Customs, to name just a few 'regulatory' law enforcement agencies, are in a similar situation. They can prosecute breaches of health and safety, pollution and tax laws respectively. But more frequently they attempt to secure compliance with the law by encouragement, advice, warnings and improvement notices. As with the policing of demonstrations, the criminal law is used primarily when regulatory methods fail. Regulatory strategies can be used at later stages too. There are, for example, huge numbers of orders and registers available so that sex offenders and other dangerous offenders can be monitored and controlled (see *Chapter 12*, by Blandford and Beech); and prisoners are generally subjected to supervision and licence conditions after release from prison.

It follows that regulation can be a tool of criminal justice, just as criminal justice can be a tool of regulation. Indeed, the criminal justice system can be seen as a set of 'tools' including surveillance and covert action, stop-search, civil-penal orders, compliance mechanisms, controls/detention (such as 'kettling'), arrest, sanctions (including prosecution), enforced compensation, etc. These can be chosen, almost at will by enforcement agencies to deal with a range of issues including 'normal' crimes, 'regulatory' crimes, anti-social behaviour, suspected terrorist activities, illegal immigration, disorder, oppositional activity, etc. One way of reading the chapters that follow is to see how different tools are used for different purposes in relation to different criminal and quasi-criminal problems. A key question is whether the tools used, and the way in which they are used, are the best ways of dealing with these problems, bearing in mind their different costs.

Frameworks of Analysis: Models and Aims of Criminal Justice

Most people agree that criminal justice systems should have aims on these lines:

- prevention of crime;
- reduction of re-offending;
- sanctioning offenders;
- respecting victims and witnesses;
- protecting the innocent;
- rights and liberties to be curtailed only proportionately, not disproportionately in relation to suspected crimes;
- where possible, adversely affecting only people directly involved in crime;
- using scarce resources that could be put to better use proportionately, not disproportionately; and
- public involvement and trust in criminal justice.

There are two main problems here. First, these aims often conflict with each other, at least some of the time. For example, if resources were limitless more offenders could be apprehended while using repressive measures less; but scarce resources lead the police to cut corners by often restricting suspects' rights and using stop-search, arrest and interrogation powers in either discriminatory or indiscriminate ways. These conflicting aims therefore have to be prioritised. Second, many of these aims are not really aims. The best way of protecting innocent people, for example, is to simply not use coercive powers against anyone who might be innocent and to not prosecute except where guilt is certain. But this would be intolerable, as criminal justice powers would then rarely be invoked. Thus, the final five aims in the list are actually constraining principles or values that limit the actions of criminal justice agencies in pursuit of the first four.

The point of frameworks of analysis (models) is that they aim, in part, to prioritise particular aims or values in order to make sense of the overall criminal justice system.

Due process and crime control

The principle of 'innocent till proven guilty' drives the laws, policies and practices of 'due process'-based criminal justice systems. Suspects and defendants have extensive rights and the innocent are protected at the expense of convictions. By contrast, 'crime control'-based systems prioritise conviction of the probably-guilty. Most European criminal justice systems claim to be largely 'due process'-based, but in reality are largely 'crime control'-based.[2] Packer, who coined these terms, argued that no system corresponds entirely with the due process or crime control positions. Instead, each system sits somewhere on a spectrum with due process and crime control at each end.[3]

Since 'due process' is not an aim, but a set of procedural standards, both models have crime control aims, constrained by due process procedures. Thus the difference between the two models is a matter of balance between the two ends of the spectrum. Many commentators[4] are rightly concerned that there is no basis on which to judge whether a particular 'balance' is struck well or not, particularly when one is usually considering the balance between an increased probability of conviction against reduced civil liberties (and vice-versa).

There is also another 'balance' problem. In the world of tax evasion, health and safety, pollution, etc, the issue of civil liberties rarely arises. But, depending on the context, 'regulatory' agencies can prevent processes or businesses running. They therefore have potentially powerful tools with financial and economic consequences that go far beyond the bottom line of a particular business (closing down major businesses or creating an environment that leads them to re-locate has major effects on employment, for example). On the other hand, these agencies have limited resources, so investigation and the invocation of these powers at any one time has to be considered against what else could be done with the resources those actions would consume.[5]

Balances are therefore constantly being struck by enforcement agencies: between the cost of enforcement action in a particular instance (cost to the

---

2. *Criminal Justice* (2010), Sanders A, Young R and Burton M (4th ed, OUP).
3. *Limits of the Criminal Sanction* (1968), Packer H, Stanford UP.
4. For example, *The Criminal Process* (2005), Ashworth A and Redmayne M (3rd ed, OUP).
5. See, for example, *Law as Last Resort* (2003), Hawkins K, Oxford: OUP and *Enforcing Pollution Control Regulation* (2009), Abbot C, Oxford: Hart.

agency, to the 'offending' individual, firm or organisation, and to employees and consumers connected to the 'offenders') and the likely harm done by the offence(s) in question.

The Packer model does not seem able to incorporate this issue, nor concerns for victims, for the spectrum is two-dimensional with only suspect/accused concerns at one end and concerns of the state at the other. A key feature of the freedom model that will be outlined later is that it does take these matters into account.[6]

Clearly Packer's models do not provide us with an adequate basis for formulating criminal justice aims. To establish 'crime control' as the primary aim means that concern for both the accused and the victim will always be secondary and there is no coherent basis for calibrating 'how much' due process (or the rights of victims) should intrude on crime control. And financial and human costs are largely neglected issues. However, in a world of scarce resources agencies will always attempt to become more efficient. While 'crime control' is a dominant aim this will usually mean eroding costly due process obstacles (such as comprehensive access to free high quality legal advice for suspects; rights to jury trial; full disclosure to the defence of evidence collected by the police). With most public spending activities facing cuts of 20% or more from 2011, we are seeing this happen already in 2010. However, expensive crime control measures, such as excessive use of prison, are also being questioned (e.g. by the Justice Secretary in July 2010). We shall see that the freedom model seeks efficiencies based on principle rather than expediency, and in the conclusion and the final chapter we briefly explore the prospects for a happy combination of the two.

Human rights

Ashworth and Redmayne[7] argue that the crime control aim of securing as many convictions as possible can be tightly constrained by human rights principles (drawn from the European Convention on Human Rights (ECHR)) instead of merely compromised to a varying extent by due process standards.

---

6. For a rare example of resources being taken into account, albeit differently from here, see also 'The uneasy relationship between criminal procedure and criminal justice' (1997), Stuntz, Yale *Law Journal* 107: 1.
7. *The Criminal Process* (2005), Ashworth A and Redmayne M (3rd ed, OUP).

They suggest that we resolve conflicts between different rights (e.g. of the accused and of victims), and between the protection of rights and the aim of bringing cases to effective trial, by: absolutely forbidding some law enforcement practices regardless of their overall social benefits (e.g. torture or inhuman treatment: ECHR Article 3); allowing some other practices only in exceptional circumstances (that is, derogation from e.g. Article 5 ECHR restrictions on detention); and balancing less strong rights (e.g. privacy: Article 8 ECHR) against social or political considerations.

There are a number of problems here: there are very few 'absolute' rights; the circumstances under which states may derogate are unclear; derogation and Article 8-type balancing of rights against other considerations is no different in principle from due process/crime control balancing (though it is true that principles such as proportionality are being applied with increasing sophistication); many 'rights', especially when the courts fill the gaps left by the ECHR, are vague, as with the 'human rights' of victims (see later); and for human rights to underpin all the important elements of the criminal justice system the network of human rights would have to go far beyond the ECHR.

Finally, the human rights approach has little to say about the balancing of resource costs of law enforcement against the costs of crime. The criminal justice system cannot operate without making decisions on priorities, for — as with the National Health Service, for example–the demands on law enforcement agencies far exceed the supply of their time and resources, and will always do so. An adequate model of the criminal justice system has to incorporate this consideration. This is a problem for 'normal' crime such as theft, burglary, public order, prostitution, drug abuse, anti-social behaviour, etc. as well as 'regulatory' crime. The police and other agencies *do* prioritise, but not always intelligently. For example, powers of arrest have been increased in recent years, allowing the police to pick off 'low hanging fruit'. This is 'efficient' in improving their 'figures', but at the expense of tackling more serious crime, such as rape which has been subject to much public discussion recently.

But to deny the value of human rights ideas in criminal justice, as elsewhere, would undermine the benefits that human rights thinking in general, and the ECHR in particular, have brought. Governments have been constrained, and the most extreme crime control measures have been limited.[8] Thus Gearty defends the underpinning of law and legal processes with human rights but he acknowledges that the term can have no fixed concrete meaning.[9] It follows that 'human rights' have no autonomous existence outside democratic politics and that positive laws cannot generally be 'read off' from them. In other words, there is no 'right' or 'wrong' answer to whether stop-search should be allowed without individualised suspicion. It is a political question that should be informed by respect for fellow humans. Human rights provide a minimal floor below which protections cannot fall (an important protection for people in states that are more authoritarian than the UK), but in seeking concrete aims for criminal justice we need to look beyond human rights.[10]

Compliance approaches

It is usually assumed that 'crime control' means 'bringing offenders to justice' by prosecution and punitive sentencing. However, the UK has for many decades operated a differentiated approach to low and high-level offending. Serious crime is indeed dealt with ever more punitively. But alternatives to prison, and indeed to prosecution, such as warnings, restorative justice (RJ), fixed penalties and ASBOs for relatively minor crime committed by non-prolific offenders have increased hugely in recent years.[11] This is particularly, though by no means exclusively, true of 'regulatory' crime, which is generally seen — wrongly in my view — as low-level. Regulatory agencies are not unconcerned about crime control in the broader sense of preventing crime and reducing re-offending. Far from it. This is what the 'compliance approach' — which characterises regulatory theory — is supposed to be

---

8. See, for example, measures in July 2010 restricting stop-and-search without reasonable suspicion following recent ECtHR rulings: Porter, 'Bravo Theresa May and the new spirit of freedom' *Guardian*. 14 July 2010.
9. *Can Human Rights Survive?* (2006), Gearty C, CUP.
10. Discussed more fully in *Criminal Justice* (2010) Sanders A, Young R and Burton M (4th ed, OUP), ch 1.
11. 'Defending the Criminal Law: Reflections on the Changing Character of Crime, Procedure, and Sanctions' (2008), Ashworth A and Zedner L, *Crim Law & Phil*, 2: 21 and 'Street Policing after PACE: the drift to summary justice' (2008), Young R in Cape E and Young R (eds), *Regulating Policing*, Hart. On RJ see *Chapter 8* of this work by Doolin.

about. There are, in principle, more similarities than differences between, for example, 'compliance' approaches for health and safety offences and RJ for low-level property offences. And probation supervision is increasingly a matter of securing compliance with conditions rather than aiding resettlement and reintegration (see *Chapter 6* by Farrow et al).

But there are also important differences between the approaches of police and non-police agencies. Regulatory crime is very rarely prosecuted, while the police and Crown Prosecution Service (CPS) adopt compliance approaches for a minority of 'normal' crimes. The regulatory code for non-police agencies requires regulators to justify any strong enforcement action, while the Code for Crown Prosecutors requires police and CPS to justify not prosecuting. The suffering of victims of 'normal' crime is invoked to justify punitiveness for 'normal' criminals, while the victims of 'regulatory' offences are largely ignored.[12] Victims of health and safety offences, for example, should benefit under the Code of Practice for Victims of Crime but, scandalously, they do not.[13] And there is little evidence that the desire to control 'normal' crime is matched by a similar zeal in relation to 'regulatory' crime[14] — largely because of the different cost balances highlighted earlier in relation to these two types of crime.

As Braithwaite[15] argues, we should integrate compliance and punitive approaches in respect of all types of crime, both in our theoretical thinking and in policy-making. Neither compliance nor punishment should, in themselves, be seen as aims of criminal justice; rather, they are sets of tools that should be chosen on the basis of their effectiveness — not just in securing quanta of compliance, but in securing compliance regarding the crimes with most impact and in the most cost-effective way.

---

12. 'Victims of corporate crime' (2007), Whyte D in Walklate S (ed), *Handbook of Victims and Victimology*, Cullompton: Willan.
13. See 'Reconciling the apparently different goals of criminal justice and regulation: the 'freedom' perspective' (2010) Sanders A in *Regulation and Criminal Justice* Quirk H, Seddon T, Smith G (CUP).
14. For example, *One Death Too Many* (2009), Donaghy R, Department for Work and Pensions, TSO, Norwich, Cm 7657.
15. *Restorative Justice and Responsive Regulation* (2002), Braithwaite J (OUP).

Victim-centred approaches

We have seen that inability to take victims into account is one of the failings of the crime control/due process approach. Although the human rights approach advocated by Ashworth/Redmayne puts that omission right, simply throwing 'victims' into an ever-growing pot of aims exacerbates the problem of prioritisation. Thus they welcome the European Court of Human Rights' decision[16] to extend Article 6 'fair trial' rights to victims. But legislation to restrict the use of sexual history evidence in rape trials — an important element in creating fair trials for rape victims — was found to conflict with the Article 6 'fair trial' rights of the accused, creating an insoluble dilemma.[17] Some people argue that the answer is to create a victim-centred criminal justice system in which all the other aims would be subordinated. Government rhetoric claims to be doing just this (without acknowledging that these aims might clash with crime control aims).[18] A pure victim-rights approach would allow victims to determine all decisions. There would be no due process or human rights protections for the accused. Vengeful (and falsely accusing) victims would be able to insist on arrest and prosecution when there was no evidence, and on wildly disproportionate sentences. This could not be countenanced. A human rights back-stop would be required if only to comply with our international obligations, but a backstop would, by definition, provide only minimal protection. Disparity—and consequent discrimination and unfairness—would be rife, and the interests of the community in reducing re-offending would also be sidelined.

Consequently, when victim-rights approaches are advocated, they are generally combined with other approaches. Beloof, for example, advocates a 'three model' approach to understanding criminal justice.[19] This combines Packer's two models with one that promotes the interests of victims. Like the human rights approach, this simply throws concerns for victims into

---

16. *Doorson v The Netherlands* (1996) 23 EHRR 330.
17. A (No 2) [2001] UKHL 25. See, 'Judicial perspectives on the use of s 41 and the relevance and admissibility of prior sexual history' (2005), Kibble N, *Criminal Law Review*, 190.
18. See, for example, *Justice for All* (2002), Home Office, Cm 5563 and, more recently, 'Justice system should put victims first, says Jack Straw' Mulholland and Travis, *Guardian* 27 October 2008.
19. 'The 3rd model of criminal process: the victim participation model' (1999), Beloof J, 2 *Utah LR* 289.

an unprioritised pot of aims. It takes an analytical model that sets out to illuminate irreconcilable conflicts of values and adds to it a further set of irreconcilable elements.

A New Framework: The 'Freedom' Approach

All the approaches discussed so far have an instinctive appeal to anyone concerned about criminal justice, whatever their particular viewpoint may be. So the problem is not whether or not we agree that this multiplicity of aims and values are important—in the main, we all do—but in deciding how to prioritise one over another.

What is the point of protecting victims, offenders and, indeed, anyone affected by crime and the criminal justice system? We could say that it is primarily to protect and enhance freedom. We make it a crime to thieve or assault because the losses and hurts they cause are (among other things) losses of freedom: to enjoy one's possessions, to walk the streets without fear, and so forth. We seek to convict thieves and violent offenders in the hope that the punishment or treatment they receive will reduce their re-offending, and reinforce everyone else's law-abiding instincts and behaviour. In the same way, we can ask what the point is of protecting suspects and defendants, innocent or guilty. Again, protection is not an aim in itself, but a means to the end of promoting their freedom. We insist that the police must obey the rule of law because when they do not do so we no longer feel that we live in a free society.

This means that, in theory at least, the problem of allocating priority to conflicting aims is solved if, in relation to any one incident or problem, we prioritise the aim that is likely to enhance freedom the most. What is most likely to enhance freedom will vary from circumstance to circumstance. Under this model, the freedom of victims as well as the freedom of people accused of crime is valued. These freedoms sometimes compete (as in the 'fair trial' examples given earlier), but they can work often together. Once a crime is committed the harm it causes is usually irreversible, so the application of state power to apprehend and sanction the alleged offender may do nothing to redress the balance. For example, less than one-tenth of all stop-searches lead to arrest, and less than one-half of all arrests lead to caution or prosecution.[20] These applications of power therefore reduce freedom for suspects in exchange for little gain. State power through criminal justice should only be used if it is likely to enhance more freedom than it erodes. Moreover, reducing the use of criminal justice powers allows the money saved to enhance the lives (indeed, the positive freedom) of everyone through improved health, education, housing and so forth. Not only would this be freedom-enhancing in itself, but these welfare improvements could do more to reduce crime—i.e. to enhance the freedom of potential victims—than arrest and prosecution.

Ayres and Braithwaite's 'pyramid' of sanctions[21] is applicable, whereby the least intrusive sanctions are at the base, while the most intrusive are at the apex, and sanctions move up a level only in response to failure to comply and repeated offending. Prosecution both uses more resources than do alternatives, and encroaches more on the freedom of the suspect than do alternatives. Unless there are obvious gains to freedom by moving up the pyramid, there is no good reason to do it. This is the 'compliance' approach by another name, but applied to police-enforced as well as regulatory crime.

However, some 'alternatives' are more freedom-reducing than prosecutions. As Cohen[22] observed many years ago, and Ashworth and Zedner warned more recently, apparently 'soft' alternatives are sometimes more coercive and controlling than swift punitive sanctions. Modern examples include penalty notices for disorder,[23] and ASBOs. Frequently, 'alternatives' are actually additions. Less obviously, measures against companies that lead to shut down, removal to other jurisdictions or reduced activity might be as hugely harmful to the freedom of innocent people as it is for the offenders for whom we may have less sympathy. But these examples show the need to (a) be clear about what elements in the pyramid are genuinely 'higher' and 'lower' than others, and not be misled into thinking that 'regulation' is nec-

---

20. *Police Powers and Procedures England and Wales 2007/08* (2009), Hand T and Dodd L in Povey D, Smith K (eds), Home Office Statistical Bulletin 07/09, London: Home Office.
21. *Responsive Regulation* (1992), Ayres R and Braithwaite J, OUP.
22. *Visions of Social Control* (1985), Cohen S, Polity.
23. 'Street Policing after PACE: the drift to summary justice' (2008), Young R in Cape E and Young R (eds), *Regulating Policing*, Hart.

essarily less coercive than 'criminal justice'; and (b) develop alternatives that are proportionately intrusive and do not harm innocent people (e.g. state takeover of offending companies instead of shut-down). We also need to consider the extent to which coercive measures are used against individuals and particular sections of society, as documented in *Chapter 7* by Ahmed and Spalek, for example. No-one would argue that that the rudeness and disdain so often shown by police to marginalised sections of the population breaches human rights. But if low-level disrespect is frequent and systemic, it can be as corrosive as an arrest without cause or a denial of the right of silence.

It is true that this approach involves a form of balancing similar to the due process/crime control and human rights approaches. But it has a methodology that due process/crime control lacks, and a reach that human rights approaches lack. Human rights has nothing to say about resource allocation, jury trial, the length or content of prison sentences or how to balance pollution risks against job losses.

'Freedom' also applies to the substantive criminal law. For example, Child and Hunt (*Chapter 3*) express a due process concern about the increasing number of risk-based laws that criminalise activity that is far short of actual harmful activity (e.g. possession of information that might be of use to terrorists). Their appeal to traditional notions of criminal law is limited in power since many such laws have existed for a long time (e.g. possession of offensive weapons; behaviour that could cause distress to householders). Nor is there any human rights-based objection to such laws. From a freedom point of view though, the objection is obvious: unless such laws can be shown to reduce harmful behaviour, the erosions of freedom they entail, and the police resources they consume, are unjustifiable. If, on the other hand, it can be shown that they achieve their objectives, the fact that they do not conform to traditional notions of 'proper' criminal law would be viewed by most as of little consequence.

Take also Elliott's concern about the criminalisation of the purchase of sexual services from women who are coerced into prostitution or exploited (*Chapter 4*). These new laws are, again, offensive to traditional lawyers because lack of knowledge of the coercion or exploitation is no defence, but they are not contrary to human rights or completely deficient in due process protections. On the other hand, coerced prostitution is an evil that should be tackled. A more effective method would surely be to create a licencing system for sex workers working alone or in co-operative groups. Purchasing the services of other sex workers could then be criminalised with less loss of freedom for sex workers and their clients, better protection for those being exploited and less use of resources by the police. This also shows how regulatory tools can often be used to solve problems more effectively than criminal justice tools. A similar critique could be made in relation to ASBOs (see Lynch in *Chapter 5*): the legal form, as such, tells us nothing about whether yet another extension of state power is justifiable, and crime control/due process and human rights approaches have insufficient bite.[24]

To summarise, the freedom approach means restricting the reach of the criminal law; using less intrusive measures where they would be as effective as more intrusive measures; enhancing those rights of victims that are least at the expense of those for the accused; and using the least resource-intensive measures: instead of monetary compensation, services for victims plus better information about progress of cases, involvement in restorative processes, etc—not involvement in decision-making, victim impact statements etc which tend to be retributive in effect.[25]

Regulating Criminal Justice

Packer recognised the potential for abuse of state powers when he formulated his models. One reason why the due process model incorporates exclusionary rules, for example, is that they are powerful deterrents against police abuse of power. Other methods of controlling the way police power is used include civil and criminal sanctions, complaints procedures, and supervision/monitoring of officers. The human rights perspective has little to say about such matters. Thus when human rights are breached by the police, as

---

24. This is the problem with the critique of this type of new law (and many others) by Ashworth A and Zedner L, 'Defending the Criminal Law: Reflections on the Changing Character of Crime, Procedure, and Sanctions' (2008), *Crim Law & Phil*, 2: 21.
25. 'Vengeance, victims and the identities of law' (1997), Sarat A, 6 Social and Legal Studies 163 and 'Victim Participation in an Exclusionary Criminal Justice System' (2002), Sanders A, in Hoyle C and Young R (eds), *New Visions of Crime Victims*, Hart.

in many recent stop-search and covert policing cases, the courts have had few sanctions. What would be criminal and/or tortuous if done by ordinary people remains subject to no sanctions when done illegally by the police. Sometimes evidence is excluded or cases are terminated for abuse of process, but only in the most serious cases of abuse. In short, it is as important to regulate the exercise of power as it is to restrict the number and extent of powers. Though few people argue for an extreme version of due process whereby every minor breach of a rule would lead to exclusion of evidence or prosecution of the police, the reality is that much police power is largely unregulated.[26] Only the freedom perspective provides a coherent way of balancing competing demands.

As with the earlier discussion, the key principles are the valuing of the freedom of suspects and cost-effectiveness. There are some criminal and civil laws, as well as exclusionary mechanisms, but these are all expensive blunt instruments of limited effectiveness. One would expect complaints mechanisms to be more effective, but as these remain police-dominated, civil claims are still remarkably popular. This indicates how ineffective the alternatives are. The main regulatory control is supervision and monitoring, largely in the form of a plethora of forms: custody sheets, stop-search records, etc. But it is the very police who are being regulated and monitored — the officer conducting the stop-search, the custody officer who authorises detention and is responsible for the welfare of detainees — who complete the forms. This is self-regulation taken to an extreme. And it is largely ineffective.[27]

But police power cannot be eradicated. Shearing argues that instead of (ineffectually) attempting to rid the world of power, we should empower the weak. This would enable those outside the 'power nodes' — such as 'communities' — to hold the powerful to account. Regulation could become more plural, and the resulting 'nodal governance' would disperse power.[28] This is, in

---

26. On 'street' policing, see Ahmed and Spalek (*Chapter 7* of this work); on arrested suspects, see *Police Custody* (2010), Skinns L, Willan.
27. *Criminal Justice* (2010) Sanders A, Young R and Burton M (4th ed, OUP), ch 2, 4, 5, 6, 12.
28. 'Reflections on the refusal to acknowledge private governments' in Wood J and Dupont B eds *Democracy, Society and the Governance of Security* (CUP, 2006). There is now a considerable body of 'regulation' literature which there is no space here to discuss. See, for example, 'Networked governance and the post-regulatory state?' (2006), Crawford A, *Theoretical Criminology*, 10: 449, and the papers collected in Quirk H, Seddon T and Smith G (eds), *Regulation*

many ways, what *Part II* of this book is about. The empowering of communities is juxtaposed against regulation by the state because the community is considered to have more potential to tackle its own problems—in this case, criminal problems. The community understands its problems better than a distant state can, and has the self-interest to do something about them.

This approach can be applied to the police station itself. The obvious way of regulating the station more effectively would be for those whose job it is to protect the interests of suspects to monitor and supervise them i.e. legal representatives and friends/family of suspects. Legal representatives attend police stations when requested by suspects, and if the suspected offence is sufficiently serious, but only for a short period of time and on terms dictated by the police. Why not accommodate defence lawyers in police stations? The only acceptable objection—unless one is an extreme crime control adherent—would be cost. But since prosecutors are now stationed in police stations to help the police, the problem is clearly not cost per se, but priorities. And friends/family have even fewer rights to attend and monitor, something that could be changed at almost no cost. The freedom approach, in other words, could lead to a form of 'anchored pluralism' to control the police, whereby control of the police would be dispersed away from the police 'power node', making the rights of suspects more meaningful than now.[29] This would be a form of community empowerment, where 'community' is constituted by professional groups and suspect family/friendship networks as well as by geographical entities.

Conclusion

Without an approach that prioritises aims coherently, crime control aims dominate over other concerns; human rights get reduced to minimal safety nets and/or become political footballs; and economic and political forces

---

and Criminal Justice (CUP, 2010).

29. 'Can coercive powers be effectively controlled or regulated? The case for Anchored Pluralism' (2008), Sanders A, in Cape E and Young R (eds) *Regulating Policing*, Hart. This argument draws on the regulation literature noted above.

are allowed to shape rationales for differential enforcement that make no sense in moral or human terms.

- The freedom approach allows us to:
- incorporate a fluid notion of human rights;
- prioritise constitutionally agreed aims;
- limit the scope of substantive criminal law and coercive powers;
- regulate police power cost-effectively; and
- integrate the way 'normal' and 'regulatory' crime and other social problems are dealt with.

All victims of serious misfortune would be given consideration, according to the scale of their suffering and in view of what is needed to ensure they retain genuine freedom, not according to whether they fall into one politically-motivated category or another. In short, criminal justice agencies (defined broadly) should have mutually consistent policies and practices, and they should be required to treat equal harms and every person equally. Thus 'criminal justice' and 'regulation' are part of the same enterprise. Policies and practices characteristic of one should be used, where appropriate, in the other. This might lead to more use of coercive law enforcement in 'regulatory' crimes, but the greater change would be in the 'criminal justice' sphere, where respect would be given greater prominence, coercion would be used more sparingly, and the least damaging and most freedom-creating 'tools' would be deployed regardless of context.

This approach would be naturally decremental. This is because every application of power is freedom-removing. State power should therefore to be justified by positive effects on freedom (rather than appeals to retribution or the 'rights' of victims). Not only would this restrict state power, and reduce the use of the most coercive (i.e. the most freedom-reducing) state power, it would also push the state into using its powers—all other things being equal—more effectively. Thus genuinely intelligence-led policing would gradually supplant mass stop, search and detention. The middle-classes may dislike the increased surveillance and record-keeping and more invasion of privacy and more extensive DNA databanks that would result. But the poor, marginalised and socially excluded—those who currently suffer most both as victims and as those against whom coercive powers are most used—would benefit. Unfortunately—by definition—the poor, marginalised and socially excluded have little influence over legislation and policy making. In normal circumstances the decremental approach would therefore be most unlikely to be adopted. However, the financial crisis has created a window of opportunity. For once, fewer resources could mean a better service. Reduced resources for police and prisons mean they could be used less. Some of the savings could be channelled into communities to help to generate the voluntary-led 'Big Society': the Prime Minister's Big Idea. In the hope that someone might be listening, this is the subject of *Chapter 14* of this book.

CHAPTER 3

RISK, PRE-EMPTION, AND THE LIMITS OF THE CRIMINAL LAW

JOHN CHILD AND ADRIAN HUNT

Introduction

At the core of state driven approaches to criminal justice is the concept of *criminalisation*. Formally speaking, the initial stage of criminalisation involves the identification of behaviour thought serious or dangerous enough to merit criminal punishment. However the mere identification of such behaviour is not sufficient to criminalise the behaviour. Rather the behaviour must be *defined* in legislation as a criminal offence. This chapter is concerned with a number of key trends and issues associated with the process of identifying behaviour thought worthy of criminalisation, as well as the process of *definition* of such behaviour as a criminal offence. Our particular focus is the use of the process of criminalisation as a tool for pre-empting harm, and therefore punishing those whose behaviour creates the risk that harm may result from their actions.

As will be explained in the next section of this chapter, the use of criminal offences as a pre-emptive tool is distinguishable from their use as an instrument for punishing those who have already caused concrete harms. The popular conception of criminalisation tends to assume it is concerned with behaviour which has caused harm; however in reality the use of the criminal law in its pre-emptive mode — that is to say defining offences which punish those whose behaviour creates the risk that harm may result from their actions—is a pervasive trend. The use of the criminal law in its pre-emptive mode involves extending the boundaries of the criminal law such that it may catch a host of behaviours and actions which are significantly divorced from actually causing concrete harms. In so doing therefore it involves a conscious choice by the state formally to regulate, control or punish actions which would otherwise fall to be controlled, if at all, by informal societal sanctions. Therefore in exploring the use of criminal offences as a pre-emptive tool we are concerned with one of the indicators of the formal boundaries of the 'criminal justice system'.

In this chapter we raise issues associated with justifications for using criminal law as a pre-emptive tool. In so doing we identify and explain a number of different ways in which criminal offences may be defined or used as instruments of pre-emption. We then proceed to examine the consequences of different approaches adopted to defining such offences with a view to examining whether the types of pre-emptive offences currently in use reflect a coherent, consistent and principled justification for criminalisation of such behaviour.

Pre-emptive Offences and Other Criminal Offences Distinguished

The paradigm of criminal law in the liberal tradition involves proscribing culpable actions of persons where those actions cause criminal harm.[1] All elements of the paradigm are the object of constant debate including questions concerning which type of harm is an appropriate target for criminalisation and what should the relationship be between culpability on the one hand and the type and seriousness of the harm caused on the other. However, one feature of the paradigm which is constant is that criminal liability arises only after the harm has been caused. Although there may be some ex ante protection through the deterrent effect of the threat of punishment, nonetheless criminal liability only arises after the victim has actually suffered the criminal harm.

It is arguable that if one accepts that these harms are sufficiently serious and wrongful to justify the imposition of criminal sanction, then it is not unreasonable to suggest that the criminal law ought to be employed to protect people from such harms being caused in the first place by facilitating official intervention before the resulting harm can arise from an offender's conduct. As Anthony Duff argues, '[a] law that condemned and punished actually harm-causing conduct as wrong, but was utterly silent on attempts to cause such harms, and on reckless risk-taking with respect to such harms, would speak with a strange moral voice.'[2]

Thus most developed legal systems have long provided for a mode of criminalisation which departs from the paradigm.[3] This mode criminalises conduct or actions where the offence in question may be characterised as 'non-consummate' because the conduct proscribed 'does not cause harm on each and every occasion in which it is performed.'[4] These offences, which

---

1. Referred to by J. C. Smith as the 'normal' mode of definition. 'The Element of Chance in Criminal Liability' [1971] Smith, *Criminal Law Review* 63.
2. *Criminal Attempts* (1996), Duff R. A, Clarendon Press: Oxford, 134.
3. For example, see 'Taking the Will for the Deed: The Mediaeval Criminal Attempt' (1992) Kiralfy, *The Journal of Legal History* 95.
4. 'The Nature and Justifiability of Non-consummate Offenses' (1995) Husak, 37 *Arizona Law Review* 151, 158.

are variously referred to as 'inchoate' [i.e. just begun], or 'precursor'[5] or 'pre-emptive'[6] or 'preparatory'[7] crimes, come in a variety of different forms. The paradigmatic pre-emptive offences are what may be termed the generally applicable inchoate offences, which target persons who attempt[8] to commit, or conspire,[9] assist or encourage[10] others to commit a principal offence. By definition, attempting, conspiring (i.e. agreeing), assisting or encouraging comes before the substantive harm results. These general inchoate offences therefore facilitate intervention at an earlier stage, with no requirement that the substantive harm results at all.

It should be recognised that there are difficult decisions to be made about criminalising conduct which is prior or preparatory to perceived or feared resulting harms. The legislature and/or the courts have to determine 'the point—within the succession of stages along the criminal path'[11] at which it is justifiable to impose criminal liability and punishment. Should criminal liability attach to early preparatory acts, or should it be confined to acts which are close in causal and time-related proximity to the feared or intended resulting harm? Imposing liability for the former certainly facilitates pre-emptive action; but it involves an even more tenuous link with the harm paradigm. Thus in the current English law of attempts, for instance, criminal liability attaches only to acts which are 'more than merely preparatory to the commission of the offence'.[12] Therefore, although attempt in English law is clearly a departure from the paradigm since it clearly allows for intervention before any harm has resulted, nonetheless there is some relationship between the conduct and the feared resulting harm in the sense that clearly the risk

---

5. *Blackstone's Guide to The Anti-Terrorism Legislation* (2nd ed. 2009) Walker C, Oxford University Press, 182.
6. 'Seeking Security by Eroding Rights: The Side-stepping of Due Process' in *Security and Human Rights* (2007) Zedner, in Goold B J and Lazarus L (eds), Hart Oxford, 259
7. 'Expanding the Boundaries of Inchoate Crimes: The Growing Reliance on Preparatory Offences' in *Regulating Deviance The Redirection of Criminalisation and the Futures of Criminal Law* (2009) McSherry, in McSherry B, Norrie A, and Bronitt S (eds), Hart, Oxford, 141.
8. Contrary to the Criminal Attempts Act 1981, section 1.
9. Contrary to the Criminal Law Act 1977, section 1.
10. Contrary to the Serious Crime Act 2007, Part 2.
11. 'Responding to Acts Preparatory to the Commission of a Crime: Criminalization or Prevention?' (2006) Ohana, 25 *Criminal Justice Ethics* 23.
12. Criminal Attempts Act 1981, section 1(1)

that the harm may result is greater the further along the path of criminal preparation the offender has progressed.

However, the catalogue of non-consummate offences available to English authorities is not confined to the general inchoate offences. It also includes:

- double/infinite inchoate General Offences: For example conspiring with someone to encourage someone else to commit a principal offence;
- bespoke inchoate offences: these are substantive offences that are defined in an inchoate form. For example, the harm associated with fraud by false representation relates to the causing of an illicit gain or loss by way of a misrepresentation. The Fraud Act 2006[13] does not require that gain or loss actually occurs as a consequence of the misrepresentation (it merely requires the person intended his or her misrepresentation to cause this harm);
- endangerment offences: focusing on risk creating conduct. For example, the offence of driving having drunk more than the prescribed limit of alcohol[14] criminalises a driver for creating the risks associated with drink driving, regardless of whether they cause any damage/harm as a consequence of their drink driving; and
- possession offences: Where persons are criminalised for mere possession of things which are considered to be dangerous and therefore may (in the future) lead to harm. For example, possession of a firearm without a certificate.[15]

Hereafter, we will refer to these offences collectively as preparatory offences.[16] Not only are these forms of inchoate liability very common within the criminal law, as we will later explore, they are also capable of biting very much earlier in the process than is the case with the general inchoate offences.

---

13. Section 2.
14. Contrary to the Road Traffic Act 1988, section 5(1).
15. Contrary to the Firearms Act 1968, section 1.
16. We employ the label 'preparatory offences' to distinguish these kinds of inchoate offences from the general inchoate offences. It is a distinction in form and labelling that is explored by McSherry in 'Expanding the Boundaries of Inchoate Crimes: The Growing Reliance on Preparatory Offences' in *Regulating Deviance The Redirection of Criminalisation and the Futures of Criminal Law* (2009) McSherry B, Norrie A, and Bronitt S (eds), Hart, Oxford, 141.

There remains considerable academic controversy about inchoate offences despite their seemingly increasing popularity with the legislature. How remote from or proximate to the anticipated or feared prospective harm may/must the conduct in question be in order to give rise to criminal liability? Is remoteness or proximity in this context to be judged by reference to causative effect; temporal factors; level or degree of danger or possibility that the harm would result or a combination of the all of the above? How relevant is the relative seriousness of the prospective harm anticipated or feared to the decision to impose criminal liability for the conduct? To what extent, if any, is the person's culpability as regards the feared resulting or anticipated harm relevant to the imposition of criminal liability? Must they intend their conduct to result in the harm, or at least be aware of the danger that it will result, or is likely to result in it; or is it sufficient that they are indifferent to, or perhaps subjectively entirely unaware of, the danger even if a 'reasonable' person would be alive to it?

In acknowledging these issues we are presented with the problem that if we maintain harm as the paradigm of the criminal law, then we must recognise inchoate liability as an exception to or (minimally) an extension of that paradigm. Therefore, to employ the criminal law to punish persons in the absence of primary resulting harms — to extend the boundaries of the criminal liability — we must identify special justifications.[17] The requirement of a special justification or a compelling reason for extending the law in this way is most expressly evident within debates surrounding the general inchoate offences. In a recent flurry of Law Commission[18] publications in this area, the Commission evidently still believes that it not only has to restate the advantages of inchoate liability in terms of pre-empting future harm, but that in certain cases it must do so in order to justify their very existence.[19] Then, having established a basis, we are led in each case through a detailed discussion of where the lines of criminal intervention should be drawn. We

---

17. It is the exploration of these 'special' justifications that we turn to in the second part of this chapter.
18. The Law Commission was established by the Law Commissioners Act 1965, with the express statutory purpose of promoting the reform of the law.
19. See, for example, *Conspiracy and Attempts: A Consultation Paper* (Law Com. Consultation No. 183, 2007) The Law Commission, Part 2.

balance the ability of the police to make a timely intervention against the opportunity of the defendant to change his or her mind: we examine whether reliance placed on the mental element of the offence (often gained through confessions) will expose the defendant to the risk of police abuse: and we examine the relative culpability of an offender as his or her conduct moves closer to the principal harm and so on. Consistent principles of liability are identified and then applied.[20]

However, as we have already identified, inchoate liability extends back considerably further than the core general inchoate offences. Therefore, in the light of our discussion above, it would be reasonable to imagine that these preparatory offences are subject to a similar level of scrutiny. In fact, as many of these offences are designed to criminalise persons at a considerably earlier stage than is the case with the general inchoate offences (hence the need for the offences at all), the justifications for their existence must surely be even more special. However, preparatory offences have too often been perceived as special exceptions that are not subject to the more general rules and not subject to the same levels of scrutiny. Indeed, it is almost as if their specialism somehow exempts them from any discussion about whether they cast the net of criminality too widely. This is a phenomenon that seems to touch the work of several academics,[21] and can be perceived in that of the Law Commission. For example, in the recent review of attempts liability, the Commission sets out a list of preparatory offences that criminalise the conduct of persons before they have reached the stage of an attempt.[22] They also observe that, aside from hypothetical examples, the list of offences is so comprehensive that they are not able to demonstrate any previous cases that fell short of an attempt that were not caught by one of these preparatory offences. Yet despite the cumulative breadth of these offences, despite their inconsistencies in terms of physical and mental elements, the Commission simply presents them as a background to their sole focus of the

---

20. This is discussed in the second part of this chapter.
21. For example, most criminal law textbooks discuss the boundaries of the criminal law in relation to general inchoate offences without more than a passing aside about other preparatory offences that will criminalise certain conduct at a considerably earlier stage.
22. *Conspiracy and Attempts: A Consultation Paper* (Law Com. Consultation No. 183, 2007) The Law Commission, Appendix C.

general offence of attempt. The problem with this is that when we reach a discussion of the boundaries of the criminal law based upon the consultation questions, we are not discussing the true boundary. Even if consultees had accepted the modest extension proposed by the Commission to create a new offence of criminal preparation,[23] such an offence would still be preceded by a collection of preparatory offences.

In the next part of this chapter, we explore the potential justifications for inchoate non-consummate offences. We analyse not only the principles governing the boundaries of attempts and conspiracies, but also those governing other inchoate exceptions to the harm paradigm. In so doing it is important not to imply that justifications have never or could never be made for the various preparatory offences. The problem is not always simply a lack of justification, but that such offences are too often viewed, and therefore appraised, within a vacuum rather than as part of a system of preparatory offences which ought to form a coherent whole. Therefore we ask whether the justifications which are offered for the general inchoate offences can be generalised across other similar offences, and if not, why not?

A Search for Coherence

A search for coherence requires a search for legal principles underpinning and shaping the expansion of the criminal law beyond the harm paradigm. As the physical part (otherwise known as the conduct element or *actus reus*) of the inchoate offences move further away from the anticipated harm, how are these offences constructed in order to justify the continued use of criminal sanctions?

The obvious starting point for this inquiry is to focus on the governing principles which the Law Commission recently identified as being relevant for the purposes of justifying the imposition of criminal liability for the general inchoate offences of attempt, conspiracy and assisting and encouraging.

---

23. *Conspiracy and Attempts* (Law Com No. 318, 2009) The Law Commission [8.1-8.82]. The Commission have presented this not as an extension, but as a return to the original intentions of the legislature.

The Commission's recent review of these offences, which resulted in recommendations for a further broadening of the law,[24] identified two separate (but interrelated) governing principles which are important within this context.

The first principle is that, although the future harm may not yet have arisen, the *actus reus* of the offence must still target conduct which (of its nature) gives rise to a sufficient cause for concern: conduct that creates a risk or danger of the ultimate harm occurring such that this justifies official intervention before it comes about. Thus, for criminal attempts, in the Commission's view, this required police to wait until a person's actions have gone beyond mere preparation towards the commission of the principal offence; they must therefore have reached a stage in the criminal pathway such that the risk of harm occurring effectively outweighs the potential that they may desist voluntarily.[25] For conspiracy and assisting and encouraging, the Commission focused on the increased likelihood of the harm coming about where people collude in their activities.[26] Thus, although a person's actions might be further removed from the eventual harm than is the case with an attempt (not going beyond mere preparation), the act of collusion itself manifests a comparable level of danger that the harm may come about, such as to justify official intervention.

The second principle focuses on the blameworthiness (otherwise known as the mental element or the *mens rea*) of the offender. Here, adopting the language of Ashworth, the Commission states that:

> ... as the form of criminal liability moves further away from the infliction of harm, so the grounds of liability should become more narrow.[27]

---

24. The broadening has focused particularly on the *mens rea* requirements of each offence. See, *Inchoate Liability for Assisting and Encouraging Crime* (Law Com. No 300, 2006) The Law Commission, and *Conspiracy and Attempts* (Law Com. No 318, 2009) The Law Commission. The former provided the basis of the Serious Crime Act 2007, Part 2.
25. This does not represent a change from the position under the current law as stated in the Criminal Attempts Act 1981, section 1.
26. *Conspiracy and Attempts: A Consultation Paper* (Law Com. Consultation 183, 2007) The Law Commission [2.11-2.19].
27. *Principles of Criminal Law* (5th ed, 2006) Ashworth, Oxford University Press, 423. Endorsed by the Commission in *Conspiracy and Attempts: A Consultation Paper* (Law Com. Consultation 183, 2007) The Law Commission [1.6-1.7] and *Inchoate Liability for Assisting and Encouraging Crime* (Law Com. No 300, 2006) The Law Commission [5.86].

Starting with the remoteness of the *actus reus* from the eventual harm, this second principle (which the Commission calls the remoteness principle) goes considerably further than the first in terms of satisfying the objectives of our current inquiry. This is not simply because the remoteness principle dictates that inchoate offences should require high threshold levels of *mens rea*. It is also because it purports to provide a basis for extending liability in an objectively measurable coherent manner: as we move further from the feared resulting harm, a higher degree of *mens rea* is required in order to maintain a broadly consistent level of culpability,[28] a level required to justify the imposition of criminal sanctions.

The normative and practical importance of this second principle (if applied consistently) and the logic of its approach should not be underestimated. Seeking to maintain a constant standard through the balancing of *actus reus* and *mens rea* requirements, the remoteness principle purports to provide a basis for safeguarding against the creation of inchoate offences that criminalise insufficiently culpable behaviour.[29] Indeed, there is a relationship between the mental element and the risk/dangerousness associated with the conduct element where the former has an impact on the latter. Engaging in particular conduct with the intention that that conduct will contribute towards the commission of a criminal offence clearly presents a greater prospect that the resulting harm (the criminal offence) will occur than might be the case if the person engaging in the conduct has some version of *mens rea* below 'intention'.

The remoteness principle ought also to operate as a basis for ensuring that offences targeting the different stages of a person's behaviour leading up to an eventual harm do not undermine one another. Thus, for a criminal

---

28. We are assuming that other variables, for example the maximum penalty for the principal offence and the wrong constituted by the *actus reus* of that offence, remain constant. For a wider discussion of the role played by these variables, see 'Crimes of Ulterior Intent' (1996) Horder in *Harm and Culpability*, Simester and Smith (eds), Clarendon Press, 153.
29. For example, if a shopkeeper sells a product intending the buyer to use that product for an illegal purpose then it is right to prosecute him for assisting the future offence. However, if the shopkeeper sells the product merely foreseeing the possibility that it might be used for such a purpose, the imposition of criminal sanctions are likely to appear unwarranted. For further discussion, see *Inchoate Liability for Assisting and Encouraging Crime* (Law Com. No 300, 2006) The Law Commission [5.87].

attempt it is always necessary for a person to intend to bring about the principal offence,[30] even if the definition of the principal offence itself does not require intention. Therefore, where it is clear that the defendant has satisfied the *actus reus* of the principal offence (brought about the harm), it will always be more appropriate for a prosecutor to charge them with that principal offence rather than with criminal attempt. Were the *mens rea* of the attempt or conspiracy or other inchoate offence to be less restrictive than that of the principal offence, prosecutors would have an incentive to charge the inchoate offence even where the harm had been brought about. This would cause problems both in terms of sentencing and fair labelling, since the charge would not reflect the full extent of the defendant's crime, and would have the potential to make the substantive offences redundant.[31]

In this manner, an apparently straightforward principle linking the remoteness of a person's conduct to the level of *mens rea* required for inchoate liability has the potential to provide the consistency and coherence that we are searching for. Just as we can identify the natural limits of the spectrum of *mens rea* (intention), so we may also identify the limits of the *actus reus*: the most remote behaviour that a person can be justifiably criminalised for on the basis of his or her intention to cause a future harm. Furthermore, in practice it can serve to discourage prosecutors from undercutting substantive offences, and contribute to the normative concerns associated with fair labelling.

However, as the physical remoteness of the general inchoate offences have already required a *mens rea* of 'intention',[32] it is arguable that it is dif-

---

30. The Criminal Attempts Act 1981, section 1. Although recklessness may in some instances be sufficient in relation to the circumstance element (see *R v Khan* [1990] 1 W.L.R. 813), this will only arise where the circumstance element of the principal offence requires a *mens rea* of recklessness or less. Further, intention is still required for the act and result elements. In this manner, the essence of the offence is still the requirement of intention.
31. The Law Commission also recognises this danger in their discussion of conspiracy, stating unequivocally that the creation of a disincentive to charge a substantive offence in favour of an inchoate alternative would 'not be right'. *Conspiracy and Attempts: A Consultation Paper* (Law Com Consultation 183, 2007) The Law Commission [4.55-4.56].
32. The exception being the reformed offences of assisting and encouraging (Serious Crime Act 2007, Part 2) that require varying levels of *mens rea* including belief as to the principal offender's future conduct and recklessness as to the future consequences and surrounding circumstances of that conduct. However, it is important to note that where the *mens rea* of

ficult to see how preparatory offences can be structured to target conduct that is further removed from the eventual harm: if 'intention' is the highest level of fault then it is arguable that the general inchoate offences should also mark the physical boundaries of the criminal law. However, as we have already explained above, the statute book contains a multitude of preparatory offences that target conduct that is more remote from harm than that targeted by the general inchoate offences.

The first category of preparatory offences targets conduct (more remote from harm than the general inchoate offences) only when the person *intends* that the eventual harm should come about. The most widely applicable example of this form of liability can be identified through double or infinite inchoate liability. This form of liability criminalises a person (D) for conduct which is a further step removed from the principal offence, for example, where D conspires with Y to encourage Z to commit an offence.[33] For liability to arise D must intend that Y should encourage Z, and must *also* intend that Z commit the principal offence. The problem here is that, although D's conduct is a further step removed from the eventual harm than is the case with conspiracy to commit the principal offence, the *mens rea* of intention is not fundamentally different from that required if D was conspiring with Y to commit the offence directly. As a result, double inchoate liability appears to be inconsistent with the remoteness principle, leading to potential problems relating to inappropriate extensions of the law and the undermining of more proximate offences.

Of course it is possible to construct a justification for double inchoate liability. In the above example, it is not sufficient that D intended Z to commit the principal offence; D must *also* intend Y to encourage Z to do so. Therefore, although the level of fault (intention) has not changed from a standard conspiracy, there are further aspects of the offence that must be intended. However, even if one were to accept this justification of double

---

the principal offence requires a higher degree of fault, D's *mens rea* will reflect that higher standard. Therefore, for the most serious offences (used as examples in much of this chapter) D will still require intention.

33. The breadth of conduct coming within this form of liability has been considerably expanded by the Serious Crime Act 2007, Part 2. Notably, for example, it is now an offence for D to assist or encourage P to form a conspiracy with another party to commit a principal offence.

inchoate liability,[34] several other preparatory offences of similar physical remoteness do not include this added double intention requirement. For example, section 25(1) of the Theft Act 1968 criminalises persons for possession of any article with the intention to use that article to commit theft or burglary. With this offence, as with others of a similar construction, the conduct element is considerably further removed than a criminal attempt for example, and yet an intention to commit the future offence is deemed to be a sufficient *mens rea*.

The problems which this approach throws up can be demonstrated by the simple example of someone (D) intentionally shooting a victim (V). In this example, when D first acquires the firearm, they may well become liable for a possession offence (possession of a firearm with intent by means thereof to endanger life);[35] as D goes beyond mere preparation towards the shooting of V, there will be liability for attempted murder;[36] and when the harm (V's death) is brought about, D will be liable for murder.[37] One can identify a raising of the *mens rea* requirement between the substantive offence and the attempt[38] (in line with the principle explained above) since liability for murder will arise if D intends to kill or intends to cause grievous bodily harm, whereas liability for attempted murder will only arise if D intends to cause death. However, there appears to be little difference in *mens rea* terms to mark the difference between attempt and the possession offence. Whilst it is not our suggestion that this behaviour with the appropriate intent ought not necessarily to be a criminal offence, it is not consistent with the remoteness principle which it is claimed ought to provide a consistent basis for deciding where to draw the line between conduct which may or may not

---

34. Although we recognise the desirability of certain forms of double inchoate liability, we are not inclined to accept this line of defence. This is because, as D moves further steps away from the eventual harm, the causal role played by his or her conduct will be significantly reduced. We do not accept that an intention that another party should play their intermediate part is sufficient replacement.
35. The Firearms Act 1968, section 16(1).
36. Contrary to the Criminal Attempts Act 1981, section 1. We are assuming that D does not have a valid defence.
37. Again, we are assuming that D does not have a valid defence.
38. For attempted murder, D must intend to cause death. An intention to cause GBH, sufficient for a substantive murder charge, will not be enough.

justifiably be criminalised. Furthermore the possession offence provides the distinct possibility of undermining more proximate offences (in this case the criminal attempt).[39]

Despite the problems just explained with this category of inchoate offences, we can identify other categories of offence which present an even more serious challenge to the coherence of the law in this area. This is because, although the majority of preparatory offences, like those just mentioned, require persons to intend to bring about a future harm, there are other offences which in addition to targeting similarly remote conduct, require a *mens rea* less than full intention. For example, section 15(2) of the Terrorism Act 2000 provides that a person commits an offence if they receive money and they either intend using that money for terrorist purposes, or have 'reasonable cause to suspect that it may be used' for such purposes. Although receiving money is considerably earlier in the criminal pathway than an attempt to provide financial support for terrorist purposes, the 'reasonable cause to suspect' requirement involves a standard of *mens rea* which is lower than intention. Therefore this offence departs considerably from the remoteness principle in relation to both *actus reus* and *mens rea* requirements, rendering it almost impossible to reconcile within our search for coherence. As such, offences within this category pose a considerable risk of inappropriate criminalisation as well as undermining other more proximate offences.

Of course, it is certainly the case that when offences within this category are examined individually, out of context with other inchoate offences, it *may* be possible to justify their existence. This is because, although they are inconsistent with principles identified generally to guide the expansion of inchoate liability, we certainly would not deny that the future harms that they are designed to prevent (focusing overwhelmingly in recent times upon terrorism and sexual offences) represent some of the most potentially serious within the criminal law. Indeed, there are several interrelated reasons that could be invoked to defend the creation of such offences that focus on the seriousness of the future harm and the difficulty of securing convictions

---

39. In the case of certain preparatory offences, it may be contended that a significantly lower maximum sentence will mitigate the chance of more proximate offences being undermined. However, this is not always the case. Each of the offences in this example, including the possession offence, carries a maximum penalty of life imprisonment.

if a higher standard of *mens rea* were to be required. However, the problem with this kind of focused justification for the offence is that it begs a simple question. If such reasons are sufficiently powerful to set aside the remoteness principle, and if it is these reasons that are guiding the outer boundaries of criminal liability, then why are they applied in such an inconsistent manner?

In order to demonstrate the inconsistency of the current law, and the absurdities that it can lead to, we may take the example of section 58(1) of the Sexual Offences Act 2003, which is useful because it is capable of coming within either of the two categories of preparatory offence just discussed. Section 58 of the Act provides:

> 58(1) A person [D] commits an offence if he intentionally arranges or facilitates travel within the United Kingdom by another person (B) and either—
>
> (a) he intends to do anything to or in respect of B, during or after the journey and in any part of the world, which if done will involve the commission of a relevant offence, [e.g. rape and sexual offences including child sex offences] or
>
> (b) he believes that another person is likely to do something to or in respect of B, during or after the journey and in any part of the world, which if done will involve the commission of a relevant offence

Section 58(1)(a) provides an example of the first category of offences, criminalising a person (D) at a very remote stage, based on his or her intention to commit a future sexual offence. Section 58(1)(b), on the other hand, comes into the second category. This is because, for D to be liable under this provision, although the *actus reus* requirement remains very remote from the eventual harm, D's *mens rea* (in relation to the potential future offence to be committed by someone else) is set at a level akin to a form of recklessness: belief in a likelihood.

Focusing first on section 58(1)(b) and the second category currently under discussion, once again one *may* be able to justify the manner in which the offence has been constructed. Clearly, the remoteness of D's *actus reus* and the lower levels of *mens rea* demonstrate an abandonment of the remoteness principle, which it will be recalled is that 'as the form of criminal liability moves further away from the infliction of harm, so the grounds of liability should become more narrow'. However, if D is willing to arrange travel for another, knowing that that person is likely to become a victim of a serious sexual assault at some stage during that journey or shortly afterwards, they certainly demonstrate a high level of culpability. The use of criminal sanction seems justified. But if this is indeed an adequate justification, why is it not extended to other future harms not catered for within this section? Murder is one of the most serious offences in English law. However, if D arranges travel for, and even travels with another person believing that it is likely that that person will be killed by someone else, D will not have committed an offence: in order to be liable for assisting the murder of B, D must (at least) believe that the conduct of that other person leading to B's death *will* take place.[40]

Turning to section 58(1)(a) which is an example of the first category of preparatory offence, here too a similar level of inconsistency is apparent. Section 58(1)(a) criminalises the same remote conduct of D (arranging or facilitating the movement of B), but this time on the basis that D *intends* to personally commit a relevant sexual offence at some point during or shortly after that journey. Again, one might make the case that such an offence is justified: if D intends to commit a relevant offence and has already started on the road towards its commission by arranging travel, why wait until he or she has actually gone beyond mere preparation towards the commission of that offence before intervening with the criminal law. However, again using the offence of murder as our point of comparison, such a justification must surely fail. If D arranges for the travel of B with the intention to kill B at some point during or shortly after that journey, there can be no criminal liability until a very late stage: since liability for attempted murder will not arise until D has gone beyond mere preparation towards the killing of B.

Given that the remoteness principle is identified as the basis for regulating or controlling the acceptable limits of the criminal law the discussion above indicates a basic inconsistency in its application, and a consequent incoherence in the approach to non-consummate offences. Of course, we are aware that the consistency argument may lead to a different conclusion. It might

---

40. The Serious Crime Act 2007, Part 2.

be argued that if the problem is merely with the consistency of application of the remoteness principle then this could be resolved by allowing all serious offences (including murder) to be covered by both categories of preparatory offence. In other words intention would not be required. The problem with such a suggestion, however, is that it would create a very strange relationship between the preparatory offences and the substantive offence itself. One could only be convicted of murder if one intended to kill or cause grievous bodily harm. Whereas one could be convicted of attempted murder, say, on the basis that one is reckless as to whether conduct [which does not actually result in death] might actually do so.

The practical confines of this chapter do not allow us to enter this secondary debate with any degree of detail. However, the recognition that this is a debate that should be waged, and the recognition that it is preparatory offences, as distinct from the general inchoate offences, which mark the true boundary of the criminal law, at least provides us with a more appropriate starting point for engaging in a coherent discussion of the issues. Issues associated with deciding the most appropriate approach conceptually to criminalising non-consummate harms, as well as allowing for a principled approach to examining how such offences individually should be defined. It is our contention that it is only when preparatory offences of this kind are recognised, not as the exception, but as fundamental parts of our criminal law, that they will be given the same level of scrutiny that is currently focused upon the general inchoate offences of attempt, conspiracy and assisting and encouraging. As we noted in relation to these general offences, reform is not simply focused upon whether we would like to be able to intervene using the criminal law, but rather it is based upon the balancing of a range of factors including the importance of individual autonomy and the confining of the criminal law to the most culpable offenders (as protected by the remoteness principle).

Conclusion

As we move ever more into an age of intelligence-led policing, the increasing role of inchoate liability may be viewed as a measure of success: the criminal law is intervening to protect the community from the risk of harm by facilitating official action before the harm is brought about. However, criminalisation requires principled justification, and theory and practice need to accord with one another. The current approach which regards the proliferation of preparatory offences, not as further extensions of the criminal law that must be subjected to the same scrutiny as the general inchoate offences, but as exceptions that can be tolerated without further examination, is not acceptable for a number of reasons. First it disengages these other inchoate offences from the remoteness principle which is the principled basis offered both as a justification for inchoate liability as well as the organising principle for defining such offences. Secondly, it serves to present an inaccurate account of where the true boundary for criminalisation lies: the true boundary is not the general inchoate offences; rather it is the forms of preparatory offence which we have examined above, which target conduct prior to that which is caught by the general inchoate offences, and in doing so may apply lower standards of *mens rea* than is the case with the general inchoate offences. In addition to the practical problem which this presents in terms of undercutting general inchoate offences, this means that we have no coherent theory which justifies the exception in the light of the apparent rule.

In arriving at this conclusion we are aware that we have not provided solutions to the problems of theoretical and practical dissonance which we have identified. This is a task which requires considerably more in terms of space and scope than the current practical constraints of this chapter allow. We have instead here contented ourselves with the more limited, but important, preliminary task of asking the question whether the first principles as conventionally offered make sense in the light of current practice. For the reasons set out above, we conclude they do not, which in turn makes it all the more incumbent on those with an interest in this field to begin to engage in a deeper and grander exploration of the conceptual basis for criminalisation, as well as a more extensive examination and systematic identification of different types of preparatory offences than has been possible within the scope of this chapter.

CHAPTER 4

CRIMINALISING THE PURCHASE OF SEXUAL SERVICES: THE USE OF STRICT LIABILITY AS A FORM OF RISK MANAGEMENT?

JESSICA ELLIOTT

Introduction

It is undisputed that coercion and sexual exploitation constitute particularly problematic aspects of the sex trade, and have the potential to adversely affect not only persons trafficked for the purpose of sexual exploitation but also migrant and domestic sex workers. In any situation where sexual services are purchased, there is the risk that the sale of these services does not take place with the full consent of the sex worker. Forced or coerced sex work is clearly a matter of social concern — this, coupled with human trafficking featuring high on the Labour government's political agenda over recent years,[1] has led to a criminal law response in the United Kingdom (UK) which comprises somewhat of an unprincipled departure from the norm, focussing on the risk of harm rather than the culpability of the purchaser.

The perceived prevalence of coerced prostitution and human trafficking for that purpose has meant that the focus in recent years has shifted from the sex worker to the client. The fact that prostitution itself is not criminalised in the UK (although a plethora of related offences[2] surround it) indicates

---

1. The Coalition government of May 2010 (comprised of the Conservative and Liberal Democrat Parties) makes no specific mention of trafficking or prostitution policy in the manifesto, available at libdems.org.uk/latest_news_detail.aspx?title=The_Coalition%3a_our_programme_for_government&pPK=084cfed9-12f0-45da-ae34-341d01645295 (accessed 18/07/2010).
2. Including soliciting, brothel keeping and the use of cards in telephone boxes to advertise

that it is accepted that one has the right to sell sex. But, does the purchaser have the right to buy it, particularly when this 'right' or 'freedom' is juxtaposed against the risk that the seller is forced or coerced, and therefore does not consent to the provision of the services purchased? This very question is addressed by the Policing and Crime Act 2009 (PCA),[3] section 14 of which targets the purchaser of sexual services in certain situations, as a method of risk management.

A decade ago, in response to a Parliamentary question Lord Williams of Mostyn stated that:

> In considering whether new offences should be created, factors taken into account include whether: the behaviour in question is sufficiently serious to warrant intervention by the criminal law; the mischief could be dealt with under existing legislation or by using other remedies; the proposed offence is enforceable in practice; the proposed offence is tightly drawn and legally sound; the proposed penalty is commensurate with the seriousness of the offence.[4]

In the light of the above mentioned statement, this chapter provides an analysis of the strict liability offence provided within section 14[5] of the PCA — a controversial legislative measure, the enactment of which arguably requires strong justification. Examples from other jurisdictions will be drawn upon where appropriate, to illustrate the potential effects of this novel legislative move. Ultimately, this chapter questions the ability of the central State to make a positive impact through the use of the criminal law in terms of targeting purchasers of sexual services, and concludes that in the face of the unwelcome side-effects that such measures are likely to bring, the State would do better to regulate the sex trade rather than expand the reach of the criminal law in the manner illustrated by the PCA provision.

---

sexual services. The relevant provisions can be found in the Sexual Offences Act 2003, Street Offences Act 1959, Criminal Justice and Police Act 2001 and the Sexual Offences Act 1956.
3. In force from 1 April 2010 www.opsi.gov.uk/acts/acts2009/ukpga_20090026_en_1 (accessed 12/07/2010).
4. Lord Williams of Mostyn, written response to a question by Lord Dholakia, HL Debates, vol 602, WA 57 (June 18, 1999).
5. Amending the Sexual Offences Act 2003, section 53

Criminalising the Prostitute User: Tackling the 'Demand'

According to Section 51(2) of the Sexual Offences Act 2003, a 'prostitute' is:

> ... a person (A) who, on at least one occasion and whether or not compelled to do so, offers or provides sexual services to another person in return for payment or a promise of payment to A or a third person; and "prostitution" is to be interpreted accordingly.

This definition indicates that it is possible to prostitute one's self and also to be prostituted by another, illustrating the potentially coercive and exploitative nature of sex work in some circumstances. However, prostitution is not simply either the result of free will on one hand or coercion/force on the other. These are two opposite points on a spectrum along which all prostitution-related activities may be placed.

Within the past decade, international anti-trafficking legislation has entered into force in the form of the United Nations Protocol to Prevent, Suppress and Punish Trafficking in Persons, Especially Women and Children, supplementing the United Nations Convention against Transnational Organised Crime, and the Council of Europe Convention on Action against Trafficking in Human Beings.[6] Both instruments encourage state parties to adopt or strengthen legislative measures to discourage 'demand' for sexual services. Although not all were conceived specifically as anti-trafficking measures, various countries have in recent years enacted legislation which is aimed to combat sexual exploitation from the demand side. At the turn of the century, Sweden imposed a blanket ban on the purchase of sexual services in any situation.[7] This approach has subsequently been replicated in Iceland, Norway, South Africa and Korea. Other jurisdictions have taken a more qualified approach–Finland, in 2006, made an amendment to the Finnish Penal Code which criminalised the purchase of sexual services from victims of pimping or trafficking. The UK approach sits somewhere between the two.

---

6. *Council of Europe Convention on Action against Trafficking in Human Being and its Explanatory Report*, Warsaw, 16.V.2005, Council of Europe Treaty Series—No. 197.
7. Law (1998:408) Prohibition of the Purchase of Sexual Services.

Originally, proposals for measures to address demand in the UK mirrored those of the Swedish model. These proposals were welcomed by some, not least by certain MPs,[8] but were vehemently opposed by others.[9] Acceptance by the UK government and legislature that while prostitution exists, the sex worker should not be criminalised for the actual act of selling sexual services, shows a tolerant attitude to this form of 'vice' in some respects. The original proposals not only challenged the assumption that prostitution must exist (and therefore we simply have to accept it), they also appeared to be aiming to achieve a normative shift in attitudes towards prostitution.

Following a six-month review into tackling the demand for prostitution,[10] the proposals for the UK were reconsidered and presented as somewhat of a pared-down version of what was initially considered, the focus now being upon the criminalisation of the purchase of sexual services only where certain conditions are present. Some backtracking on the language to be used in the legislation was criticised.[11] The original terminology which proposed to criminalise the purchaser where the sex worker is 'controlled for gain' was amended to instead specifically target purchasers where the sex worker is — by a third party — subjected to 'force, threats (whether or not relating to violence) or any other form of coercion, or ... any form of deception.'[12] This position is now reflected in section 14 of the PCA.[13] The legislation will therefore apply, for example, in the situation where the sex worker has a pimp or has been trafficked.

The usual position in criminal law is that individual crimes are comprised of the elements of *actus reus* and *mens rea* — the conduct element and the mental element. All elements must be shown to be present before a guilty

---

8. Many examples may be found throughout Hansard; see for example Hansard HC vol 470 Column 481 (9 January 2008).
9. 'Our sex lives are our own business' (16 September 2007), Henry Porter, *The Observer* www.guardian.co.uk/commentisfree/2007/sep/16/comment.labour (accessed 11/11/2008).
10. *Tackling the Demand for Prostitution: A Review* (November 2008), Home Office. Now available at: http://webarchive.nationalarchives.gov.uk/20100418065544/http://homeoffice.gov.uk/documents/tackling-demand2835.pdf?view=Binary
11. *Smith accused over prostitute law*, BBC News, 19 May 2009 news.bbc.co.uk/1/hi/uk/8056767.stm (accessed 21/05/2009).
12. Policing and Crime Act 2009, section 14(3)(a) and (b).
13. Policing and Crime Act 2009, section 14.

verdict can be reached. However, certain crimes can be committed even in absence of *mens rea*—such crimes are categorised as 'strict liability' offences. The offence provided within section 14 PCA is one of strict liability; therefore departing from the usual position that *mens rea* must be proven in order to incur criminal liability. There is no defence of 'reasonable excuse or due diligence',[14] so that pleading ignorance (as to the status of the sex worker as forced or coerced) will not help the position of the prostitute user in terms of legal culpability, and it follows from this that those who purchase sexual services with the knowledge that the sex worker has been forced, coerced or trafficked could face being charged with rape. This implies a multi-level approach, in that those who use a controlled sex worker in ignorance will be prosecuted regardless, and those who knowingly do so may be prosecuted for the much more serious offence of rape. The new strict liability offence carries sanctions of a substantial fine, and a criminal record. This contentious legislative move reflects the aim of risk-management: within the framework of the strict liability offence, criminalisation targets the defendant even in absence of *mens rea*, in order to address the 'risk' that the sex worker may not be free from force/coercion, and therefore has not truly consented to the provision of sexual services.

Why Target the Purchaser?

Ashworth criticises governmental tendencies to create new crimes without adequate justification.[15] The PCA provision is clearly controversial. Accordingly, one might ask why such measures have been employed, and whether the reasons are sufficient to justify criminal sanction. Outshoorn recognises that 'states have traditionally tried to curb prostitution for a variety of reasons, such as preserving morals, maintaining public order, containing the spread of sexually transmitted diseases (STDs), or to protect women from sexual exploitation.'[16] On the face of it, these reasons point to eradication,

---

14. 'Is the Criminal Law a Lost Cause?' (2000), Ashworth, *Law Quarterly Review* 225, 228.
15. *Ibid*, 225.
16. 'The Political Debates on Prostitution and Trafficking of Women' (2005) Outshoorn J, *Social Politics: International Studies in Gender, State and Society* Vol 12, number 1, 141-155, 141.

particularly in terms of the coerced (and therefore non-consenting) sex worker, but it is necessary to consider whether they are sufficient to justify criminalisation, particularly in terms of the potential for adverse side effects flowing from this legislative measure.

In 1957, the Departmental Committee on Homosexual Offences and Prostitution (Wolfenden Committee) produced a report[17] which expressed the position that criminalising the purchase of sold sex was inconsistent with liberal criminal law principles, but it did at the same time identify that there were problems surrounding prostitution which needed to be addressed.[18] Sexual exploitation and forced or coerced sex work clearly fall within this category. Yet, if a prostitute is forced or coerced, then criminalisation should surely target the creation of the harms; namely the individual(s) responsible for exerting force or coercion. There is not necessarily any intended harm here on the part of the purchaser. As with other legislative 'risk-management' measures, the aim of the strict liability offence provided within the PCA is 'to "manage" sources of risk to the public by means of preventative measures.'[19] Accordingly, any purchaser of sexual services in the UK at present does so with the risk that he has, albeit unknowingly and potentially in a situation beyond his control, committed an offence.[20]

If the purchase of sold sex outright, or at least the purchase of sold sex in forced or coercive circumstances (with the force or coercion coming from the trafficker, pimp, or other relevant actor) is criminalised with an adequate sanction as deterrent, it can be argued that this sort of measure has the potential to positively target the resulting 'harm' that arises due to lack of consent, or the risk thereof. In 2005, Dempsey considered whether 'blame', as such, for harm which may occur as a result of the purchase of sexual services, was fairly imputable to 'johns' i.e. prostitute users.[21] She

---

17. *Report of the Departmental Committee on Homosexual Offences and Prostitution* (1957) Wolfenden Committee, HMSO.
18. 'Committee on Homosexual Offences and Prostitution' (1958), Hammelmann H A, *Modern Law Review*, Vol. 21, No. 1, 68-73.
19. 'Social control and "anti-social behaviour": the subversion of human rights?' (2004), Ashworth A, *Law Quarterly Review*, 263, 271–272.
20. 'Editorial—The Policing and Crime Act 2009' (2010) *Criminal Law Review*, 2, 91—92, 91.
21. See 'Rethinking Wolfenden: Prostitute-Use, Criminal Law, and Remote Harm' (2005), Dempsey M, *Criminal Law Review*, 444–455.

concluded that criminalisation of the purchase of sexual services is desirable in the following situations:

1. where the prostitute is forced and the client is aware of this;
2. where the prostitute is forced and the client is unaware of this; and
3. where the prostitute is not in any way forced or coerced.[22]

This approach would, therefore, welcome blanket criminalisation of the purchase of sexual services, such as is in place in Sweden. One of Dempsey's main arguments underpinning these conclusions was to look at solicitation for prostitute use (SPU) as an abstract endangerment offence.[23] She asserts that SPU 'creates an unacceptable risk of the harm of rape',[24] and cites in some depth von Hirsch's exploration of the criminalisation of remote harms:[25] von Hirsch states that abstract endangerment will arise where the risk of harm of the conduct 'depends on the existence of a contingency ... [and] it is not known or knowable to the actor ex ante whether that contingency will materialise in the particular situation.'[26] Therefore, the criminalisation of the purchase of sexual services is based on a contingency i.e. is the potential for collateral damage (i.e. rape, or unknown lack of consent on the part of the sex worker) sufficient to justify either outright criminalisation, as has taken place in Sweden, or criminalisation of a certain category, such as is provided for by the PCA.

Sex workers come with no promise of lack of coercion—the purchaser therefore almost always takes a risk when purchasing sex. The purchase of sexual services from one who does not consent can be considered to be a serious wrong; therefore criminalising the purchase of sexual services from forced or coerced persons may seem to be *prima facie* justified. This novel

---

22. See 'Rethinking Wolfenden: Prostitute-Use, Criminal Law, and Remote Harm' (2005), Dempsey M, *Criminal Law Review*, 448.
23. *Ibid*, 449.
24. *Ibid*.
25. See 'Extending the Harm Principle: "Remote" Harms and Fair Imputation' (1996) Andrew von Hirsch, in A. P. Simester and A. T. H. Smith (eds), *Harm and Culpability*, Clarenden Press, Oxford.
26. *Ibid*, 236.

legislative measure undeniably has some merit, but it also carries with it certain problems.

Is Criminal Sanction Justified?

Numerous arguments can be offered as to why the use of a strict liability offence such as that provided within the PCA is undesirable. The provision imposes a problematic evidential burden, it will be difficult to enforce, and evidence suggests that the deterrent value may not be as great as is anticipated. Further, there is a lack of solid empirical evidence with regard to what proportion for sex work is forced or coerced in the UK to justify the enactment of the law. Finally, there is a risk that demand sanction legislation will simply have the effect of forcing prostitution further underground, thereby increasing the risks for vulnerable sex workers. These issues will be evaluated in turn.

i) Evidential difficulties, and lack of enforceability

Regarding the structuring of the PCA, the Home Office stated that:

> Given the practical difficulties in proving whether a defendant knew if a woman was controlled or not — the new offence should be a strict liability offence, to aid prosecution and to remove any ambiguity from possible offenders minds about the potential consequences of sex with a trafficked or exploited woman.[27]

There are clear evidential difficulties inherent in criminalising solely those who had knowledge or who were 'reckless' as to whether the sex worker was forced or coerced and therefore did not consent. Following the adoption of Finnish legislation which criminalised the purchase of sexual services from trafficked or pimped persons, the first case concerning a purchaser of sexual services from such a victim ended in acquittal as the court felt that although the woman was clearly a victim of pimping and the man clearly intended to pay for sex, it could not be proven that the man was aware of

---

27. Home Office, n 10, 14.

the sex worker's status as being 'pimped'.[28] This would imply that the state of mind of the purchaser is considered under the Finnish law, which sets this law apart from the UK legislation, where there is no distinction between those who have knowledge and those who do not. By the end of 2008, the Finnish offence had resulted in no prosecutions.[29] As a result, one can see how the UK approach could potentially serve to act as a stronger deterrent.

Section 14 of the PCA imposes its own evidential burden, which may still prove difficult to discharge. A person who 'makes or promises payment' in return for sexual services from a sex worker who is forced or coerced falls within the scope of the provision—therefore, the act does not have to be completed, as a promise to pay will suffice, yet the promise of payment or the actual making of payment still needs to be proved. Further, the matter remains to be proven that the sex worker in question was forced or coerced, therefore requiring the identification of a pimp, trafficker or relevant actor applying the force or coercion. Enforcement of the Swedish law criminalising the purchase of sexual services has been very resource intensive, and there is not an overly impressive conviction rate. Charges are often dropped, with evidential difficulties being cited as a central factor.

As regards section 14 of the PCA, it has been stated that:

> Members of the police force were among the first to criticise some of the key elements of the act. The head of the Metropolitan police's anti-trafficking unit, Alan Gibson, argued that the law criminalising men who pay for sex with trafficked prostitutes would be "very difficult to enforce" and that the unit would need to commission research to discover whether the majority of sex workers were indeed controlled for gain (which was the original definition).[30]

Accordingly, not only is enforceability an issue, but the measures are also likely to lead to only a small number of convictions at best.

---

28. 'First Sex Purchase Court Case Ends in Acquittal in Salo', *Helsingin Sanomat*, (19 April 2007) www.hs.fi/english/article/First+sex+purchase+court+case+ends+in+acquittal+in+S alo/1135226667994 (accessed 01/12/2008).
29. Fiona Mactaggart, Hansard HC vol 482 Column 354 (6 November 2008).
30. 'Policing and Crime Act 2009: An act aiming to make local police forces more accountable to their communities and increase their effectiveness' (Wednesday 2 December 2009) *Guardian* www.guardian.co.uk/commentisfree/libertycentral/2009/feb/05/civil-liberties-police (accessed 03/12/2009).

ii) Lack of deterrent

Ashworth states that 'in practice, there is no shortage of examples of governments either repeatedly over-estimating the preventative efficacy of the criminal law or deliberately ignoring the poor prospects of prevention in favour of the politically symbolic effect of creating a new crime.'[31] The UK government strategy shifts the focus from sex workers to the users and abusers,[32] and the strict liability offence has clearly been motivated by the hope that purchasers of sexual services will be deterred by the potential for them to be subject to criminal sanction.[33] Although it is not for the state to cater for the demands of the purchaser, the demand will still exist. Arguably, demand sanctions will not act as sufficient deterrent to put off prostitute users. Interviews conducted among some Finnish prostitute users back up this assertion.[34] A UK-based report entitled 'It's just like going to the supermarket,'[35] which included research concerning the men who purchase sexual services from sex workers in the UK, appears to indicate largely that legal intervention has limited deterrent effect as regards the demand for sold sex. The report indicated that only 3% of respondents were concerned about coming up against the law, which indicates that criminal sanctions are not currently a particularly effective deterrent.[36] This lack of deterrent point was raised during House of Commons debate, yet was refuted by Vera Baird MP who stated that other research suggests otherwise.[37] She neglected to expand upon what this 'other research' is. According to the above mentioned report, the main deterrents cited were: concerns as regards fear of disease;

---

31. 'Is the Criminal Law a Lost Cause?' (2000), Ashworth A, *Law Quarterly Review* 225, 250
32. *UK Action Plan on Tackling Human Trafficking* (March 2007), Home Office and Scottish Executive, 54. Now available at: http://www.londonscb.gov.uk/files/resources/trafficking/uk_action_plan_on_tackling_human_trafficking.pdf
33. 'Paying for sex to be criminal offence' (November 2008), Gaby Hinsliff, *Guardian* http://www.guardian.co.uk/society/2008/nov/16/prostitution-women-lapdancing (accessed 01/12/2008).
34. 'Criminalisation of buying sex does not scare away regular clients' (7 April 2006), *Helsingin Sanomat*, www.hs.fi/english/article/Criminalisation+of+buying+sex+does+not+scare+away+regular+clients/1135219451353 (accessed 13/04/2008).
35. 'It's just like going to the supermarket: Men buying sex in East London' (2007) Coy M, Horvath M and Kelly L, Child and Women Abuse Studies Unit www.cwasu.org/filedown.asp?file=17242_LMU_Demand_Report_Text_screen-1.pdf (accessed 01/09/2008).
36. *Ibid* 15.
37. Vera Baird MP, Hansard HC vol 469 Column 448 (13 December 2007).

having a regular sexual partner; or negative feelings as a result of purchasing sex. JUSTICE state that 'we believe that—as in the case of controlled drugs—while it is possible that legal prohibition may deter some men from using prostitutes, many others—in particular those with less respect for the law in general—will not be so deterred.'[38] Based upon such evidence, criminal sanction would need to be very serious in order for measures such as the PCA provision to act as an effective deterrent.[39]

iii) Lack of empirical evidence

Lack of consent is not a given in purchase of sex situations, so arguably criminalisation of the purchase of sexual services in all situations is not desirable. The move away from a Swedish-style model (as originally proposed for the UK) is partly based upon Jacqui Smith's (then Home Secretary) grudging acceptance that some sex workers argue that they have consented.[40] If there is no consent by the woman, then there is a serious criminal offence, and criminality should be established in the ordinary way. What appears to have happened here is that the ambiguities of the forced, coerced, and therefore 'lack of consent' element and the evidential difficulties of proving the defendant's knowledge have resulted in the creation of a crime of strict liability which operates indirectly and without discrimination,[41] which is a contentious development.

If neither lack of consent nor harm can be taken as given in a purchase of sexual services situation, outright criminalisation of said purchase cannot be justified: it can be argued that not all purchasers should be subject to criminal sanction because of the potential for remote harm as a result of their purchase of sexual services. However, criminalisation of the purchase of sexual services from an individual who is forced or coerced is potentially much more defensible—it allows the purchase of sexual services to take

---

38. 'Policing and Crime Bill: Briefing on Second Reading, House of Commons' (2009), *JUSTICE*, 4.
39. The sanction is contained within section 14 PCA, which states that 'A person guilty of an offence under this section is liable on summary conviction to a fine not exceeding level 3 on the standard scale.' A level 3 fine currently stands at £1,000 in the UK.
40. 'Paying for sex to be criminal offence' *Guardian* available at www.guardian.co.uk/society/2008/nov/16/prostitution-women-lapdancing (accessed 18/11/2008).
41. 'Editorial—The Policing and Crime Act 2009' (2010) *Criminal Law Review*, 2, 91—92, 92.

place, but flags up the issue of sexual exploitation i.e. the potential that the sex worker is coerced and therefore does not consent.

Lack of solid empirical evidence (or the presence of conflicting evidence) as to the proportion of forced/coerced sex work in the UK, however, undermines justifications for the enactment of the strict liability offence. Prostitution is not always a 'patriarchal tool of oppression'[42] and women and girls are not always 'induced and kept in prostitution'.[43] Some are, in fact, autonomous actors, capable of making a rational economic choice to work in the sex sector. Lack of solid empirical research and evidence means that we have little idea as to what realistic proportion of the sex sector is comprised by these autonomous actors, or by forced/coerced or even trafficked sex workers. This provides a real stumbling block for drawing conclusions as to the magnitude of forced prostitution in this country.[44] This problem is further evidenced by figures used in the current UK debate as regards criminalisation: according to Jacqui Smith, 'up to 70% of prostitutes were controlled by pimps or had been trafficked into the country'.[45] Yet, a representative of the English Collective of Prostitutes stated that the government had 'made up' these figures and that most prostitution is consensual.[46] Other sources compound the lack of solid statistics–for example, it was stated in the Commons in 2007 that 'There are 25,000 sex slaves operating in Britain.'[47] The commentator made no further comment to clarify how this number was arrived at, or whether this estimate refers to prostitutes in general or only those subject to forced prostitution. Further to this, the recently reported 'failure' of Pentameter 2[48] to find and prosecute any actual traffickers in the

---

42. 'The Swedish Law that Prohibits the Purchase of Sexual Services: Best Practices for Prevention of Prostitution and Trafficking in Human Beings' (October 2004), Ekberg G, *Violence against Women* 1191.
43. *Ibid.*
44. See M Dempsey, n 21.
45. 'Prostitute users face clampdown', BBC News (19 November 2008) news.bbc.co.uk/1/hi/uk_politics/7735908.stm (accessed 23/11/2008).
46. *Ibid.*
47. Denis MacShane MP, Hansard HC vol 465 Column 432 (25 October 2007).
48. See statistics on Pentameter 2 available at http://www.soca.gov.uk/about-soca/library/cat_view/95-ukhtc?start=10 or http://www.cps.gov.uk/Publications/docs/pentameter_0706.pdf

UK[49] could indicate that trafficking for sexual exploitation into the UK has been overestimated.

iv) Adverse consequences for sex workers: Forcing prostitution underground

Following the enactment of the blanket ban on the purchase of sexual services in Sweden, some sources report a decrease in street prostitution in particular.[50] This may be indicative of the law having a positive effect, but the alternative conclusion is that it may be indicative of prostitution being forced underground or moving to less visible, off-street premises. The decline in street prostitution may simply represent a redistribution of those working in the sex sector, a 'reshuffling', as Clausen[51] refers to it. Similarly, if the demand sanction legislation in the UK is to have any marked effect, it is likely to be that of forcing prostitution further underground — more clandestine means of making the transaction will be sought to render it less visible from and further beyond the reaches of the law. In the report mentioned above,[52] the information given by the respondents indicates that the vast majority of transactions took place in an off-street setting; only 6.6% of respondents reported purchasing sex on the street only, and a further 25% reported purchasing sex in both street and off-street contexts.[53] Approximately half stated that their preferred premises for the transaction to take place was a private flat.[54]

---

49. 'Inquiry fails to find single trafficker who forced anybody into prostitution' (20 October 2009), Nick Davies, *Guardian*, www.guardian.co.uk/uk/2009/oct/20/government-trafficking-enquiry-fails (accessed 22/10/2009).
50. Information gathered by the Swedish National Board of Health and Welfare (SNBHW) indicated that the number of known street prostitutes in Sweden halved in the year following the demand sanction legislation coming into force — see 'Purchasing Sexual Services in Sweden and the Netherlands: Legal Regulation and Experiences, An abbreviated English version, A Report by a Working Group on the legal regulation of the purchase of sexual services' (issued on 8 October 2004) Justis- og Politidepartementet (Ministry of Justice and the Police) 9 www.regjeringen.no/upload/kilde/jd/rap/2004/0034/ddd/pdfv/232216-purchasing_sexual_services_in_sweden_and_the_nederlands.pdf (accessed 01/07/2010).
51. 'An Assessment of Gunilla Ekberg's account of Swedish prostitution policy' (January 2007), Clausen V, 3. Available from: http://www.sexworkeurope.org/de/resources-mainmenu-189/category/5-sex-work-demand
52. M Coy, M Horvath and L Kelly, n 35.
53. *Ibid*, 13.
54. *Ibid*, 13.

Any form of sanction for prostitute users has the potential to decrease the visibility of the trade. The effect of the legislation is simply that it creates extra problems for an already vulnerable cross-section of society, and may have the effect of increasing the risks (of, for example, violence) to the same. Perhaps we are creating a new problem through trying to solve a pre-existing one. Liberty[55] state that:

> The aim of the changes, according to a Home Office memo, is "to send a clear message that the Government will protect the vulnerable." However, many groups, including coalitions of sex workers, have raised concerns that the implementation of such legislation will actually increase the dangers for trafficked women and migrant workers in the sex trade, whose lack of papers will leave them even more vulnerable to abuses within underground prostitution rings.[56]

The evidence and commentary suggests that the effect of demand sanction-style legislation upon existing sex workers is not necessarily to their benefit.

Prior to the enactment of the blanket demand sanction legislation on Sweden, the criminalisation of sale and/or purchase of sexual services had been proposed and considered at various points over recent decades, yet it had always been rejected on the basis that the activity in question would be forced underground, and that there would be resulting evidential problems and questions of definition, as well as increased risks for the parties involved.[57] There is a need to weigh up the likelihood of increased prevention (which is yet to be established in the UK) against the unwelcome side effects of the strict liability offence, such as worsened working conditions for sex workers, and ill-effects for punters who may have had no ill intent

---

55. An independent human rights organisation.
56. 'Home Office anti-prostitution proposals flawed and dangerous' (22 October 2008), UK Liberty ukliberty.wordpress.com/2008/10/22/home-office-anti-prostitution-proposals-flawed-and-dangerous (accessed 21/11/2008).
57. 'Purchasing Sexual Services in Sweden and the Netherlands: Legal Regulation and Experiences, An abbreviated English version, A Report by a Working Group on the legal regulation of the purchase of sexual services' (Issued on 8 October 2004) Justis- og Politidepartementet (Ministry of Justice and the Police) 9 www.regjeringen.no/upload/kilde/jd/rap/2004/0034/ddd/pdfv/232216-purchasing_sexual_services_in_sweden_and_the_nederlands.pdf (accessed 01/07/2010).

at all. The sanctions are not hugely onerous,[58] but there will undeniably be a social impact upon the criminalised prostitute user. The law can also be criticised on the basis that the unknowing purchaser lacks moral culpability when compared to those who purchase sexual services from a forced or coerced sex worker with knowledge of her status, yet due to the evidential difficulties of proving knowledge[59] both will be deemed equally as culpable in a legal sense. Bearing in mind the adverse effects, are these measures proportional to the risk? If the 'risk' or 'harm' is difficult to determine in the face of a lack of empirical evidence, then the discussion is circular, and we return to the previous point.

Conclusion

To return to the quote provided at the start of this chapter by Lord Williams of Mostyn regarding factors to be taken into account when creating new offences, it was stated that it should be considered whether:

> the behaviour in question is sufficiently serious to warrant intervention by the criminal law; the mischief could be dealt with under existing legislation or by using other remedies; the proposed offence is enforceable in practice; the proposed offence is tightly drawn and legally sound; the proposed penalty is commensurate with the seriousness of the offence.[60]

It is questionable as to whether the strict liability offence created by section 14 of the PCA satisfies all of these criteria, not least with respect to the potential difficulties as regard to enforceability of the offence, but also because, as stated by Nicky Adams of the English Collective of Prostitutes, 'there were (already) existing laws to deal with situations where a woman was subjected to violence or coercion.'[61]

---

58. A level 3 fine.
59. Evidenced by the Finnish experience, n 28.
60. Lord Williams of Mostyn, written response to a question by Lord Dholakia, HL Debates, vol 602, WA 57 (18 June 1999).
61. *Ibid*.

The approach taken by the PCA is unsound, for the myriad reasons discussed in the preceding sections. Kinell suggests that 'clients, far from being a tiny minority of men, with abnormal desires and predilections for violence, are a substantial subsection of the male population, broadly representative of it on most demographic variables, with fairly mundane reasons for engaging in commercial sex, and rarely violent.' Therefore, the creation of the harms, such as the individual exerting the force or coercion, should be targeted, rather than the unknowing client. The PCA provision may have been conceived with good intentions, but the problems surrounding it, the difficulty inherent in enforcing and policing such provisions, and the potential for adverse side effects outweigh the reasons for the enactment of such legislation.

There is a need to weigh up the relevant considerations—are the issues targeted frequent and pervasive enough to justify criminalisation, bearing in mind the negative ramifications of legislative measures such as those employed in Sweden and the UK? Lack of sound empirical evidence as to the proportion of forced, coerced and trafficked sex workers in the UK renders this question difficult to answer. The UK approach also sends out somewhat of a mixed message–it appears to accept that sexual services can be consensually bought and sold, and it criminalises the purchase of sexual services outside of a consensual forum, yet does not provide a recognised forum for the consensual sale and purchase to take place in. If the criminal law should be administered in the fairest possible way, and so that it protects and enhances freedom,[62] then the use of demand sanctions in the form of the UK strict liability offence does not meet this standard. The legislation leaves no room for 'reasonable belief' (of the ignorant or 'innocent' purchaser) in consent, which could be envisaged if a regulated sex sector existed with criminalisation of the purchaser being employed where sexual services were purchased outside of the regulated setting. Sanders (*Chapter 2*) refers to the idea of the criminal justice system as a 'tool-kit'. It is submitted here that the state has opted, in this instance, for the incorrect 'tool'; criminal sanction was chosen, whereas regulation of the sex sector would have been a preferable move. The undesirable side effects of demand sanction legislation

---

62. See Sanders, *Chapter 2* of this work.

adversely affect those who are most vulnerable — the sex workers themselves. Morally, section 14 of the Policing and Crime Act 2009 appears to be on the right track. Practically, this is questionable. In the face of the matters discussed throughout this chapter and the negative ramifications of the use of demand sanctions, it is acceptable to remain sceptical on this matter.

CHAPTER 5

THE ASBO: REGULATING BEHAVIOUR AND MANIPULATING LAW

THERESA LYNCH

Introduction

Research confirms that persistent anti-social behaviour can have a significant impact on the lives of a minority of people, particularly those living in inner cities and areas of social deprivation.[1] As a response to such behaviour the Labour Party implemented the anti-social behaviour order (ASBO). Whilst in government (2 May 1997 - 6 May 2010) the ASBO remained a focal point of Labour's policies on crime and anti-social behaviour.[2] Following the election of a Conservative-Liberal Coalition government an emphasis on small-government and 'Big Society' has been advocated and has led to a commitment to review the ASBO.[3] The imminent review of the order can be seen as part of a wider policy on crime and anti-social behaviour which aims to provide citizens with the tools needed to help play a greater role in crime-fighting in their area.[4] It remains uncertain whether these develop-

---

1. For example, see *Anti-Social Behaviour Strategies: Finding a Balance* (2005), Millie A, Jacobson J, McDonald E and Hough M, York: Joseph Rowntree Foundation.
2. This chapter uses the term 'ASBO' to cover ASBOs issued after application either by magistrates' courts (acting in their civil capacity) or by county courts. It also covers ASBOs issued following conviction for a criminal offence (CrASBOs) either by magistrates' courts (acting in their criminal capacity) or the Crown Court.
3. 'Time to "move beyond" ASBOs, Says Home Secretary May' 28 July 2010, *BBC News UK*: www.bbc.co.uk/news/uk-10784060.
4. See the speech: Let's Mend our Broken Society (2010), Cameron D, www.conservatives.com/ News/Speeches/2010/04/David_Cameron_Lets_mend_our_broken_society.aspx; 'Theresa

ments signal the death of the ASBO. What is clear is that concerns about the ASBO can be seen as more than political manoeuvring.

A major criticism of the ASBO is that it is a fusion of civil and criminal law and is best described as a two-stage order. The first stage of ASBO proceedings is civil (the order) and second stage is criminal (breach).[5] In terms of social control the mix of the civil and criminal law was seen as an attempt to take maximum advantage of legal forms, and was controversial from the outset.[6] This legislative technique, of which there are numerous examples,[7] has been dubbed the 'two-step prohibition.'[8] Several approaches have previously been advocated for amending the rules which govern the ASBO, including turning the two-stage order into a completely civil process.[9] However, this chapter will focus on the first stage of the ASBO (civil stage).

I will question whether the civil status which allows the state to avoid standards of due process traditionally required for criminal intervention can be justified? It is contended that the civil label allows the state to avoid various procedural protections associated with criminal proceedings enshrined in the European Convention on Human Rights (ECHR). It will be argued that Article 6 (the right to a fair trial) ECHR which provides extra protection in criminal cases should apply to the first stage of ASBO proceedings. The chapter will begin with a brief history of the development of the ASBO. This discussion will include the rationale for the ASBO in England and Wales and explain what the ASBO is and how it works. The second part of this

---

May unveils radical police shake-up plans', *Telegraph.co.uk*, 26 July 2010: www.telegraph.co.uk/news/newstopics/politics/7911537/Theresa-May-unveils-radical-police-shake-up-plans.html

5. Crime and Disorder Act 1998 (CDA), section 1(1) and (10).
6. 'Overtaking on the Right' (1995), Ashworth A, Gardner J, Morgan R, Smith A T H, von Hirsch A and Wasik M, *New Law Journal*, 145, pp. 1501-1502; Neighbouring on the Oppressive: the Governments Community Safety Order Proposals' (1998), Ashworth A, Gardner J, Morgan R, Smith A T H, von Hirsch A and Wasik M, *Criminal Justice*, 16 (1), pp.7-14.
7. For example,: non-molestation orders under the Family Law Act 1996; protection from harassment orders under the Protection from Harassment Act 1997; control orders under the Prevention of Terrorism Act, football banning orders under the Football Spectators Act 1989; and drinking banning orders under Violent Crime Reduction Act 2006.
8. 'Regulating Offensive Conduct through Two-Step Prohibitions' (2006), Simester A P, and von Hirsch A, in *Incivilities: Regulating Offensive Behaviour* (2006), von Hirsch A, and Simester A P, (eds.), Oxford: Hart Publishing, pp.173-195.
9. See 'Should the ASBO be civilized?' (2010), Hoffman S and Macdonald S *Criminal Law Review*, 6, pp. 457-473.

chapter will focus on a critique of the civil status of the ASBO and the final part will consider the possible effects of a criminal classification.

The ASBO: Background and Context

The ASBO can be traced back to 1995 when the Labour Party proposed a remedy to combat persistent incivilities which would be available to anyone proven to have been persistently distressing others in the community.[10] In its embryonic form the ASBO was called, 'the community safety order'. The community safety order was a civil order similar to an injunction, with civil standards of proof[11] but with a criminal sanction for breach. Following Labour's election victory in 1997 the community safety order was renamed the ASBO and found pride of place in section 1 of the Crime and Disorder Act 1998 (CDA).[12] The ASBO was implemented to tackle a broad range of behaviour which includes that which may not be suitable for criminalisation but could cause fear, distress, and misery. Examples of anti-social behaviour include: harassment and intimidating behaviour; behaviour that causes alarm or fear; noisy neighbours; drunken and abusive behaviour; vandalism and other deliberate damage to property; dumping rubbish or litter, drug-dealing in parks, and burglaries. Much of the behaviour listed here is clearly criminal and could have been targeted by existing legal instruments without recourse to the ASBO.[13] However, the ASBO was also implemented to address the

---

10. *A Quiet Life* (1995), Labour Party, London, p.8. See also Labour's (1996) paper entitled: *Labour's Plans for Tackling Criminal, Anti-Social Behaviour in Neighbourhoods*, Labour Party: London.
11. Every allegation must be established to a particular standard of proof which is set by law. The criminal standard of proof is 'beyond reasonable doubt.' The civil standard of proof is 'on the balance of probabilities.'
12. The Crime and Disorder Act 1998 came into force on 1st April 1999. Since its enactment the 1998 Act has been amended by numerous pieces of legislation such as the Police Reform Act 2002; the Anti-social Behaviour Act 2003; the Serious Organised Crime and Police Act 2005; and the Criminal Justice and Immigration Act 2008.
13. Forerunners of the ASBO included local authorities' powers both to apply for injunctions against public nuisance and, in their capacity as social landlords, to prevent anti-social behaviour by injunctions against tenants. Echoes of the ASBO are also to be found in the civil injunctions and restraining orders against harassment that became available following the

problems associated with the criminal procedures in place for prosecuting persistent minor offences. Prior to the ASBO the Labour Party considered these procedures to be too lengthy and too heavily weighted in favour of the accused.[14] For example, in the prosecution of repeat offences of a relatively minor nature the likely result was that each single offence would receive only a small punishment. The problem with such a punishment was that it did not correspond to the cumulative impact of those crimes on their victims or society generally. Added to this was the fact that prosecution of these low-level crimes was at times impossible because of witness intimidation. The ASBO, however, would allow orders to be imposed without frightened or intimidated people being required to give direct evidence. Furthermore, breach of an ASBO can result in a prison sentence of up to five years. This maximum sentence is far in excess of the maximum sentences available to magistrates in their criminal capacity or even the statutory maxima for typical anti-social crimes such as threatening behaviour.

The ASBO was designed as a community-based initiative which would enable local people to become actively involved in protecting the community through the collection of evidence and by helping to enforce any breaches of the order. The Labour Party recognised that communities needed more protection from anti-social behaviour but their policies conceived that the weakness of these communities was a moral failing, induced by the presence of a selfish and uncivil minority, upon which enforcement must be imposed. The idea that communities have somehow lost the ability to deal with bad behaviour by informal means drives much government rhetoric on the issue of anti-social behaviour. The plight of the community was used by the Labour Party to justify the state controlling anti-social behaviour from the top down. Richard Sennett has claimed that 'Asbos don't work because they come from the top down.'[15] He claims that: 'Good behaviour is instilled by family life'[16], and not government enforcement policies. In fact Sennett welcomes the end of the ASBO. Like many critics of the ASBO, Sennett

---

implementation of the Protection from Harassment Act 1997.
14. *A Quiet Life* (1995), Labour Party, London, p.8.
15. 'The ASBO is an icon of New Labour's negligence' (30th July, 2010) *Guardian* (http://www.guardian.co.uk/commentisfree/2010/jul/30/asbo-icon-new-labour-negligence).
16. *Ibid.*

suggests that they were introduced as a tool to reform offending individuals and have failed in this regard. However, ASBOs are not and never have been an instrument of moral reform for society or the individual but a tool to help regulate anti-social behaviour and reduce fear in those communities subject to such behaviour. Furthermore, there has been a shift from an initial over-emphasis on the use of enforcement tools (such as the ASBO) towards a more balanced approach in the methods used to control anti-social behaviour which includes several supportive interventions which are often used to avoid legal measures being taken.[17]

The statutory definition of anti-social behaviour can be found in section 1(1)(a) CDA which describes such behaviour as 'acting in a manner that caused or was likely to cause harassment, alarm or distress to one or more persons not of the same household as the defendant.' Some commentators have strongly criticised this statutory definition for being excessively broad and vague.[18] Anti-social behaviour appears in a 'pyramid of different kinds and degrees of incivility, where only the tip is the painfully sharp experience, compared with a wide base of mere distaste or annoyance.'[19] These distinctions are lost on a broad definition and approach that extends control and regulation to ever increasing categories of anti-social behaviour. Since 2003 begging, prostitution and graffiti have been added to the list of behaviours deemed anti-social, reflecting a wider sanitising agenda.[20] This broad statutory definition of anti-social behaviour has allowed for a gradual form of mission creep and the ASBO is now being used far beyond its original purpose extending its use to the most bizarre circumstances.[21] An application for an

---

17. Examples include: warning letters and anti-social behaviour contracts (ABCs).
18. 'Overtaking on the Right' (1995), Ashworth A, Gardner J, Morgan R, Smith A T H, von Hirsch A and Wasik M, *New Law Journal*, 145, pp. 1501-1502; Neighbouring on the Oppressive: the Governments Community Safety Order Proposals' (1998), Ashworth A, Gardner J, Morgan R, Smith A T H, von Hirsch A and Wasik M, *Criminal Justice*, 16 (1), pp.7-14; and 'A Suicidal Woman, Roaming Pigs and a Noisy Trampolinist: Refining the ASBO's Definition of Anti-Social Behaviour' (2006), Macdonald S, 69 *Modern Law Review*, pp. 183-213.
19. *Making People Behave: The Politics of Behaviour* (2005), Burney E, Cullompton: Willan, p.9.
20. See generally, the Anti-Social Behaviour Act 2003.
21. See, for example, the case of Mrs Cartwright who was given an ASBO for loud sex sessions. 'Neighbour with Sex ASBO Arrested For Noisy Sex Sessions' (2010) *DailyTelegraph*. www.telegraph.co.uk/news/newstopics/howaboutthat/7494294/Neighbour-with-sex-Asbo-arrested-for-noisy-sessions.html.

ASBO may now be made to the magistrates' court,[22] county court[23] or Crown Court.[24] There are now several 'relevant authorities' which can apply for an ASBO.[25] The Environment Agency was added to this list in 2005 and other 'relevant authorities' include registered social landlords and social housing action trusts. Individuals over the age of ten may be issued with an ASBO.[26]

There were 16,999 ASBOs issued in the period 1 April 1999 to 31 December 2008.[27] Of the total number issued in this period 9,247 (55%) were breached at least once with 6,804 (40%) breached more than once.[28] Of the 9,247 ASBOs breached at least once, 53% were given an immediate custodial sentence. As Chakrabati has suggested, like the traditional criminal justice system, ASBOs have achieved what the Labour Party never set out to achieve—'namely, higher levels of incarceration. Even in relation to those ASBOed for recognisable low-level crime, the five-year breach penalty can lead to the inadvertent raising of custody tariffs for what was originally very low-level offending.'[29] The ASBO is routinely used against children and young people, which is particularly concerning given that the statutory provisions for support are limited.[30] The targeting of children and young people has led to concerns about the possibility of custodial net-widening.[31] In the period 1 April 1999 to 31 December 2008 it was reported that 1,253 young people (ten-to-17 year olds) have received a custodial sentence for breach of an ASBO with forty-nine% of ten-to-17 year olds who breach their ASBOs receiving a custodial sentence of over three months and up to

---

22. CDA, section 1(3).
23. CDA, section 1B, as inserted by Police Reform Act 2002, section 63.
24. CDA, section 1C, as inserted by Police Reform Act 2002, section 64.
25. A 'relevant authority' is defined in CDA, section 1(1A), Crime and Disorder Act 1998 (Relevant Authorities and Relevant Persons) Order 2006 (SI 2006/2137).
26. CDA section 1(7).
27. ASBO Statistics- England and Wales (2008). These statistics can be found at http://rds.homeoffice.gov.uk/rds/antisocial1.html, Table 1.
28. *Ibid*, Tables 7, 11 and 9.
29. 'ASBOmania' (2008), Chakrabati S, and Russell J, in *ASBO Nation: The Criminalisation of Nuisance (2008), Squires P, (ed.)*, Bristol: Policy Press, p.315.
30. Statutory support for young persons subject to an ASBO includes: parenting orders, (CDA, s8); one year reviews of ASBO issued to those under 17 years of age, (CDA, s.1J) and individual support orders (CDA, s.1AA).
31. See 'The Use of ASBOs Against Young People in England and Wales: Lessons from Scotland' (2007), Macdonald S and Telford M, 27 *Legal Studies*, pp. 604-629.

four months.[32] Furthermore, the use of publicity campaigns to inform communities of ASBOs issued against people currently operate with few or no restrictions and local authorities regularly publish the names of local youths who have had ASBOs issued against them.[33] Naming those youths subject to an ASBO 'cannot be separated from "shaming", and shame by itself, without any reintegrating process, is likely to be counter-productive resulting in rejection of the ethical standpoint of the accusers.'[34]

Courts are able to make limitless prohibitions when imposing an ASBO. The prohibitions are designed to prevent repetition of the behaviour in question, limited only by the fact that prohibitions must be considered necessary to protect others from further anti-social acts.[35] The ASBO prohibitions have no maximum length but have a minimum duration of two years. The Home Office, the Judicial Studies Board and the Court of Appeal, have encouraged the use of preventative prohibitions, such as curfews, exclusion zones and non-association clauses.[36] However, the widespread use of preventative prohibitions has been the subject of critical scrutiny.[37] Preventative prohibitions have been questioned in light of their potential incompatibility with the ECHR. There are various Convention rights which could be infringed by the prohibitions of an ASBO, especially those found in Articles 8-11. For example, an ASBO which bans individuals from a particular area may well infringe their Article 8 right to a private or family life if it means they cannot visit members of their family who live within that area or if they are banned

---

32. ASBO Statistics - England and Wales (2008). These can be found at http://rds.homeoffice.gov.uk/rds/antisocial1.html, Table 12.
33. See *Stanley, Marshall and Kelly v Commissioner of Police for the Metropolis and Chief Executive of London Borough of Brent* [2004] EWHC 2229. *Cf.* Council of Europe's Commissioner of Human Rights Gil-Robles reiterated by his successor Hammarberg (2008). A Report by Mr. Alvaro Gil Robles, Commissioner Human Rights, on his visit to the United Kingdom, Strasbourg: Council of Europe, 83.
34. *Making People Behave: The Politics of Behaviour* (2009), Burney E, Cullompton: Willan, 108.
35. CDA, section 1(6).
36. *A Guide to Anti-Social Behaviour Orders* (2006), Home Office, COI: London; *Anti-Social Behaviour Orders: A Guide For the Judiciary* (2007), 3rd edn. London: Judicial Studies Board. See also *Boness* [2005] EWCA Crim 2395; [2006] 1 Cr. App. R. (S.) 120, p.690.
37. See 'How Offensive Can you Get?'(2006), Duff R, and Marshall S, in *Inciviliities: Regulating Offensive Behaviour*, (2006), Simester A, and von Hirsch A, (eds.) Oxford: Hart publishing, p. 58.

from talking to certain people. The problem with this argument is that it is limited by the fact that all these rights are conditional and can be overridden on the grounds of 'democratic necessity in the interests of national security or public safety, for the prevention of disorder or crime ... or for the protection of the rights and freedoms of others'.[38]

The Civil Classification of the ASBO: Subverting the Right to Fair Trial

The House of Lords upheld the civil classification of section 1(1) CDA (the first stage of the ASBO) in the case of *Clingham v Kensington and Chelsea Royal London Borough Council* and *R (McCann) v Manchester Crown Court*.[39] Academic writers have criticised the civil classification of the first stage of the ASBO proceedings.[40] Simester and von Hirsch have warned that using the civil law to tackle criminal behaviour blurs the difference between the civil and criminal laws, associating the former with condemnation of culpable wrongdoing and risking a "loss of clarity of the criminal law's distinctively moral voice'.[41] Critics assert that the civil label also allows the state to subvert various procedural protections associated with criminal proceedings enshrined in the ECHR.[42] The key human rights element is whether Article

---

38. Article 8(2), ECHR.
39. [2002] UKHL 39. The two cases were unrelated but raised overlapping issues. Both cases involved the power of the magistrates' court, under section 1(1) CDA, to impose an ASBO.
40. See 'Social Control and Anti Social Behaviour: The Subversion of Human Rights?' (2004), Ashworth A, *Law Quarterly Review*, 120, 263-29; 'The Nature of the Anti-Social Behaviour Order - R (McCann & Others) v Crown Court at Manchester' (2003), Macdonald S, 66(4) *Modern Law Review* 630-639; *Making People Behave: The Politics of Behaviour* (2009), Burney E, Cullompton: Willan and 'Regulating Offensive Conduct through Two-Step Prohibitions' (2006), Simester A P, and von Hirsch A, in *Incivilities: Regulating Offensive Behaviour* (2006), von Hirsch A, and Simester AP, (eds.), Oxford: Hart Publishing, 173-195.
41. *Ibid*, p.189.
42. 'Regulating Offensive Conduct through Two-Step Prohibitions' (2006), Simester A P, and von Hirsch A, in *Incivilities: Regulating Offensive Behaviour* (2006), von Hirsch A, and Simester AP, (eds.), Oxford: Hart Publishing, pp.173-195; 'Social Control and Anti Social Behaviour: The Subversion of Human Rights?' (2004), Ashworth A, *Law Quarterly Review*, 120, 263-29; 'An Elephant on the Doorstep: Criminal Policy without Crime in New Labour's Britain' (2000), Rutherford A, in *Criminal Policy in Transition* (2000), P Green, and A

6 (the right to a fair trial) of the ECHR regarding procedures in criminal cases applies to the first stage of ASBO proceedings. As Ashworth points out, states are not permitted to get around the safeguards provided by the ECHR simply by declaring a process to be civil rather than criminal.[43] However, orders labelled preventative (such as the ASBO) are normally regarded as civil rather than criminal.

As Ashworth writes, 'preventive measures may be seen as manifestations of the "risk society", in which the aim is to "manage" sources of risk to the public.'[44] In the case of the ASBO, the aim of the Labour Party was to 'manage' the risk of certain types of behaviour from occurring by targeting the individual perpetrators of this behaviour through the ASBO.[45] However, the ASBO was also a significant step in the direction of 'preventive justice'[46] which can be explained as the use of civil law to control people's actions because of what they might do in the future, rather than punishing them through the criminal courts for what they have done in the past. It is only at the breach stage of an ASBO that the legal safeguards and standards of due process (which Sanders introduces in *Chapter 2*), traditionally required for criminal intervention, apply. These safeguards serve to protect the liberty of those subject to criminal proceedings, both in preserving freedom of lawful action and in ensuring that people are not wrongly convicted and punished. But because these safeguards can make it difficult to impose sanctions on wrongdoers, there has been a modern tendency to resort to hybrid orders

---

Rutherford, (eds), Hart Publishing; 'Anti-Social Behaviour Orders: An Infringement of the Human Rights Act 1998?' (2002), Hopkins Burke R, and Morrill R, 11 *Nottingham. Law Journal, p.1*; 'Anti-social Behaviour Orders - a Nail in the Coffin of Due Process?'(2005), Ireland S, 2 *Justice Journal*, 94; and Hybrid Law and Human Rights- Banning and Behaviour Orders in the Appeal Courts' (2006), Pearson G, 27 *Liverpool Law Review*, 125.

43. 'Social Control and Anti Social Behaviour: The Subversion of Human Rights?' (2004), Ashworth A, *Law Quarterly Review*, 120, 289.
44. *Ibid*, 272. See also, *Housing Urban Governance and Anti-Social Behaviour: Perspectives, Policy and Practice* (2006), Flint J (ed.), Bristol: Policy Press.
45. The media now often refers to Britain as an 'ASBO nation'. For example see: Bright M, Asthana A and Thompson L (2005), 'Welcome to ASBO Nation', June 12, 2005, *The Observer*, www.guardian.co.uk.
46. For a more detailed discussion of this concept see 'Seeking Security by Eroding Rights: The Side-Stepping of Due Process' (2007), Zedner L, in Lazarus L and Goold B (eds.), *Security and Human Rights*, Cullompton: Willan Publishing, 255-277.

such as the ASBO. By leaping the criminal barrier (as the Protection from Harassment Act 1997 passed by the Conservatives had done), Labour had set the template for punishment disguised as prevention. The question then is: is the ASBO solely preventative or is it in effect a form of punishment? This was the question upon which the appellants in *Clingham* and *McCann* came to the House of Lords. The matter in dispute in this latter case was the use of hearsay evidence[47] upon which the ASBOs had relied. It was argued that the nature of the orders was punitive in context and inextricably linked to the fact of criminal punishment if breached. The Law Lords disagreed.

In the case of *McCann*, the House of Lords considered there to be four issues for determination.

- First, there was the question whether, as a matter of domestic classification, the proceedings in place for the first stage of the ASBO under section 1(1) CDA should be viewed as criminal or civil.
- Second, there was the question whether ASBO proceedings involve a criminal charge so as to entitle a defendant to the protections afforded by Article 6(3) ECHR.
- Third, there was the issue whether hearsay evidence is admissible in proceedings under section 1(1) CDA.
- Finally, there was the issue of which standard of proof was to be applied by the courts in the first stage of ASBO proceedings.

In relation to the first issue, the House of Lords unanimously agreed that ASBOs are correctly classified as civil orders.[48] Counsel for the appellants in *McCann* had argued that the proceedings leading to the making of an ASBO should be considered together with the fact that, if the order is breached, criminal proceedings may be brought under section 1(10) CDA which carry a maximum prison sentence of five years. Lord Steyn dismissed this stating: 'These are separate and independent procedures. The making

---

47. The rules relating to hearsay evidence restrict the extent to which statements made out of court will be admitted as evidence. For criminal law see statutory provisions contained in the Criminal Justice Act 2003, sections 114-117 and for the civil hearsay rules see the Civil Evidence Act 1995, sections 1-7.
48. See Lord Steyn, *Clingham* and *McCann*, para: [22] and Lord Hutton para: [94].

of the order will presumably sometimes serve its purpose and there will be no proceedings for breach. It is in principle necessary to consider the two stages separately.'[49]

Despite Lord Steyn's assertions, it is difficult to view the proceedings under section 1(1) CDA as 'separate and independent' from the possible subsequent criminal proceedings under section 1(10) CDA. This difficulty arises because findings of fact from the proceedings for the making of the ASBO may later form the basis of the sentence that is imposed in the criminal proceedings. When sentencing for breach, the court takes into account the course of conduct which attracted the order in the first place, not simply the action constituting the breach. Retrospectively, the whole record of anti-social behaviour becomes criminalised. The penalty for breaching the order may be higher than if the conduct had been the subject of a successful criminal prosecution.[50] Child and Hunt discuss the limits of the criminal law in *Chapter 3*. They argue that there is a lack of coherence in the extension of the criminal law. The ASBO is the ultimate example of this, and stretches the criminal law to the extreme. The Labour Party and the House of Lords may claim that section 1(1) CDA proceedings are outside of the problem because they are not criminal, however, as the second part of this chapter will explain this is only in form rather than substance.

On the second issue, the House of Lords decided that section 1(1) CDA proceedings do not involve a criminal charge. In reaching this conclusion, the House of Lords decided that only the protections under Article 6(1) ECHR would apply to the first stage of ASBO proceedings. Article 6(1) ECHR provides 'that in the determination of his civil rights and obligations or of any criminal charge against him, everyone is entitled to a fair and public hearing within a reasonable time by an independent and impartial tribunal established by law.' The decision that section 1(1) CDA proceedings do not involve a criminal charge was directly linked to the conclusion that the ASBO was preventative in purpose and, therefore, incapable of inflicting a punishment. Following this decision the House of Lords concluded that the extra protections available under Article 6(3) ECHR would not apply to section

---

49. *Clingham* and *McCann*, para; [23].
50. See *R v H, Stevens and Lovegrove* [2006] EWCA Crim 255.

1(1) CDA proceedings and an individual's right under Article 6(3)(d) ECHR to cross-examine witnesses was therefore not applicable to section 1(1) CDA.

In considering the third issue the House of Lords decided that hearsay evidence would be admissible in section 1(1) CDA. Permitting hearsay evidence in section 1(1) CDA allows professional witnesses (such as police officers) to provide a statement on behalf of a witness or witnesses who remain anonymous. Hearsay evidence must be relevant to the matters to be proved. The House of Lords argued that the failure to admit hearsay evidence 'would greatly disturb the balance which section 1 of the Crime and Disorder Act 1998 seeks to strike between the interests of the individual and those of society.'[51] However, Ashworth has argued that this balancing approach fails to reflect the substance of the case law of the European Court of Human Rights (ECtHR) stating that 'Lord Hutton repeats the error of the Privy Council in *Brown v Stott* in assuming that rights coming within Art. 6 can simply be "trumped" by public interest considerations'.[52] It has accordingly been suggested that the rule against hearsay evidence should apply to section 1(1) CDA.[53]

Following the decision in *McCann*, section 116 of the Criminal Justice Act 2003 and the recent case law of both the Court of Appeal[54] and ECtHR[55] has recognised that exceptions may be made to the hearsay rule in criminal proceedings for witnesses who have been intimidated.[56] Intimidated witnesses are witnesses whose quality of evidence is likely to be diminished because they are in fear or distress about testifying. It is for the court to decide whether the quality of a witness's evidence is likely to be diminished. Section 116(2) of the Criminal Justice Act 2003 provides five conditions ((a)-(e)) in which a statement not made in oral evidence in criminal proceedings is

---

51. Lord Hutton, *Clingham* and *McCann*, para: [113].
52. 'Social Control and Anti Social Behaviour: The Subversion of Human Rights?' (2004), Ashworth A, *Law Quarterly Review*, 120, 290-291.
53. See 'Should ASBOs be civilized?' (2010), Hoffman S, and Macdonald S, *Criminal Law Review*, 6, 461.
54. *Horncastle* [2009] UKSC 14.
55. *Al-Khawaja & Tahery v United Kingdom* (2009) 49 EHRR 1.
56. Additionally, CDA, section 11 as inserted by section 143 Serious Organised Crime and Police Act 2005 provides that special measures formerly reserved for criminal hearings can be used in anti-social behaviour cases.

admissible. Of most relevance here is (2)(e) which provides that if 'through fear the relevant person does not give (or does not continue to give) oral evidence in the proceedings, either at all or in connection with the subject matter of the statement, and the court gives leave for the statement to be given in evidence'. Leave will be given if the court considers that the statement ought to be admitted in the interests of justice. The relaxation of the hearsay rules in ASBO hearings has removed one of the major obstacles to successful prosecutions of this kind of behaviour under the criminal law and, thus, undermines many of the policy considerations underpinning the *McCann* decision.

Finally, on the fourth issue for consideration, despite endorsing the use of hearsay evidence in both *Clingham* and *McCann*, the House of Lords imposed a strict rule for its interpretation which was equivalent to the criminal standard of proof.[57]

In reaching their decision on the civil status of the first stage of the ASBO in the case of *McCann*, the House of Lords also considered the case law of the ECtHR. However, the House of Lords has been criticised for being 'selective in the parts of the Strasbourg judgments it chose to apply.'[58] Of particular importance to their decision was the case of *Engel v The Netherlands (No 1)*.[59] *Engel* established three criteria to be used by the ECtHR when determining if a penalty introduced in a member state is civil or criminal:

- the domestic classification of the legal proceedings;
- the nature of the offence; and
- the nature, degree and severity of the penalty.

A finding that the ASBO is civil in domestic law serves only as a starting point[60] and, if the ECtHR were to pass judgment on the correct classification of the first stage of the ASBO proceedings, it would also assess the second

---

57. See Lord Steyn, *Clingham* and *McCann*, para: [37].
58. 'ASBOs: Criminal Penalties or Civil Injunctions?' (2003), Bakalis C, *Cambridge Law Journal*, 62 (3) , 584.
59. (1976) 1 EHRR 647, paras: [82–83].
60. See *Benham v United Kingdom* (1996) 22 EHRR 293, para: [56].*Cf.* Lord Steyn, *Clingham and McCann* para: [67]; Lord Hope of Craighead, para: [51] and Lord Hutton, paras: [94-98].

and third *Engel* criteria.⁶¹ Based on the second and third criteria, the ECtHR may conclude that the ASBO is in substance criminal. This argument is of course speculative as there has not yet been an appeal to the ECtHR challenging the civil classification of the order.

Scrutiny of the Strasbourg jurisprudence reveals that in determining the second *Engel* criteria; the 'nature of the offence' the ECtHR would take into account two factors. Firstly whether or not the behaviour complained of is in essence criminal and the secondly whether the behaviour is something that is prohibited under the criminal law in most member states.

If the behaviour in question is punished by the criminal law (either within the member state or in other member states), then characterising the procedure as disciplinary or regulatory or administrative or civil will not work, and the proper classification as far as the ECtHR is concerned will be criminal.⁶² On occasions where the behaviour triggering the proceeding does not clearly fall within the category of what might broadly be classified criminal, the ECtHR considers a second factor: the character of the rule. An example of this is the case of *Benham*⁶³ where the ECtHR was assessing the applicability of Article 6(3) to non-payment of the community charge. In this case, several factors persuaded the ECtHR that they were dealing with a criminal charge. The ECtHR looked at factors such as the procedure in question; the fact that liability to pay applied to all citizens, and that the proceedings were brought by a public authority under statutory powers of enforcement.⁶⁴ The House of Lords in *McCann* did not assess any of the above principles when determining the nature of the offence because they failed to maintain a distinction between the second and third *Engel* criteria (nature of the offence and the nature, degree and severity of the penalty). The House of Lords found that the ASBO did not constitute a penalty under the third *Engel* criterion and this led all three judges (on slightly different

---

61. The effect of the second and third *Engel* criteria is alternative and not cumulative (*Garyfallou AEBE v Greece* (1997) 28 E.H.R.R, 344), and so a conclusion of criminal by the ECtHR on either of these latter two criteria would be decisive.
62. See *Welch v United Kingdom* (1995) 20 EHRR. 247, para: [27].
63. *Benham v United Kingdom* (1996) 22 EHRR 293, para: [56].
64. *Human Rights in Criminal Proceedings* (2005), Trechsel S, and Summers S, Oxford: Oxford University Press, p.20.

bases) to decide that, as far as this second *Engel* criterion was concerned, section 1(1) CDA was also not criminal.[65] As Bakalis has explained: 'By saying that the nature of the offence is determined by reference to the penalty involved effectively makes the second *Engel* criterion redundant'.[66] It also meant that the House of Lords did not go on to scrutinise closely the behaviour which constitutes anti-social behaviour and its relationship to existing criminal offences. Bakalis has argued that: 'Given the convergence between anti-social behaviour and criminal behaviour, it would certainly be open to the ECtHR to find that the behaviour proscribed under section 1(1) CDA is indeed criminal in nature'.[67] The House of Lords' interpretation and application of the second *Engel* criterion is therefore open to question.

When passing judgment on the third *Engel* criteria (the nature, degree and severity of the penalty), the House of Lords decided that the ECtHR makes a distinction between sanctions that are punitive in purpose (and thus criminal penalties within the context of Article 6 ECHR) and those that are merely preventive and, therefore, not criminal in nature.[68] This decision was based on the reliance which Lords Hope and Hutton placed on the cases of *Guzzardi*[69] and *Raimondo*.[70] The problem with this decision is that the House of Lords failed to recognise that the ASBO may operate as both a preventative and punitive remedy. In the cases of *Guzzardi* and *Raimondo*, the Italian legislation in question was dealing with suspects on remand and, consequently, the preventive nature of the provisions was very clear since the applicants would be punished for their past behaviour once their trial took place. As Bakalis asserts: 'The purpose of ASBOs is not quite as clear as this.'[71] When the Labour Party first proposed the ASBO (then named the community safety order), Labour themselves said that the principal aim of

---

65. See *Clingham* and *McCann* [2002] UKHL 39; paras: [30], [61] and [102].
66. 'ASBOs, Preventative Orders and the European court of Human Rights' (2007), Bakalis C, *European Human Rights Law Review*, 4, p.432.
67. *Ibid*, 434.
68. See *Clingham* and *McCann*, para: [72] and [109].
69. *Italy v Guzzardi* (1981) 3 E.H.R.R. 333.
70. *Italy v Raimondo* (1994) 18 E.H.R.R. 237.
71. 'ASBOs, Preventative Orders and the European court of Human Rights' (2007), Bakalis C, *European Human Rights Law Review*, 4, 434.

the new order is punitive and preventative.[72] In any case, even if the preventive nature of ASBOs was beyond doubt, the European Human Rights case law on this point has moved on since *Raimondo* and *Guzzardi*.

For example, the case of *Steel v United Kingdom*[73] involved the procedure for binding-over for breach of the peace which is classified as a civil order under UK law but was found by the ECtHR to be criminal for the purposes of Article 6 ECHR.[74] In *McCann*, the House of Lords made a distinction between binding over for breach of the peace and the imposition of an ASBO. The judges rejected the relevance of *Steel* on the basis that a power of arrest is attached to a refusal to be bound over whereas, in the case of ASBOs, imprisonment can only follow once a separate procedure under section 1(10) CDA is undertaken.[75] In other words, their rejection of *Steel* as a relevant authority was a natural consequence of their de-coupling of the two procedures under section 1(1) CDA (application) and section 1(10) CDA (breach). However, even if we accept this decoupling, Bakalis asserts that the House of Lords' 'rejection of *Steel* as a relevant authority is still questionable'.[76] Although it is indeed the case that the ECtHR was influenced by the power of arrest attached to the binding-over procedure, it is wrong to draw the conclusion from this that a power of arrest or threat of imprisonment is a necessary pre-condition before a finding by the ECtHR that a particular measure is punitive.

The ECtHR is keen to assess the potential detriment that a measure might have on an individual's life. For example, in *Malige*,[77] the deduction of points from a driving licence was understood to be a criminal sanction even though no mention was made of any powers of arrest. The ECtHR said 'although the deduction of points has a preventative character, it also has a

---

72. *A Quiet Life*, (1995), Labour Party, London, 8.
73. (1999) 28 E.H.R.R. 603.
74. There are many parallels between the binding over procedure for breach of the peace and ASBOs: both involve a finding that the defendant has breached the peace or acted antisocially and the threat of imprisonment for refusing to be bound over or to abide by the terms of the order.
75. See *Clingham* and *McCann*, para: [74] and [106].
76. ASBOs, Preventative Orders and the European Court of Human Rights' (2007), Bakalis C, *European Human Rights Law Review*, 4, 436.
77. *Malige v France* (1999) 28 E.H.R.R. 578.

punitive and deterrent character and is accordingly similar to a secondary penalty.'[78] In *Welch*,[79] the threat of imprisonment was only one of a number of factors taken into account when determining the punitiveness of confiscation orders. The ECtHR commented that 'whatever the characterisation of the measure of confiscation, the fact remains that the applicant faced more far-reaching detriment as a result of the order than that to which he was exposed at the time of the commission of the offences and for which he was convicted.'[80] Similarly, the terms of an ASBO can be (and often are) far-reaching and so the effect of an ASBO being imposed on an individual can be drastic, particularly as the orders apply for a minimum of two years and any prohibitions can apply to the whole of England and Wales. The judges did not make any observation with regard to the appropriateness or proportionality of the prohibitions laid down in the orders in *Clingham* and *McCann* (which in McCann excluded three brothers aged 13, 15 and 16 from their home neighbourhood), merely accepting that the conditions were needed to protect people in the area from further anti-social acts by them.

Given the ECtHR's insistence on the need to look at the reality behind the imposition of sanctions rather than focusing on semantic discussions as to whether the procedure is punitive or preventative, it is far from clear that the ECtHR would reach the same conclusion as the House of Lords on the classification of section 1(1) CDA. It is likely that the 'potentially wide-ranging terms and broad discretion given to judges in imposing the prohibitions of an ASBO may well persuade the European Court that section 1(1) is a penalty and hence criminal in nature.'[81]

---

78. Malige, para: [39].
79. *Welch v United Kingdom* (1995) 20 E.H.R.R. 247.
80. *Welch*, para: [30].
81. ASBOs, Preventative Orders and the European court of Human Rights' (2007), Bakalis C, *European Human Rights Law Review*, 4, 438.

A Criminal Classification: Re-asserting the Right to a Fair Trial?

It is arguable that the impact of a criminal classification of the first stage of ASBO proceedings would be minimal in that it would not prevent states continuing to adopt the two-stage process as a form of social control. However, it would require states to guarantee the protections offered to defendants under Article 6(3) ECHR. In the context of ASBOs, Article 6(3)(d) ECHR is of particular relevance as it will put limits on the extent to which hearsay evidence can be used when applying for such orders. Classifying the ASBO as criminal could also have implications for the publication of the names of those against whom an order has been imposed. A finding by the ECtHR that ASBOs are criminal, although not determinative of the issue (as the right to not have one's name published is not guaranteed under Article 6 ECHR), may well strengthen the case in favour of applying such restrictions. At a more fundamental level, a finding that the application stage for an ASBO is criminal could engage Articles 5 and 7 ECHR and trigger arguments about the requirements for legal certainty.[82] For, example the criminal classification would assist in ensuring that the prohibitions contained in an ASBO are suitably certain so as to give fair warning to citizens to know how to behave. Whether or not behaviour which causes harassment, alarm or distress is sufficiently well-defined is very much open to question. If such a challenge were made, the government would no doubt point to the decision in *Steel* where it was held that the concept of breach of the peace was sufficiently clear so as to satisfy the requirements of legal certainty. However, section 1(1) CDA can be distinguished from breach of the peace in a number of ways. The ECtHR was influenced by the fact that the term, 'breach of the peace', has been clarified by the UK courts over a number of years to cover acts which would provoke violence. In comparison the definition of anti-social behaviour is not agreed and the wording under section 1(1) CDA is far wider than acts which provoke violence.

---

82. See further, *Principles of Criminal Law* (2009), Ashworth A, 5th edition, Oxford: Oxford University Press, 76-78.

The two-stage order is an innovative tool that tests the very boundaries of the ECHR. A successful appeal to the ECtHR will not prohibit states from using the two-stage order, but it could dilute the benefits of overriding the criminal law and will ensure that Convention rights can no longer be subverted. None of this is to suggest that preventative orders such as the ASBO are undesirable in themselves; it is, however, to insist that they be subjected to proper procedural scrutiny in order to ensure that declared rights are not undermined.

Conclusion

Under the banner of anti-social behaviour the Labour Party encroached upon the regulation of traditional community problems and created novel means (such as the ASBO) to regulate anti-social behaviour. The ASBO has allowed the state to manipulate the law and operate outside of its usual criminal law model. I have argued in this chapter that the civil classification of the first stage of the ASBO proceedings allows the state to circumvent the fundamental legal safeguards of the criminal law and to subvert the right to a fair trial provided for by Article 6 ECHR. Following the relaxation of the criminal rules of hearsay evidence the necessity of a civil classification of the first stage of the ASBO proceedings is questionable. Furthermore the House of Lords' decision in *McCann* can also be criticised for paying insufficient regard to both the nature of the conduct that may result in the imposition of an ASBO and the impact and consequences of the prohibitions contained in an order. The decision also disregards the possibility that an ASBO may be imposed for both preventative and punitive objectives. It remains to be seen whether the measures used to tackle anti-social behaviour 'move beyond the ASBO'. What is clear is that hybrid nature of the ASBO is in need of a review.

CHAPTER 6

MANAGING RISK AND CHANGING PRIORITIES FOR PROBATION PRACTICE AND YOUTH JUSTICE

KATHRYN FARROW, GILL KELLY AND BERNADETTE WILKINSON

Previous chapters have discussed significant shifts, in the legal context towards the criminalisation of risk, or, as McNeill suggests, a move towards a concern with 'protecting potential future victims'.[1] In relation to those that have previously offended, the focus is now on reducing the offender's risk, with less attention paid to helping the offender lead a better life for their own sake: 'rehabilitation recast not as an end but as a mechanism for reducing crime'.[2] This shift, together with other changes, has had a major impact on practice in community criminal justice agencies.

This chapter will provide an account of how risk-led approaches are operationalised in criminal justice agencies, including an exploration of risk assessment tools, relevant processes, procedures and management arrangements. It explores the extent to which risk assessment processes and offender management are illustrations of a more centralised and standardised system of criminal justice. It asks who these developments have been for, and contrasts the growing technicality of practice and the performance driven culture within agencies, with the reality that practitioners need to establish and sustain relationships with individual offenders within their communities. It also poses the question about whether an increasing emphasis upon

---

1. 'What Works and What's Just?' (2009) McNeil, F. *European Journal of Probation*, Vol. 1, No. 2, 21, 23.
2. *Ibid*, 21.

risk avoidance militates against the strengths-based approaches that are now being recommended to support sustainable desistance from offending.[3]

Risk and Community Protection

A focus on risk with the associated community protection approach to risk management has, particularly for those offenders considered to pose a high risk of harm to others,[4] been associated with an increase in restrictive approaches. These measures have included indeterminate sentences and greater surveillance and control of those offenders in the community.[5]

More generally, for all offenders, not just those posing a high risk of harm, the National Offender Management Service in England and Wales[6] has the following aims:

- protect the public;
- reduce re-offending;
- punish offenders;
- rehabilitate offenders; and
- ensure victims feel justice has been done.

Rehabilitation is towards the bottom of this list; the emphasis on public protection and crime reduction has led to a greater stress on control and enforcement, with increased imprisonment as a result.[7] The Youth Justice Board for England and Wales (YJB), within their vision, places the aim that

---

3. See, for example, 'The Good Lives Model and conceptual issues in offender rehabilitation' (2004), Ward T and Brown M, *Psychology, Crime and Law*, vol 10, no 3, and *After Crime and Punishment* (2004), Maruna S and Immarigeon R, Cullompton: Willan.
4. *A Review on the Research Literature on Serious Violent Sexual Offenders; Research monograph* (2000) Connelly C and Williamson S, 1-121.
5. For more detail, see Criminal Justice Act 2003, Criminal Justice and Immigration Act, 2008; also MAPPA Guidance in Scotland 2008, England and Wales, 2009.
6. National Offender Management Service (2010). Available at www.noms.homeoffice.gov.uk (accessed 22nd February 2010).
7. *Prison Populations Projections 2006-2013* (2006), De Silva N, Cowell P, Chow T and Worthington P, London: Home Office.

'more offenders are caught, held to account for their actions, and stop offending' ahead of 'children and young people receive the support they need to lead crime-free lives'.[8] In the field of crime prevention interventions with children and families based on their risk of future offending have increased, access to resources for troubled young people being increasingly accessed through a criminal justice route and as a consequence, with larger numbers of young people being criminalised. These developments are viewed differentially as Morgan (2008) notes, 'the critics' 'net widening' is the government's 'closing the justice gap'.[9] Others describe the 'problematisation' of and response to anti-social behaviour by young people as overly emphasising 'discipline, punishment and containment' and failing to recognise the anti-social environments in which many live.[10]

The reasons for these changes in priorities are complicated but risk as a dominant political and societal discourse has played a significant role. Risk is generally couched in negative language, as something that people need be protected from rather than recognising that risk-taking can be positive in terms of empowering people and society to have choice and move forward.[11] Commentators like Beck[12] and Giddens[13] have suggested that societies are increasingly characterised by fear and anxiety and are facing a range of risks unknown in earlier generations. Waiton suggests that the growth of attention on crime reflects a failure of politics to engage productively with these new realities, with politicians seeking to cast themselves as protectors of the weak and vulnerable public.[14] Risk has come to the fore in the context of an increased fear of crime; the political process has played a part in both feeding and responding to that fear. Walklate and Mythen suggest 'that neo-

---

8. *Mission, vision and values* (2009) Youth Justice Board, www.yjb.gov.uk/en-gb/yjb/MissionVisionandValues (accessed 22nd February 2010).
9. 'Children, young people; criminalisation and punishment' (2009), Morgan R, in Barry M and McNeill F (eds) *Youth offending and youth justice*, London: JKP, 61.
10. *Rougher justice: anti-social behaviour and young people*, (2005) Squires, W. and Stephen, D. Cullompton: Willan.
11. *Risk And Risk Taking In Health And Social Welfare* (2004), Titterton M, London: JKP.
12. *Risk Society: Towards a New Modernity* (1992), Beck U, London: Sage.
13. *BBC 1999 Reith Lectures* (1999), Giddens A, BBC Radio Four.
14. *Policing after the crisis: Crime, safety and the vulnerable public: Punishment Society* (2009), Waiton S, 11; 359.

liberal politicians have become practised in nurturing and harnessing fear as a tool to reinforce political strategy and to legitimate law and order policies'.[15] However, such an overt emphasis on public protection has within it the potential seeds of its own destruction with the public losing confidence in the risk management system itself.[16] By promising to protect, government increases the sense that there is something to be feared. However, the nature of human behaviour means that our ability to predict and influence the actions of others is limited;[17] thus even in the best run justice system offending will occur and people will be harmed, making organisational failure inevitable. As Kemshall notes 'the risks facing us constantly outstrip the tools and technologies used to assess and tame them'.[18] This preoccupation with risk and fear of organisational failure has had an impact on probation and youth justice practice and on their agencies. It has clearly affected offenders themselves, not least for those serving more and/or longer prison sentences as a result. It has also affected society as a whole, changing views about who is responsible for how people behave towards one another. Higher expectations of organisations deemed responsible for protecting society and managing its risk can hinder the efforts of those organisations when they try to support the reintegration of offenders back into their communities.[19]

Impact on Practice

Practice in criminal justice has changed very significantly. The emphasis on public protection has resulted in much closer inter agency relationships between police and probation, for example, in supervising high risk offenders

---

15. 'How scared are we?' (2008), Walklate S and Mythen G, *British Journal of Criminology*, Vol. 48, 219.
16. 'Defensible Decisions for Risk: Or "It's the Doers Wot Get the Blame"', (1998) Kemshall H, *Probation Journal*, 45 (2) 67-72.
17. 'Risk Rationalities in Contemporary Social Work Policy and Practice', (2010) Kemshall H, *British Journal of Social Work*, 40(4) 1247-1262.
18. *Understanding risk in criminal justice* (2003), Kemshall H, Berkshire: Open University Press, 8.
19. *Towards Effective Practice in Offender Supervision* (2009), McNeil F. Glasgow: Scottish Centre for Crime and Justice Research, available at www.sccjr.ac.uk/documents/McNeil.

in the community through MAPPA arrangements.[20] However, despite growth in partnership working and the involvement of a much wider range of service providers in work with offenders,[21] the focus for most workers is linking with other professionals not on engagement with communities themselves.

Practice change has also been driven by other influences, including the significant impact of an evidence based approach. This requires agencies to invest resources in processes that have some proven effectiveness in reducing crime. Although a contested concept, 'evidence based practice' seems on the surface to be self-evidently 'what we should do'.[22] In reality evidence based practice—ensuring robust research informs what people do—is not unproblematic as it is dependent on the available research base. Any body of research will have been influenced by many forces, including the demands of policy makers and others who are funding research efforts. The interests of academics will support some research strands over others and of course some phenomenon are more susceptible to the 'gold standard' of research often favoured by government.[23]

How the evidence base is used and put into practice also makes a difference as can be seen in the development of the principles of Risk, Need and Responsivity (RNR) in relation to offender treatment and management. Risk, in this model, relates to the likelihood of reoffending or recidivism and the research-based view is that the more intensive interventions (length and frequency) are best reserved for higher risk offenders. Risk of harm to others is also a focus of attention for practitioners and the two types of risk can sometimes be unhelpfully conflated in discussions about risk and offending. Need, in this context, concerns the target of interventions and is defined as those

---

20. *Strengthening Multi-Agency Public Protection Arrangements (MAPPA)* (2005), Kemshall H, Wood J, Mackenzie G, Bailey R and Yates J, London: Home Office. This issue is explored more fully in *Chapter 12*.
21. 'Multi-agency practice: experiences in the youth justice system' (2008) Souhami A, in Green S, Lancaster E and Feasey S (eds) *Addressing Offending Behaviour: Context, Practice and Values*, Cullompton: Willan.
22. *Using evidence: How research can inform public services* (2007), Nutley S, Walter I and Davies H, Bristol: Policy Press.
23. See, *Using evidence: How research can inform public services* (2007), Nutley S, Walter I and Davies H, Bristol: Policy Press and 'Offending Behaviour Programmes: emerging evidence and implications for practice' (2004) Roberts C in Burnett R and Roberts C (eds) *What Works in Probation and Youth Justice, Developing evidence based practice*, Cullompton: Willan.

needs which are most closely associated with a person's offending behaviour. It is argued that these should be the primary focus for work with offenders (given the aim of the justice system to reduce offending). Responsivity is a developing concept and seeks to specify the characteristics of interventions which are most likely to have a positive effect upon offenders.[24] Responsivity includes the content and methods used and the manner in which they are delivered by practitioners. The concept places an onus upon practitioners to put in place interventions with which the individual offender is able to engage constructively.

Evidence based practice and the RNR concepts has been seen as offering real potential and welcomed by many practitioners. The principles of Risk and Need can help practitioners manage offenders' risk more rationally and focus their assessments and interventions more effectively on issues directly associated with offending. The principle of Responsivity stressed both the importance of the methods used and the need for flexible approaches which would take account of the different characteristics and capacities of offenders. The RNR approach was intended to be seen in its entirety with the principles complementing each other; they '…do not necessarily work on their own but need to be implemented together'.[25]

Early practitioner enthusiasm was evident in the 'What Works?' conferences of the early 1990s, at which the principles of effective practice were promoted alongside the importance of committed and well-trained staff. As interest in the 'What Works?' agenda gained momentum, its messages about effective practice began to chime with developing strategic and operational priorities. Probation bodies in England and Wales incorporated effective practice principles into their service developments. However in interpreting and operationalising messages from research they chose to focus attention on structured programme provision, largely group based and delivered via

---

24. 'Enhancing adherence to Risk-Need-Responsivity: Making quality a matter of policy' (2006), Andrews D A, *Criminology and Public Policy*, 5, 595–602; *Offenders in Focus: Risk, Responsivity and Diversity* (2007), Farrow K, Kelly G and Wilkinson B, Bristol: Policy Press and 'Exploring the Black Box of Community Supervision' (2008), Bonta J, Rugge T, Scott T, Bourgon G and Yessine A K, *Journal of Offender Rehabilitation*, Vol. 47(3), 248–270.

25. *Assessment, Planning Interventions and Supervision: Source Document* (2007), Youth justice Board, available from www.yjb.gov.uk/publications (accessed 22nd February 2010).

programmes that have gone through a significant process of accreditation. This focus on the technical aspects of effective practice arguably marginalised and underestimated the significance of other elements particularly those associated with responsivity.[26]

Whilst there is evidence of the effectiveness of accredited programmes, particularly in relation to specific groups of offenders,[27] the overall impact on offending of programmes has not been as great as had been hoped. Roberts acknowledges that programmes do have an impact on some offenders but argues that 'for the majority, the programmes *by themselves,* are unlikely to deliver the outcomes in reducing offending that have been expected of them'.[28] Wikstrom links effectiveness (or not) with the rigour and quality of its implementation and delivery.[29] Other commentators[30] argue that the emphasis on structured programmes has been at the expense of individual work with offenders which recognised their diversity of experience[31] and more directly facilitated their re-integration back into local communities, for example, employment, housing and debt.

---

26. See discussion in *Offenders in Focus: Risk, Responsivity and Diversity* (2007), Farrow K, Kelly G and Wilkinson B, Bristol: Policy Press and 'Exploring the Black Box of Community Supervision' (2008), Bonta J, Rugge T, Scott T, Bourgon G and Yessine A K, *Journal of Offender Rehabilitation*, Vol. 47(3), 248–270.
27. See for example, 'The Principles of Effective Correctional Treatment Also Apply To Sexual Offenders: A Meta-Analysis' (2009), Hanson, Bourgon, Helmus and Hodgson, *Criminal Justice and Behavior*, 37, 477-481.
28. 'Offending Behaviour Programmes: emerging evidence and implications for practice' (2004) Roberts C in Burnett R and Roberts C (eds) *What Works in Probation and Youth Justice, Developing evidence based practice*, Cullompton: Willan ,156 (emphasis as in the original).
29. Wikstrom, P, and Treiber, K. (2008), *Offending Behaviour Programmes: Source document*, London: YJB.
30. See, for example, 'Social Capital and offender reintegration: making probation desistance-focussed' (2004), Farrall S, in Maruna and Immarigeon (eds.), *After Crime and Punishment*, Cullompton: Willan and *Towards Effective Practice in Offender Supervision* (2009), McNeil F. Glasgow: Scottish Centre for Crime and Justice Research, available at: www.sccjr.ac.uk/documents/McNeil.
31. *The Assessment and treatment of women offenders: An integrative perspective* (2006), Blanchette K, and Brown S L, Chichester: Wiley, and *Offenders in Focus: Risk, Responsivity and Diversity* (2007), Farrow K, Kelly G and Wilkinson B, Bristol: Policy Press.

Risk Assessment Tools

Risk assessment tool have been developed to enable interventions and the allocation of resources to be structured in response to estimations of risk. These tools are designed to help practitioners to distinguish between different levels of risk in order to classify offenders. There are a number of different tools in existence[32] but all are designed to contribute to a similar outcome: identifying the appropriate level of risk category an individual falls within so that decisions can be made about the type and intensity of interventions. Higher risk offenders attract greater intensity of supervision, whilst lower risk individuals can be supervised with a lighter touch.

To achieve this classification most tools adopt scoring systems to reflect the judgement of those making assessments.[33] They are rooted in a risk factor approach to predicting offending behaviour drawing on longitudinal and other studies that have investigated the correlation between a range of risk factors and the incidence of offending behaviour.[34] Briefly, these tools gather and record information in a structured way about research derived risk factors and use that information to determine the likelihood of re-offending and, where relevant, an offender's potential for seriously harming others.[35] Information, systematically collected, informs two types of assess-

---

32. For example, OASys and LSI-R for adults offenders and *Asset* and YSLI-R in youth justice.
33. The OASys assessment tool has been evaluated (See *A Compendium of research and analysis on the Offender Assessment System (OASys) 2006-2009* (2009), Debidin M (ed.), Ministry of Justice Research Series 16/09). A new version, *OASys* Release 4.3.1 2009 was deployed at the end of August 2009. The research base and design of *Asset* is in *Assessment, Planning Interventions and Supervision: Source Document* (2007), Youth Justice Board, available from www.yjb.gov.uk/publications (accessed 22nd February 2010).
34. See 'Key Results from the first forty years of the Cambridge Study in Delinquent Development' (2003), Farrington D, in Thornberry T P and Krohn M D (eds) *Taking stock of delinquency: and overview of Findings from Contemporary Longitudinal Studies*, New York: Kluwer; *Criminal Careers and Life Success: new findings from the Cambridge Study in Delinquent Development* (2006), Farrington D, Coid J, Harnett L, Jolliffe D, Soteriou N, Turner R and West D. Research Findings 281, London: Home Office; 'Social Inclusion and Early Desistance from Crime' (2006), Smith D J, *Edinburgh Study of Youth Transitions and Crime Research Digest* No 12, University of Edinburgh and 'Theory and method in the Edinburgh Study of Youth Transitions and Crime' (2003), Smith D J and McVie S, *British Journal of Criminology*, 43(1) 169-195.
35. See *Assessment, Planning Interventions and Supervision: Source Document* (2007), Youth Justice

ment: actuarial and clinical. In actuarial assessment, statistical calculations are used to predict the likelihood that an offender will be reconvicted based on reconviction rates for large populations with similar characteristics, in like situations. Some of the most significant actuarial information is static, including age, gender and criminal history which do not change. OGRS (the Offender Group Reconviction Scale) and early tools (sometimes termed as second generation tools) are actuarially based. Actuarial information is important in terms of risk classification but does not help in planning subsequent interventions. Clinical assessment which tends to focus upon dynamic risk factors; offending related needs or influences, that if addressed, may reduce the likelihood of the behaviour of concern and therefore support risk planning.[36] Increasingly assessments (third and fourth generation tools) have also included the identification of dynamic risk factors and support structured professional judgment.[37]

The tools now commonly used in England, Wales and Scotland in practice with adults and young people who offend all contain elements of professional judgement. They play a dual role in both classifying offenders into risk levels that inform the level and nature of interventions to be offered, but also guide the content of those interventions in order to address the most significant influences on offending behaviour.

The impact of risk assessment tools has been substantial. As well as supporting a more accurate approach to estimating future risk and enabling service delivery to be targeted at the identified risks, they have increased the consistency of assessments and the range of information gathered in the course of risk assessment.[38] However, this has not been unproblematic.

Board, Appendix 2 for a selection of risk factor research. Available from www.yjb.gov.uk/publications accessed 22nd February 2010. And *Offenders Risk of Serious Harm: a Literature Review* (2002), Powis B, Home Office RDS, Occasional Paper No 81, London: Home Office.

36. See *Risk Assessment and Management of Known Sexual and Violent Offenders: A review of current issues* (2001), Kemshall H, Home Office paper 140, 14-16 and *Understanding the Community Management of High Risk Offenders* (2008), Kemshall H, Berkshire: Open University Press.

37. *Standards and Guidelines for Risk Management* (2007), RMA (Risk Management Authority), Paisley: RMA. Available at www.RMAScotland.gov.uk. And 'Risk and need assessment' (2008), Bonta J and Wormith S J, in McIvor G and Raynor P (eds) *Developments in social work with offenders*, London: JKP.

38. *Role of Risk and Protective Factors* (2005), Sutherland A, Merrington S, Jones S, Baker K and

Arguably, while they have improved the range and quantity of information considered and recorded, they have been less successful in improving the analysis and understanding of the information in the context of each offender's life and situation.[39] Prediction remains a problem. For example, whilst it may be possible to calculate statistically that an offender with a particular offending profile has a 60% chance of reconviction when compared with others with a similar profile, it is not possible to say whether the offender in question is in the 60% who will be convicted or the 40% who won't.[40] There is a concern that a mere gathering of information about risk factors fails to move beyond correlation to understanding causality.[41] Furthermore, because of the time demands involved in completing risk assessment, what Kemshall calls 'the demand to maintain workflow',[42] practitioners look for evidence which confirms past judgements rather than looking for new or contradictory evidence and do not always update it when circumstances change. Critics of risk-led developments have drawn attention to a narrowing focus of concern, individualising risk, holding individual offenders responsible for their actions[43] and taking attention away from social influences.[44] Others have emphasised what they see as an overly negative and deficit led approach with insufficient attention to strengths and protective factors. Ward and Brown, in articulating their 'Good Lives Model', argue that the negative orientation associated with a risk-based paradigm, is actually an obstacle to constructive engagement with offenders.[45] Identifying the posi-

---

Roberts C, London: Youth Justice Board.
39. See 'Re-visioning risk assessment for human service decision making' (2004), Schwalbe C, *Children and Youth Services Review*, 26, 561-576; 'Risk, uncertainty and public protection: assessment of young people who offend' (2007), Baker K, *British Journal of Social Work*, Vol. 8 No.3, 1463-1480 and 'Serious Further Offences: An exploration of risk and typologies' (2009), Craissati J and Sindall O, *Probation Journal*, Vol. 56, No. 1, 9-27.
40. *Understanding the Community Management of High Risk Offenders* (2008), Kemshall H, Berkshire: Open University Press.
41. *Offending Behaviour Programmes: Source Document* (2008), Wikström P and Treiber K, YJB.
42. 'Risk Rationalities in Contemporary Social Work Policy and Practice' (2010), Kemshall H, *British Journal of Social Work*, 9.
43. *Understanding the Community Management of High Risk Offenders* (2008), Kemshall H, Berkshire: Open University Press.
44. *Towards Effective Practice in Offender Supervision* (2009), McNeil F. Glasgow: Scottish Centre for Crime and Justice Research, available at www.sccjr.ac.uk/documents/McNeil.
45. 'The Good Lives Model and conceptual issues in offender rehabilitation' (2004), Ward T and

tive resources available to individuals, the protective factors in their lives, is essential to being able to promote long-term desistance from offending not merely short-term risk management and containment.[46]

Risk-led Approaches

Probation and now the Youth Justice Service in England and Wales have moved towards organising service delivery based on a risk-led approach to practice. These approaches are framed in legislation (Criminal Justice Act 2003; Criminal Justice and Immigration Act 2008) and then in service design and delivery (including policies and guidance). The intention is, in relation to both adults and young people, for the court 'to be able to provide each offender with a sentence that best *meets the need of the particular case*, at any *level of seriousness*, and for *sentences to be more effectively managed* by the correctional services...'.[47] In practice, the aim is that the intensity (content and frequency of contact) of supervision will be tailored in light of the assessed level of likelihood of reoffending and risk to the public; that offenders are subject to differential supervision, with higher risk offenders attracting more practitioner time and resources, and interventions being more appropriately targeted. For offenders this should mean that the demands that are made of them will be in line with the risks that they pose rather than the more broadly standardised requirements that risk-led approaches were intended to replace and that organisations can allocate resources more rationally. This may disadvantage some lower risk offenders who may not 'qualify' for certain programmes or resources. Whilst practitioners have some flexibility in how they use their time and the methods they use, critics (for example, Phoenix) point to the increasing centrality of the technologies of risk assessment in

---

Brown M, *Psychology, Crime and Law*, vol.10, no.3, 243-57.
46. *After Crime and Punishment: Pathways to offender reintegration* (2004), Maruna S and Immarigeon R, Cullompton: Willan and *Towards Effective Practice in Offender Supervision* (2009), McNeil F. Glasgow: Scottish Centre for Crime and Justice Research, available at www.sccjr.ac.uk/documents/McNeil.
47. Criminal Justice Act (2003), Home Office, London: HMSO (*our italics*).

determining levels of intervention and the consequent 'standardisation of provision and delivery'.[48]

Managerialism and the Growth of Information Technology

These risk-led and evidence-based influences on practice in criminal justice agencies, as elsewhere in the public sector, have also been affected by the rise in managerialism, the growth in information technologies and related demands for the recording, sharing and monitoring of information. These developments link to a more target driven approach to the management of services,[49] to judgements of quality and to the accountability of practitioners to organisations and standards rather than to individual service users.[50] Technology, organisational and governmental information demands drive each other. Being able to gather information easily, particularly numerically, increases the desire of managers and policy makers to have ready access to that information and tighten control over the services they are responsible for. The more services are measured and monitored the more this feeds a demand for yet more information, particularly if the process of measurement uncovers areas of poor practice or failure in relation to processes and procedures. When this is happening in a climate of fear about crime and the criticisms that will result if, for example, someone on supervision kills, the demand for monitoring becomes even more pressing.

There is an expectation now in the public sector, and elsewhere, that someone will be held accountable for failures in risk management. Organisations are therefore increasingly concerned with managing organisational risk.[51] Practitioners operating within such an organisation are likely to be

---

48. 'Beyond Risk Assessment: The Return of Repressive Welfarism' (2009), Phoenix J, in Barry and McNeil (eds) *Youth offending and youth justice*, London: Jessica Kingsley Publishers, 117.
49. 'Target Practice in Probation: Take Aim for a Reappraisal' (2007), Whitehead P, *British Journal of Community Justice*, 5(2) 83-95.
50. 'Accountable and Countable: Information Management Systems and the Bureaucratization of Social Work' (2009), Burton J and Van den Boeck D, *British Journal of Social Work*, 39, 1326-1342.
51. *The Risk Management of Everything* (2004), Power M, London: DEMOS. www.demos.co.uk.

worried about their own job security and status and this may reduce their willingness to take risks, or to challenge organisational practices.

Certainly, there are increased demands on practitioners to record their work and the time spent at the computer screen has grown as opposed to the time spent in interactions with offenders. A survey conducted by the Ministry of Justice revealed that on average direct contact with offenders was 24% of staff time with 41% being spent on computer activity.[52] The sense of autonomy felt by those same practitioners and their managers has decreased, with more time spent adhering to agreed procedures and evidencing the defensibility of their decision making.[53]

Most practitioners in community criminal justice, in our experience, would not want to lose the benefits of the developing knowledge base about the influences that are relevant to offending behaviour and about what might work in helping to reduce it that have come from the risk factor and effectiveness approaches. Many would not want to lose the accountability of practitioners for the services they deliver. However, many are frustrated and over whelmed by procedural requirements and want the opportunity to develop greater skills and understandings in strengths based approaches and in engaging offenders as agents in their own journey to a different life. Just as offenders need to develop self-efficacy, practical and realistic confidence in their capacity to sustain change, so do practitioners. There is also a need to develop effective communities with both the capacities and confidence to collaborate in the reintegration of a potentially 'vilified group'.[54] Developing this sense of efficacy in offenders, practitioners and communities and their shared responsibility in responding to risk is necessary if the management of risky behaviour is not just something that agencies do or fail to do.

---

52. 'Only 24% direct contact time–its official!' NAPO News, Dec/Jan 2010 Issue 215.
53. See 'Risking legal repercussions' (1996), Carson D, in Kemshall H and Pritchard J (eds), *Good Practice in Risk Assessment and Risk Management*, Vol. 1, London: JKP; 'Practising in a context of ambivalence: the challenge for youth justice workers' (2002), Eadie T and Canton R, *Youth Justice*, Vol. 2, No. 1, 14-26; 'Still committed after all these years? : Morale in the modern-day Probation Service' (2004), Farrow K, *Probation Journal*, Vol.51 No.3, 206-220 and 'Defensible Decisions for Risk: Or 'It's the Doers Wot Get the Blame'" (1998), Kemshall H, *Probation Journal*, 45(2) 67-72.
54. *Towards Effective Practice in Offender Supervision* (2009), McNeil F, Glasgow: Scottish Centre for Crime and Justice Research, available at www.sccjr.ac.uk/documents/McNeil.

Impact on Offenders

Practitioners are expected by HM Inspectorate of Probation to use both constructive and restrictive approaches to managing risk posed by offenders.[55] The former, designed to help offenders make changes that reduce their likelihood of further offending, include such elements as finding employment or helping them to develop self-management skills. Restrictive approaches include monitoring and surveillance of an offender's behaviour and imposing restriction over their movements in order to control their access to offending opportunities. This is similar to Hornquist's use of the concepts of productive and repressive power.[56] He suggests that power is being exercised in all attempts by the state, or dominant groups to intervene in the lives of others. To illustrate this in the prison context, productive power would be involving prisoners in education or treatment groups that require their active engagement. Repressive power has been exercised by incarcerating them in the first place and may be used further by forcing their attendance in programmes. Clearly a balance needs to be struck with both of these ways of thinking about work with offenders. For some offenders a degree of restriction and coerced cooperation may be needed, but for real change to occur the offender needs to be engaged productively as a stakeholder within that process.[57]

Arguably criminal justice agencies have spent too little time thinking about how to ensure that constructive elements of risk management really engage offenders as stakeholders rather than being experienced as slightly more benign aspects of repressive control. Despite the inclusion of Responsivity as one of the RNR principles, less attention has been paid to actively engaging the offenders themselves in the process of change.[58] This may help to explain some of the experiences of practitioners in criminal justice agencies as they encounter increasing repressive organisational power and become less

---

55. See *Public Protection & Safeguarding an Inspectorate perspective* (2009), Bridges A, London: HMIP.
56. *The Organised Nature of Power: On Productive and Repressive Based on Consideration of Risk* (2007), Hornqvist M, Stockholm University.
57. 'What Works and What's Just?' (2009), McNeil F, *European Journal of Probation*, Vol. 1, No. 2, 21-40.
58. See 'Risk and need assessment' (2008), Bonta J and Wormith S J, in McIvor G and Raynor P (eds) *Developments in social work with offenders*, London: JKP.

confident in their ability to deliver services that are individually responsive.[59] While there is little hard evidence to draw on, practitioner skills and efficacy beliefs[60] are being built around organisational requirements, procedures and processes rather than around skills in working with offenders and making confident professional judgements about individuals and their situations.

In turn this has altered offenders' experiences of community supervision, with more time and attention being paid to the processes of assessing and classifying them and less time spent resolving the problems that they bring to their supervision appointments on the basis that many offender concerns are not necessarily seen as directly linking to the offending behaviour and as such are not a priority. Their subsequent allocation to standardised interventions (which are often delivered through group programmes rather than individually) may also undermine the sense of continuity and commitment for the offender. Heavy emphasis on enforcement and breach procedures (should the offender fail to comply with supervision requirements) reinforces the idea that 'NOMS exists to provide a *service* to the law abiding public… and not *for* offenders but to manage them for us'.[61]

Conclusion

Petrunick raises the idea of who should be controlling the most potentially dangerous offenders, the few professional experts, or the many, as part of the communities in which they live.[62] At its worst the latter could result in vigilantism, but is it possible to find a balance? Should we be seeking approaches that help offenders both to become part of their communities and still hold them accountable for their actions?

---

59. 'Still committed after all these years? : Morale in the modern-day Probation Service' (2004), Farrow K, *Probation Journal*, Vol.51 No.3, 206-220.
60. For a more detailed explanation, see *Self-Efficacy* (1997), Bandura A, New York, NY: W.H. Freeman.
61. 'Commodification and offender management' (2007), McCulloch T and McNeill F, *Criminology and Criminal Justice*, 7(3), 231 (emphasis as in the original).
62. 'Managing Unacceptable Risk: sex offenders, community response and social policy in the United States and Canada' (2002), Petrunik M, *International Journal of Offender Therapy and Comparative Criminology*, 46(4): 483-511.

This chapter has explored the development and application of risk assessment tools and the impact risk-led approaches have had on practitioners, agencies and offenders within the system. It has explored concerns that risk management processes are becoming too centralised and pre-occupied by the technical detail, thus paying insufficient attention towards seeing offenders within a wider context as part of communities. The discourse of risk has emphasised the need to assess and manage risk effectively to protect people *from* risk rather than also recognising that risk-taking is essential in moving people and society forward. Maybe the balance to be redressed now is between protection and containment of unacceptable risk and helping people (offenders, practitioners and communities) to take or live with informed risks.[63] This will require criminal justice agencies to engage with communities' anxieties about crime, taking seriously their insecurities whilst at the same time helping them to understand the process of rehabilitation and their potentially pivotal role in supporting desistance.[64] The processes and procedures that have grown up around risk provide a helpful framework within which to undertake this dialogue. Practitioners and communities need education and support in order to have the confidence to make this happen.[65]

---

63. The Child Sex Offender Public Disclosure Pilots were part of an initiative which aimed to explore how practically to achieve this balance. It is described and evaluated in *Child Sex Offender Review (CSOR) Public Disclosure Pilots:a process evaluation* (2010), Kemshall H, Wood J, Westwood S, Stout B, Wilkinson B, Kelly G and Mackenzie G, London: Home Office Research Report 32.
64. *Towards Effective Practice in Offender Supervision* (2009), McNeil F, Glasgow: Scottish Centre for Crime and Justice Research, available at www.sccjr.ac.uk/documents/McNeil.
65. See *Chapter 10* for an example of this practice development.

CHAPTER 7

(IN)SECURITY, RISK, MUSLIM COMMUNITIES, POLICING AND THE 'NEW TERRORISM'

SHAMILA AHMED AND BASIA SPALEK

Introduction

There has been an unprecedented research and policy focus upon Muslim minorities over the last ten years or so, with studies exploring questions of identity, citizenship, religiosity and activism. In the vast majority of the research and policy literature the specific issue of victimisation has been neglected, partly because the research that is being funded largely focuses upon state-led understandings of security rather than community-focussed approaches, despite official assurances that individuals' safety is a key policy and practice concern. This chapter specifically examines a hitherto neglected area: the ways in which state tactics, discourses, policy and interventions under 'new terrorism' and the subsequent 'war on terror' have impacted Muslim minorities' feelings of (un)safety in the UK. Particular attention is paid to how counter terrorism legislation, which is based on a preventative, pre-crime discourse, has shaped Muslim minorities' perceptions of community safety, fear of crime and feelings of security.

The chapter explores the complexities of 'new terrorism', detailing how the 'war on terror' has produced a disjuncture in understanding and perceptions between the state and state authorities and Muslim minorities. First, the state centric approach to 'new terrorism' is discussed whereby it is argued that the state management of risk and the prevention of violent extremism has constructed Muslim minorities as constituting 'the problem' of terrorism. Second, it is explored how the 'war on terror' has re-configured understandings and experiences of state authorities, particularly perceptions and experiences of the police. Third, the issue of Islamophobia and racism are discussed in relation to both counter-terrorism legislation and wider societal dynamics. It is suggested that Muslim minorities' feelings of (un)safety now include a fear of the police, with the regulatory and risk dominated framework of preventing terrorism perceived as state victimisation. It is, therefore, important to highlight that although the 'new terrorism' discourse, as constituted by mainstream policy makers, academics and other influential bodies, has presented the rationale of counter-terrorism legislation and policies as creating a safer society, for Muslim minorities' this rationale has produced a sense of (un)safety.

Finally, the chapter will explore the work of the Muslim Contact Unit, a counter-terrorism policing unit based on principles of community policing, in order to highlight that, despite the difficult broader context of state victimisation, some innovative approaches are being undertaken between the police and Muslim communities. This is because efforts to counter 'new terrorism' are increasingly drawing upon community-based initiatives based upon engagement and partnership work between police officers and members of Muslim communities, in the UK, in some parts of Northern Europe, North America and in other international contexts. Communities are being seen as key partners in countering the threat of 'new terrorism', and community policing models are increasingly being drawn upon, and utilised.[1] This chapter contributes to the central concern of this book, the contrasting paradigms of central state approaches and local initiatives through considering the response of the regulatory state to preventing terrorism and exploring

---

1. 'Policing Uncertainty: Countering Terror through Community Intelligence and Democratic Policing' (2006) Innes M, *Annals of APSS* 605, 1-20; *Hearts and Minds and Eyes and Ears: reducing radicalisation risks through reassurance-oriented policing* (2007) Innes M, Abbotts L, Loew T and Roberts C, Cardiff University: Universities' Police Science Institute; 'Countering Terror: Violent Radicalisation and Situational Intelligence' (2008) Lowe T and Innes M, *Prison Service Journal* Issue 179, 3-10; 'Canadian Muslims, Islamophobia and National Security Royal Canadian Mounted Police' (2008) Hanniman W, *International Journal of Law, Crime and Justice* Vol. 36 (4) 271-285; 'Partnering for Prevention' *PfP* (2008) Ramirez D, Accessed on April 25, 2010 at www.ace.neu.edu/pfp; 'Muslim Communities, Counter-terrorism and De-radicalisation: a reflective approach to engagement' (2008) Spalek and Lambert, *International Journal of Law, Crime and Justice* Vol. 36 (4) 257-270.

local contexts within which some decentralised, innovative approaches and practices are being developed to facilitate engagement and partnerships between Muslim communities and police.

'New Terrorism' Discourse and the Pathologisation of Muslim Minorities

There are many factors that are essential to understanding the contemporary realities that shape Muslim minorities' experiences and perceptions and it is through deconstructing the 'war on terror' that lived realities and emotively charged sentiments can be understood. Since 9/11 the prevention of al-Qaeda inspired and/or instigated terror-related crimes has become a significant policy issue internationally, in countries across Europe, South Asia, North America, the Middle East and Australasia. Government officials and security experts worldwide have used the terminology of the 'new terrorism' to convey the sense of a heightened risk from terrorist activity faced by western liberal democratic states.[2] It was the placement of 'new terrorism', the attribution of risk to the crime of terrorism and the subsequent response of the state which mark a departure from previous forms of terrorism.

The phrase 'war on terror' was used by the G. W. Bush administration in response to the 9/11 terrorist attacks[3] and has become a discourse that defined the attacks, identified the enemy and framed the response taken by nation states, most notably the UK and America to the terrorist attacks of 9/11. The attacks were constructed as a new form of global terrorism, in which terrorism was constructed as the dark side of globalisation and as the evil enemy of the world.[4] This new form of global terrorism gave way to not only the attachment of new identities to those whom compromise the enemy of the

---

[2]. 'Criminology and Terrorism' (2006) Mythen G and Walklate S, *British Journal of Criminology*, 46 (3) 379-398.

[3]. What is the 'War on Terror?' John Judis *The New Republic Online*, June 5, 2006 Available at www.carnegieendowment.org/publications/index.cfm?fa=view&id=18409&prog=zgp&proj=zusr

[4]. *Terrorism, Risk and International Security: The Perils of Asking 'What If?'* (2008), Mythen G and Walklate S, Security Dialogue, 39 (2): 221–242; 'Globalization, ethnicity and racism: An introduction' (2008), Bosworth M, Bowling B and Lee M, *Theoretical criminology*, 12(3): 263—273.

world but also the construction of the inhumane, pathological, self autonomy lacking, and incapacitated terrorist. According to Brah, a 'suicide bomber' is not a given but is socially constructed.[5] Findlay[6] argues the suicide bomber is de-humanised, as lacking respect for the lives of innocent victims while Tadros[7] and Stohl[8] both argue such a definition has the purpose of placing terrorist activity outside the political process. It is through constructing terrorism as being outside the political process and humanity that principles of liberalism and human rights are legitimised as not existing. In this way, the suspects of terrorism 'suffer the pain of being denied their own humanity,'[9] and it is this construction that now impacts upon Muslim minorities' feelings of (un)safety.

The construction of the terrorist within the 'new terrorism' discourse has accelerated the need for the identification of the suicide bomber and has helped to homogenise and essentialise those possessing Islamic identities– Muslim minorities. It is on a global context that Islam has been singled out as being the major threat to Western democracies and civil society,[10] with Howell[11] referring to the 'unhealthy construction of Islam as enjoying a special affinity with terrorism'. The focus on 'Islamist' terrorism and Islamic identities had central to it that Islamic identities represented an unprecedented threat and risk to the world and one that had to be eradicated through international wars, Iraq and Afghanistan. Within the nation state 'new terrorism' was used to justify national security measures which were based on state surveillance and the need for measures which incapacitated those deemed to be potential terrorists.

---

5. *Identity, Ethnic Diversity and Community Cohesion* (2009), Brah A, Sage Publications Ltd.
6. 'Terrorism and relative justice' (2007), Findlay M, *Crime, Law and Social Change*, 47: 57—68.
7. 'Rethinking the presumption of innocence' (2007), Tadros V, *Criminal law and philosophy*, 1: 139-231.
8. 'Networks, terrorists and criminals: the implications for community policing' (2008), Stohl M, *Crime, Law and Social change*, 50: 59—72.
9. Cited in *Constitutive Criminology at Work: Applications to Crime and Justice* (1999), Henry S and Milovanovic D, State University of New York Press, 8.
10. 'The politics of engagement between Islam and the secular state: ambivalences of 'civil society'' (2004), Turam B, *The British Journal of Sociology*, 55 (2): 258-281.
11. 'The Global War On Terror' (2006), Howell J, *Development and Civil Society*, 128.

'New Terrorism' Discourse and Counter-terrorism Legislation

The threat of 'Islamist' terrorism has been used by the state to justify punitive measures on the basis of suspicion and risk, measures that violate human rights. The UK response to 'new terrorism', as McCulloch and Pickering argue, has been to extend and redefine beyond reasonable suspicion because under this legislation the police can stop and search without the need for an objective basis, and therefore base suspicion on a suspects personal characteristics[12].

The UK has a history of terrorism legislation (Prevention of Violence Act 1939, the Prevention of Terrorism (Temporary Provisions) Act 1989 and Northern Ireland (Emergency Provisions) Act 1996) which has been in place for over 30 years. This legislation was introduced to counter the terrorist threat associated with the Irish Republican Army (IRA) and extended the powers of the state agencies, such as the police. First, as Hillyard states Northern Ireland was a site for extending surveillance through developing new technologies.[13] Second, the purpose of the legislation and arrests under this terrorist legislation was to gather intelligence, gain informers and screen the Irish community.[14] Finally, it was through the attribution of suspicion onto Irish communities that policies such as 'shoot-to-kill' were practiced by the British Army and Royal Ulster Constabulary, and Hillyard (1993) argues this legislation was part of a larger strategy of exceptional measures used to target Irish people.

Although there is a long history of legislation to combat terrorism, Mythen and Walklate contend 'new terrorism' conveys the actions of extreme Islamic fundamentalist groups and has therefore been distinguished and set apart from the terrorist violence practiced by organizations such as the IRA.[15] Pan-

---

12. 'Pre-Crime and Counter terrorism: Imagining future crime in the "war on terror"'(2009), McCulloch J and Pickering S, *British Journal of Criminology*, 18: 121-135.
13. Cited in 'Policing and Terrorism' (3003) Matassa M and Newburn T, in Newburn T (ed) *Handbook of Policing*, Devon: Willan Publishing, 467-500.
14. *Suspect Community: People's Experiences of the Prevention of Terrorism Acts in Britain* (1993), Hillyard P, London: Pluto Press.
15. 'Terrorism, Risk and International Security: The Perils of Asking 'What If?' (2008), Mythen G and Walklate S, *Security Dialogue*, 39 (2): 221-242.

tazis and Pemberton, drawing on Hillyard's study of Irish people's experience of the Prevention of Terrorism (Temporary Provisions) Act 1974 (and subsequent amendments) evidence how Muslim minorities have replaced the Irish now forming the 'suspect community'.[16]

'New terrorism' has accelerated the existence of otherisation and criminalization through the introduction of exceptional legislation which gives the police greater autonomy and power. The Terrorism Act was passed in 2000, and the Anti Terrorism, Crime and Security Act 2001 (ATCSA) went into force on December 13, 2001. However, in 2005, Part 4 of the ATCSA 2001 was replaced with a system of control orders under the Prevention of Terrorism Act 2005 (PTA). The PTA 2005 is one of the most controversial pieces of legislation to emerge because the Act allows for control orders to be made against any suspected terrorist, whether a UK national or a non-UK national, or whether the terrorist activity is international or domestic. The control orders are therefore of a preventive nature, and as such are designed to restrict the activities of suspects who officials fear pose a threat if left unmonitored. The Terrorism Act 2006 was drafted as a response to the July 7 2005 London bombings and while at Bill stage this legislation was criticised for several provisions, most notably an extension of detention without charge from 14 days to 3 months (later reduced to 28 days after a Commons defeat). The period of detention that this Act legitimizes far exceed the period of detention used by any other European state member.[17] According to Klausen each piece of legislation has extended the police's powers.[18] Within the 'war on terror' there has been acceleration in pre-crime as Zedner argues; the pre-crime logic of security[19] has overshadowed the post

---

16. 'From the "old" to the "new" suspect community: Examining the Impacts of Recent UK Counter-Terrorist Legislation' (2009), Pantazis C and Pemberton S, *British Journal of Criminology*, 49, 646–666.
17. *Terrorism pre-charge detention comparative law study* (2007) Liberty. Available at www.liberty-human-rights.org.uk/policy/reports/comparative-law-study-2010-pre-charge-detention.pdf
18. 'British Counter-Terrorism After 7/7: Adapting Community Policing to the Fight Against Domestic Terrorism' (2009), Klausen J, *Journal of Ethnic and Migration Studies*. Vol. 35, No. 3, 403-420.
19. 'Pre-crime' means that suspects do not actually have to commit a crime to be criminalised and further the traditional evidence-based criminal justice processes are not applied as suspicion without the need for evidence can lead to punitive measures such as house arrest and detention.

crime orientation of criminal justice.[20] Further, there has been a growth in criminalising activities and associations on the basis of prevention[21] and the emphasis on pre-empting threats and security has meant that punishment or restrictions can be imposed without traditional practices of procedural law being applied.[22] Ericson has thus argued that counter-terrorism legislation comprise of counter laws because they are 'laws against law' which erode traditional principles, standards and procedures of criminal law.[23]

It is the lack of human rights protection afforded to suspects of terrorist activity, the fact that suspicion and risk alone can justify the use of house arrest and detention, the power of the police to religiously profile in pre-empting threats under the pre-crime logic of counter terrorism policing, which has produced a significant shift in perceptions of the police and which has produced feelings of (un)safety. This is an important issue, given that in the UK the government's main counter-terrorism policy, CONTEST 2, stresses the need for community involvement in countering 'new terrorism'.[24] Pantazis and Pemberton have argued that 'it is difficult to see how such skilful, yet ultimately fragile 'soft approaches' can thrive, when the full weight of state suspicion and the brutality of 'hard' methods have fallen on these communities'.[25] According to Demos, the targeting of particular minority ethnic communities makes trust-based relationships more necessary but less feasible than ever.[26] Therefore, the next section focuses specifically on the issue of the role of community policing within a counter-terrorism context.

---

20. 'Pre-crime and post criminology?' (2007), Zedner L, *Theoretical Criminology*, 11 (2): 261-281.
21. For further discussion of this, see *Chapter 2* of this work.
22. For example, punishment in the form of house arrest can be used without a trial having taken place. Within this context state authorities have portrayed criminal trials as a risk to national security because intelligence could be compromised through a criminal trial.
23. Cited in 'Pre-Crime and Counter terrorism: Imagining future crime in the "war on terror"' (2009), McCulloch J and Pickering S, *British Journal of Criminology*, 6.
24. 'Anti-Social Behaviour Powers and the Policing of Security' (2010), Spalek B and McDonald L, *Social Policy and Society*, Vol. 9 (1), 123-133.
25. 'From the 'old' to the 'new' suspect community': Examining the Impacts of Recent UK Counter-Terrorist Legislation' (2009), Pantazis C and Pemberton S, *British Journal of Criminology*, 21.
26. *The Activist Police Force*, (2007), London: Demos.

'New Terrorism', Policing and Community Engagement

According to Virta, community-based policing is still very much prominent in policing agendas.[27] Rather than there having been a paradigm shift from community-based policing to intelligence-led policing, both styles of policing co-exist, albeit there being different emphases on the different styles in different contexts. Police services engage with communities as part of a wider strategy of securing community-based intelligence so as to respond to local, regional, national and international security risks.[28] In England and Wales there now exists a burgeoning policing infrastructure that links community-based policing with intelligence-led policing in relation to the prevention of terrorism, with Prevent indicators and police performance measures being used to assess the effectiveness of any initiatives and engagement work that is being undertaken.[29] However, to date there has been little empirical investigation of community-based policing within a counter-terrorism context, even though this raises many questions. As a result, there is little empirical investigation into, or understanding of, what community-based policing within a counter-terrorism context involves, of the kinds of issues that police officers and communities confront in this context, and whether community policing and intelligence-led policing models may clash and serve to undermine each other? As Ratcliffe has argued, 'where community policing aims primarily for police legitimacy and is organisationally bottom-up and community centered, intelligence-led policing aims for crime reduction, is top-down and hierarchical'.[30] Moreover, within the context of counter-terrorism, Hanniman argues that the intelligence-led policing model can be linked to national

---

27. 'Community policing meets new challenges' (2008), Virta S, in: Virta S (ed) *Policing Meets New Challenges: preventing radicalization and recruitment*, Finland: University of Tampere Department of Management Studies, CEPO, 15-41.
28. 'Neighborhood policing and community safety: Researching the instabilities of the local governance of crime, disorder and security in contemporary UK' (2007), Hughes G and Rowe M, *Criminology & Criminal Justice*, Vol 7(4).
29. 'Policing the "new extremism" in 21st Century Britain' (2010) Gregory F, in Goodwin and Eatwell (eds) *The 'New' Extremism in 21st Century Britain*, London: Taylor & Francis.
30. Cited in 'Community policing meets new challenges' (2008) Virta S, in Virta (ed) *Policing Meets New Challenges: preventing radicalization and recruitment Finland: University of Tampere Department of Management Studies*, CEPO, pp 15-41.

security policing strategies which derive their authority from the state or government, and so do not require public consent or support.[31] In this context, community members are encouraged to watch and share information on suspicious neighbours or friends with police—community members are viewed as informants by state authorities, rather than partners. Local police may also be encouraged to use their community policing programmes and relationships to penetrate local communities and provide intelligence. These strategies, Hanniman argues, can rapidly alienate a community.[32] At the same time, community policing itself has been criticised for being nothing more than a public relations exercise, or for being a form of 'soft power' in trying to get communities to follow wider political agendas.[33]

The developments above raise deeper questions for community-based practices within a counter-terrorism context in relation to policing. If drawing upon Virta's conceptualisation of community policing as promoting community-based problem-solving strategies to address the underlying causes of crime, and building police legitimacy, then within a counter-terrorism context the question of what this means needs to be raised.[34] Virta's conceptualisation of community policing emphasises community policing as promoting community-based problem solving strategies to address the causes of crime, however, within the counter terrorism context such a conceptualisation of community policing becomes complex with secrecy, security and risk intruding and thus destabilising community-police relations. For instance, within a counter-terrorism context, the promotion of community-based strategies to address the underlying causes of terrorism raises the question of which communities and which community groups are best placed to work with police? Moreover, if those groups best placed to counter terrorism are deemed 'suspect' by policy makers and influential commentators, then how does this impact upon any attempts at engagement and partnership made by

---

31. 'Canadian Muslims, Islamophobia and National Security Royal Canadian Mounted Police' (2008), Hanniman W, *International Journal of Law, Crime and Justice*, Vol. 36 (4), 271-285.
32. *Ibid.*
33. 'Policing Uncertainty: Countering Terror through Community Intelligence and Democratic Policing' (2006), Innes M, *Annals of APSS* 605, 1-20.
34. 'Community Policing' (2006), Virta S, in McLaughlin and Muncie (eds), *The Sage Dictionary of Criminology*, 2nd edition, London.

police officers? What does building police legitimacy look like within a counter-terrorism context? If community empowerment is an important aspect to building police legitimacy then what does empowerment mean within a counter-terrorism context? These are just some questions that are raised.

A focus upon the work of the Muslim Contact Unit (MCU) offers a rare insight into the role of community-based policing within a counter-terrorism context. The MCU was established after 9/11 by two Special Branch police officers within the Metropolitan Police Service with long-standing experience in community engagement within a counter-terrorism context, where community engagement might be considered to consist of:

> The process of enabling the participation of citizens and communities in policing at their chosen level, ranging from providing information and reassurance, to empowering them to identify and implement solutions to local problems and influence strategic priorities and decisions.[35]

Since January 2002, and against the grain of the 'war on terror', the MCU has built partnerships with minority, often marginalised, Muslim community groups—particularly Salafi and Islamist groups—in London with a view to empowering their efforts to counter al-Qaida propaganda and recruitment strategies on their own terms, in one case reclaiming a mosque from Abu Hamza's hard-core extremist supporters.[36] The MCU has also been engaging with wider sections of Muslim minorities in London within a counter-terrorism context, for example, through its interaction with members of the Muslim Safety Forum. There have been two in-depth studies of the work of the MCU.[37] Both these studies highlight the complexities to trust-building in the context of 'new terrorism', which community-based policing models will increasingly need to take into account. Establishing

---

35. *Engagement in Policing: Lessons from the literature* (2004), Myhill A, London: Home Office, 4.
36. 'Empowering Salafis and Islamists Against al-Qaida: A London Counter-terrorism Case Study' (2008), Lambert R, *Political Science and Politics* 41 (1), 31-35; *London Police and Muslim Londoners: Countering al-Qaida in Partnership* (2010), Lambert R, Unpublished PhD, University of Exeter.
37. *Police-Muslim Engagement and Partnerships for the Purposes of Counter-Terrorism: an examination* (2009), Spalek B, El-Awa S and McDonald L, Birmingham: University of Birmingham; *London Police and Muslim Londoners: Countering al-Qaida in Partnership* (2010), Lambert R, Unpublished PhD, University of Exeter.

trust between police and community members involves a sophisticated level of policing which draws upon the cultural intelligence of police officers. The skills that police officers require within this context are perhaps more easily acquired through specialist counter-terrorism units based upon the model of the MCU. Although national security, 'high level', policing is traditionally linked to 'hard' policing styles in terms of the use of informants and surveillance techniques, the studies by Spalek et al[38] and Lambert[39] focus upon the work of the MCU which has been underpinned by principles of community policing, and as such the unit has utilised 'softer' community based models of counter-terrorism.

This research illustrates that there is space for important community-focussed work within specialist counter-terrorism policing units, but this work needs to be carefully implemented, with the establishment of trust between police and community members being a core goal.

At the same time, it is important to highlight the many stresses to police-community engagement within the 'new terrorism' context. Controversial counter-terror operations that have resulted in physically and psychologically harming those deemed 'suspect', such as the Forest Gate incident in 2006 when a man was shot on the basis of intelligence, have severely eroded trust between Muslim communities and the police. Previous research has established that trust and confidence in the police can be seriously undermined in situations where communities feel that they are being over-policed.[40] A

---

38. *Police–Muslim Engagement and Partnerships for the Purposes of Counter-Terrorism: an examination* (2009), Spalek B, El-Awa S and McDonald L, Birmingham: University of Birmingham.
39. *London Police and Muslim Londoners: Countering al-Qaida in Partnership* (2010), Lambert R, Unpublished PhD, University of Exeter.
40. 'From Resistance to Rebellion' (1981), Sivanandan A, Race *and Class*, 111-152; 'Striking Back' (1982), Bridges L and Gilroy P, Marxism *Today*, 34-35; *Police and people in London :the PSI report* (1985), Smith D and Gray J, Aldershot : Gower; 'Ethnic Minorities, Crime and Criminal Justice: a study in a provincial city' (1992) Jefferson T, Walker M and Seneviratne M, in Downes (ed), *Unravelling Criminal Justice*, London : Macmillan 138-164; *The Stephen Lawrence Inquiry, Report of an Inquiry by Sir William Macpherson of Cluny* (1999), Macpherson report, London: Stationery Office, Parliamentary papers, Cm 4262-I; *Widening Access: improving police relations with hard to reach groups* (2001), Jones T and Newburn T, Police Research Series Paper 138, London: Home Office; 'To Serve and Protect?: The Experiences of Policing in the Community of Young People from Black and Other Ethnic Minority Groups' (2007), Sharp D and Atherton S, *British Journal of Criminology*, 47: 746–763; 'Disproportionate and Discriminatory: Reviewing the Evidence on Police Stop and Search' (2007), Bowling B and

breakdown of police-community relations can have serious consequences for policing, and in the context of counter-terrorism can halt the flow of vital information from communities, considered a key issue within the CONTEST 2 strategy.[41] At the same time, power dynamics that take place at a global level between different nation states and the intersections of Islam and the post 9/11 'new terrorism' discourse can impact upon local contexts of engagement and partnership work between communities and the police. Participants in the studies by Spalek *et al*[42] and Lambert[43] spoke about how, from its conception, the 'war on terror' has been perceived by many as a war on Islam, causing reluctance within Muslim communities to help the police.

MCU officers have worked towards creating spaces for the development of initiatives aimed at countering terrorism through approaching the prevention of terrorism as a public safety issue that goes beyond politics and, therefore, beyond the 'war on terror' and its associated 'war against Islam'. To do this, officers must have a good working understanding of the wider politicised context and Muslim communities' experiences and perceptions of this in order to then be able to develop and support initiatives: initiatives that might be criticised by certain politicised factions in wider society for being 'radical' or constituting a threat to democracy but which have as their core aim the prevention of terrorism. It appears that engagement between the police and Muslim minorities cannot be separated out from the wider context, a context whereby Muslim identities have been otherised and stigmatised, as will be explained in the next section below in relation to risk. The work of organisations such as MCU is not only important because relations between Muslim communities and the police have become strained and fragile as a result of the 'war on terror', but also because of the increas-

---

Phillips C, *Modern Law Review*, 70, 6, 936–961.

41. *Suspect Community: People's Experiences of the Prevention of Terrorism Acts in Britain* (1993), Hillyard P, London: Pluto Press; 'The "war on terror": Lessons from Ireland, Essays for civil liberties and democracy in Europe' (2005), Hillyard P, *European Civil Liberties Network*, www.ecln.org/essays/essay-1.pdf.

42. *Police-Muslim Engagement and Partnerships for the Purposes of Counter-Terrorism: an examination* (2009), Spalek B, El-Awa S and McDonald L, Birmingham: University of Birmingham.

43. *London Police and Muslim Londoners: Countering al-Qaida in Partnership* (2010), Lambert R, Unpublished PhD, University of Exeter.

ing marginalisation of Muslim communities experience at the societal level, as shall now be explored.

Muslim Communities' Perceptions of Risk and (in)Securities

In the war against terror Afshar *et al.* argues that Muslims have been attributed with fear, terrorism and discord and such a construction has not remained at the level of discourse but has impacted feelings of security and (in)security in society.[44] Muslim communities, in particular, have been deemed as being 'at risk' from terrorism and so have experienced the brunt of counter-terrorism policies and practices.[45] The introduction of, and use of, counter terrorism legislation has led many Muslims to see the 'war against terrorism' as a 'war against Islam'[46]. It is because, as McCulloch and Pickering[47] state, the 'preventive' counter-terrorism framework is concerned with targeting and managing through restricting and incapacitating those individuals and groups considered being a risk that Muslim minorities are fearful of the police. Through sharing certain ethnic, religious and cultural characteristics with the 'suspect population,' feelings of (un)safety and fear are compounded by feelings of vulnerability, as it is the presence of such traits which determines (as Zedner puts it) 'those within and without protection',[48] leading to the criminalisation of those who are believed to commit 'imagi-

---

44. 'Feminism, Islamophobia and Identities' (2005), Afshar H, Aitken R and Franks M, *Political Studies*, 53: 262-283.
45. *German Anti Terror Law and Religious Extremism* (2005), Bakir S and Harburg B, Berlin: HIA; *The Rules of the Game: Terrorism, Community and Human Rights* (2006) Blick A, Choudhury T and Weir S, York: Joseph Rowntree Foundation; 'The New Integrationism, the State and Islamophobia: Retreat from Multiculturalism in Australia' (2006), Poynting S and Mason V, *International Journal of Law, Crime and Justice* 36 (4): 230-246; 'Muslims: Citizenship, security and social justice in France' (2008), Body-Gendrot, *International Journal of Law, Crime and Justice*, Vol. 36 (4), 247-256; *Police-Muslim Engagement and Partnerships for the Purposes of Counter-Terrorism: an examination* (2009), Spalek B, El-Awa S and McDonald L, Birmingham: University of Birmingham.
46. *British Anti-Terrorism: A Modern Day Witch-hunt* (2005), Ansari F, Islamic Human Rights Commission.
47. *Pre-Crime and Counter terrorism: Imagining future crime in the 'war on terror'* (2009), McCulloch J and Pickering S, British Journal of Criminology. 18: 121-135.
48. 'Pre-crime and post criminology?' (2007), Zedner L, *Theoretical criminology*. 11(2), 274.

nary future harms'.[49] It follows that because there is no due process and there is a pre-occupation with attributing risk, innocent people will suffer because, as Mythen and Walklate argue, innocent people are rendered risk repositories by virtue of sharing some or other of the characteristics of the 'typical terrorist.'[50]

Policing activity under the counter terrorism legislation tends to receive media coverage and this coverage has also detailed police abuse. A case which has been cited frequently in the press and by groups representing Muslims is that of a Muslim man who was detained by the police in London. The man was forced to prostrate with his arms in cuffs, and asked, 'where is your god now?' It is alleged that the detainee suffered over forty injuries including a black eye and severe bruising'.[51] Fear amongst the suspect population could, therefore, be related to the legitimate punitive nature of this legislation with illegitimate police abuses of power further compounding feelings of (un)safety. According to Ansari,[52] draconian anti-terrorism measures such as internment and control orders are demonising the Muslim community in Britain with Fekete[53] similarly stating the effects of heavy handed police raids on Muslim meeting places and homes is of primary concern to the Muslim community in the UK. The 'war on terror' has acted to produce a considerable amount of concern and this concern is very much the product of what counter terrorism legislation legitimises and the power of the police under this legislation. As Wellar states, 'since the system, (criminal justice system) embodies aspects of the power of the state, ordinary people who are caught up in it for one reason or another can feel especially vulnerable. Such vulnerability can be exacerbated by the experience of unfair treatment on the basis

---

49. 'Pre-Crime and Counter terrorism: Imagining future crime in the 'war on terror"' (2009), McCulloch J and Pickering S, *British Journal of Criminology*, 2.
50. 'Terrorism, Risk and International Security: The Perils of Asking 'What If?'' (2008), Mythen G and Walklate S, *Security Dialogue*, 39(2), 13.
51. *The impact of anti terrorism powers on the British Muslim population* (2004), Liberty, http://www.liberty-human-rights.org.uk/policy/reports/impact-of-anti-terror-measures-on-british-muslims-june-2004.pdf, 5.
52. *British Anti-Terrorism: A Modern Day Witch-hunt* (2005), Ansari F, Islamic Human Rights Commission.
53. 'Anti-Muslim Racism and the European Security State' (2004), Fekete L, *Race and class*, 46 (1): 3-29.

of religion'.[54] Research by Spalek, et al. [55] has found that suspicion has grave consequences upon individual's and their family's life including job losses, family breakdown, mental health issues and ostracisation from their wider communities. Therefore, there is a wider form of punishment; the punitive measures have an impact beyond the suspect. Feelings of vulnerability and fear from the police have led to a sense of insecurity amongst Muslim minorities and what is of most concern is perhaps because Muslim minorities are suspicious of the police, attacks are not reported to the police. The Institute of Race Relations found that even though the 'police quote a 600% rise in attacks, the majority of people don't report an attack to the police because there is the belief that the police, on the whole, are anti-Muslim'.[56] However, although feelings of (un)safety now very much include the police, it could be argued that the 'war on terror' and subsequent impact on society has further enhanced Muslim minorities feelings of (un)safety, fear and marginalisation where societal relations are concerned.

Scraton and Chadwick state, 'once institutionalised sexism, heterosexism and racism provide legitimacy in interpersonal discrimination,'[57] with Sheridan stating, 'negative images of Muslims promoted by the media and by political leaders may serve to build or provide evidence for existing Islamophobic prejudices'.[58] The construction of Islamic identity in the 'war on terror' could be interpreted as elite encouragement with the institutional Islamophobia embedded in counter terrorism legislation providing legitimacy for interpersonal discrimination against Muslims. Research does suggest that the 'war on terror' has impacted perceptions of Muslims in society and societal relations. In April 2005, a Home Affairs Select Committee report concluded that relations between British Muslims and the wider community

---

54. *Religious Discrimination in England and Wales* (2001), Wellar P, Feldman A and Purdam K, Home Office Research Development and Statistics Directorate: 51.
55. *Police-Muslim Engagement and Partnerships for the Purposes of Counter-Terrorism: an examination* (2009), Spalek B, El-Awa S and McDonald L, Birmingham: University of Birmingham.
56. *Community responses to the war on terror IRR briefing paper no 3* (2007), Institute of Race Relations, 4. www.irr.org.uk/pdf/IRR_Briefing_No.3.pdf.
57. Cited in *Understanding Criminology: Current theoretical debates* (2003), Walklate S, Open University Press: 30.
58. 'Islamophobia Pre and Post September 11th, 2001' (2006), Sheridan L, *Journal of Interpersonal Violence*, 21 (3): 317-336: 320.

have 'deteriorated' since 9/11 and the resultant war on terrorism[59]. Research conducted by Sheridan revealed that British Muslims reported an 82.6% increase in indirect discrimination and 76.3% increase in overt discrimination, with the research suggesting religious affiliation may be a more meaningful predictor of prejudice than race or ethnicity.[60] At the societal level Muslims Islamic identity is problematic, Muslims suffer racism due to their Islamic identity—hence Islamophobia, with abuse targeted at their Islamic identity. Fear, suspicion and risk have been constructed and associated with Muslims Islamic identity and therefore, Muslims Islamic identity has become a point of concern for some people, for example, '30% of parents in one local authority area in the West Midlands refused to allow their children to go on an educational visit to a mosque because they claimed it was 'run by Al Qaeda'.[61] For Muslim minorities, feelings of (un)safety are a product of state agencies and increasing discrimination and marginalisation at the societal level. Such feelings have produced concerns amongst Muslim minorities with 60% of Muslims in the UK having considered leaving the UK since the London bombings.[62]

Conclusion

The 'war on terror' has produced feelings of (un)safety amongst Muslim minorities and these feelings exist via two avenues. Firstly, the 'war on terror' has given rise to anxiety towards the police; this is detrimental as it has shaped the extent to which Muslim minorities want to engage with the police and the extent to which they will rely on the police when they are the victim of a crime. Secondly, the 'war on terror' has influenced societal relations and therefore Muslims' feelings of (un)safety from societal interactions. Of

---

59. *Terrorism and Community Relations* (2005), Home Affairs Select Committee (cited in *British Anti-Terrorism: A Modern Day Witch-hunt* (2005), Ansari F, Islamic Human Rights Commission: 62).
60. 'Islamophobia Pre and Post September 11th, 2001' (2006), Sheridan L, *Journal of Interpersonal Violence*, 21 (3): 317–336: 317.
61. *Identity, Ethnic Diversity and Community Cohesion* (2009), Johnson N, Sage Publications 25.
62. 'Two-thirds of Muslims consider leaving UK' (26 July, 2005), *Guardian*, (cited in *British Anti-Terrorism: A Modern Day Witch-hunt* (2005), Ansari F, Islamic Human Rights Commission: 83).

particular interest is how components of the 'war on terror', risk, the construction of the suicide bomber and Islamic identities have produced feelings of (un)safety amongst Muslim minorities. This does suggest that the greater the prevalence of risk and the focus upon Islamic identities by the state, and embedded in counter terrorism legislation, the greater the extent of (un)safety and fear amongst Muslim minorities.

This chapter has demonstrated that in the era of 'new terrorism' what has increasingly become apparent is that normative frameworks are in need of transformation if understandings of UK Muslim minorities' feelings of (un)safety are to be explored. For example the concept of 'risk' has to be conceptualised as an entity which is not only part of a state dominated framework but can also be part of a reactive process which is very much part of minority perspectives and experiences of state authorities. At the same time, community-based approaches to countering terrorism, whereby communities are viewed as equal partners and not informants need to be encouraged and further explored. The 'war on terror' has produced a disjuncture and in order to challenge and reveal the harms of this discourse on minorities, the transitional impact of power from the state, to the law, to the police has to be deconstructed so that it can be understood how new forms of 'othering', are legitimised and shape minorities feelings of (un)safety.

PART II

Empowered Communities as Local Stakeholders in Criminal Justice

Having identified a number of problems in *Part I* with the centre driven approach to criminal justice, *Part II* looks to the potential of an alternative community-led approach. Of course, this approach is nothing new. Despite the predominance of state-centred approaches to crime and disorder, aspects of the community-centred alternative have found expression in a variety of areas, many of which are explored within the chapters that follow. Our question, however, is that in the light of the Conservative Party's pronouncements in favour of a 'Big Society', and in view of certain failures of the state-centred approach, how well equipped is the community approach to take a greater role in the years to come? With this in mind, the chapters in this part function both to explore the potential of community models, but also to explore the problems and inequalities that are often inherent in a localist approach.

Part II opens, through *Chapter 8* with an examination of the potential for, and challenges to, engaging and empowering communities through processes based on restorative justice. In so doing, this chapter explores some of the main issues regarding the involvement of communities in responses to crime and disorder and, as such, provides a framework for the following chapters. *Chapter 9* moves from exploring the restoration for harms done, to the role of the community (through the Safer Communities initiative) in the prevention of both criminal and community harms. Focusing in on a particular pilot project, *Chapter 10* then discusses the establishment of community justice centres, and their potential as a base for various agencies working to prevent harm and restore order in communities. The final three chapters, *Chapters 11* to *13*, go on to analyse the role and success of community responses with regard to three vulnerable or marginalised groups in society. *Chapter 11*, focusing on young people, questions the extent to which problem youth are constructed from an intolerant community. *Chapter 12* analyses the potential for the community to take a greater role in relation to convicted sex offenders, reintegrating them into community life and thereby reducing the likelihood of re-offending. Finally, *Chapter 13* highlights the positive impact of community-led responses to domestic violence, and the care for victims of domestic violence in minority communities.

CHAPTER 8

EMPOWERING COMMUNITIES THROUGH RESTORATIVE JUSTICE

KATHERINE DOOLIN

Introduction

In Britain, as in many other countries, there has been a proliferation of practices and programmes within the context of criminal justice based on what is known as restorative justice. As will be discussed in the next section, a restorative approach to justice involves a fundamental shift in the definition of, and response to, crime. It is an understanding of justice that attempts to repair the harm done to victims, to encourage offenders to take responsibility for their actions, and to reintegrate offenders into their communities. Central to achieving these aims is the involvement of these key stakeholders—the victim, the offender and the community—in decision-making processes, who try to collectively work out how to deal with the harm caused and the offending behaviour.

Victim offender mediation, conferencing and circles are the main processes associated with restorative justice. These informal, out-of-court, processes provide the opportunity, in the presence of a mediator or facilitator, for the victim and offender to come together to discuss the harm caused and ways in which reparation can be made to the victim. Conferences and circles have their roots in indigenous conflict resolution practices of the Maori people in New Zealand[1] and First Nation people in Canada[2] respectively and, underpinned by notions of collective responsibility and consensus decision-making, also encourage the participation of the family, friends and supporters of victim and offender and, in some situations, the wider community.[3] Restorative justice also has been associated with community reparation boards, panels and, although by no means universally accepted, court-based restitutive and reparative measures.[4]

While much of the expansion of restorative justice processes has occurred outside of a legislative framework, under the Labour administration of 1997 to 2010, in England and Wales, initiatives based on restorative justice principles were given statutory footing for the first time. By way of example, victim consultation and reparation to victims and the community have been advanced through diversionary and court-based measures for adult[5] and young offenders.[6] The last Labour Government also introduced referral orders[7] for young people, which involve referral to an out-of-court panel (made up of lay community volunteers and a youth offending team member)

---

1. *Restorative Justice: Healing the Effects of Crime* (1995, revised edition, 1999), Consedine J, Lyttelton, New Zealand: Ploughshares Publications, 80-96; 'Re-forming Justice: The Potential of Maori Processes' (1997), Tauri J and Morris A, 30 *Australian and New Zealand Journal of Criminology*, 149; 'Maori and Youth Justice in New Zealand' (1995), Olsen T, Maxwell G and Morris A, in Hazlehurst K (ed), *Popular Justice and Community Regeneration: Pathways of Indigenous Reform*, Westport, Connecticut: Praeger, 45; 'Translating Restorative Justice into Practice: Lessons from New Zealand's Family Group Conferencing Approach to Youth Offending' (2008), Doolin K, 4(1) *International Journal of Restorative Justice*, 1.
2. 'Restoring Justice in Native Communities in Canada' (1998), Jaccoud M, in Walgrave L (ed), *Restorative Justice for Juveniles: Potentialities, Risks and Problems for Research*, Leuven: Leuven University Press, 285.
3. For further description of restorative processes see, 'The recent history of restorative justice: Mediation, circles, and conferencing' (2008), McCold P, in Sullivan D and Tifft L (eds), *Handbook of Restorative Justice*, Abingdon: Routledge, 23; and *Youth Offending and Restorative Justice: Implementing reform in youth justice* (2003), Crawford A and Newburn T, Cullompton: Willan Publishing, 25-37.
4. *Understanding victims and restorative justice* (2005), Dignan J, Maidenhead: Open University Press, 108.
5. For example, conditional cautions introduced by Criminal Justice Act 2003, section 22.
6. For example, diversionary measures such as reprimands and warnings introduced by Crime and Disorder Act 1998, section 65; youth conditional cautions introduced by Criminal Justice and Immigration Act 2008, section 48; and youth court orders such as reparation orders introduced by Crime and Disorder Act 1998, section 67.
7. Youth Justice and Criminal Evidence Act 1999, section 1.

with the aim of agreeing a contract of behaviour, which should include an element of reparation to the victim or the wider community, and involving the young person, his or her family, and the victim in the process. Referral orders have restorative potential but the achievement in practice of restorative outcomes has been mixed.[8]

Support for restorative justice processes is also evident in Northern Ireland. Youth conferencing, which encourages the young person to take responsibility for his or her actions and attempts to involve victim, offender and community in the process, is now integrated into the youth justice system on a statutory footing.[9] Further, a number of community-based projects (similar to community or neighbourhood mediation) have been developed with the aim of being alternatives to paramilitary punishment violence.[10]

Restorative justice practices vary in the extent to which they involve the affected community. This ranges from no involvement, to the inclusion of family and friends of the victim and offender, to the use of lay volunteers, and the involvement of the local community. This emphasis on involving communities in responses to crime and disorder seems set to remain on the political agenda. The 'Programme for Government' published in May 2010 by the newly formed Conservative-Liberal Democrat Coalition government proposes Neighbourhood Justice Panels—something which they identify with restorative justice—to tackle low-level crime.[11] This would accord with

---

8. *The Introduction of Referral Orders into the Youth Justice System: Final Report* (2002), Newburn T, Crawford A, Earle R, *et al*, London: Home Office; Youth Offending and Restorative Justice: Implementing reform in youth justice (2003), Crawford A and Newburn T, Cullompton: Willan Publishing; 'Youth Crime: Whose Responsibility?' (2008), Newbury A, 35(1) *Journal of Law and Society*, 131.

9. Justice (Northern Ireland) Act 2002, s57. For an evaluation see *Evaluation of the Northern Ireland Youth Conference Service* (2005), Campbell C, Devlin R, O'Mahoney D, *et al*, Belfast: Northern Ireland Office; *Making Amends: restorative youth justice in Northern Ireland* (2009), Jacobson J and Gibbs P, London: Prison Reform Trust.

10. 'Restorative Justice and the Critique of Informalism in Northern Ireland' (2002), McEvoy K and Mika H, 42 *British Journal of Criminology* 534; 'Criminological discourses in Northern Ireland: Conflict and conflict resolution' (2003), McEvoy K and Ellison G, in McEvoy K and Newburn T (eds), *Criminology, Conflict Resolution, and Restorative Justice*, Basingstoke: Palgrave Macmillan, 45; *Justice in Transition: Community Restorative Justice in Northern Ireland* (2009), Eriksson A, Cullompton: Willan Publishing.

11. *The Coalition: our programme for government* (2010), HM Government, London: Cabinet Office, 24.

Prime Minister, David Cameron's vision of a 'Big Society' in which, as Raine and Keasey point out (*Chapter 1*), citizens and communities would become less dependent on the state and more empowered to take on responsibility for themselves in a spirit of self-help and mutual support.

With this in mind, the focus of this chapter is to consider the potential for, and challenges to, engaging and empowering communities through restorative justice. It is not to provide an assessment of examples of restorative justice practice. Rather the intention is to explore some of the main issues underpinning the involvement of communities in responses to crime and disorder through a restorative justice approach. In so doing, the inclusion of the community as a stakeholder in restorative processes raises a number of important questions, which the chapter deals with in turn. What is the nature of the community's needs and responsibilities in restorative justice? How can communities be empowered through restorative processes? What are the challenges and limitations to involving communities in restorative responses? How can a balance be struck regarding the relationship between state and community in developing restorative processes? Much of the discussion regarding the roles and responsibilities of communities, and possible challenges and limitations to community involvement in responses to crime will find resonance in some of the other chapters in this volume. In this sense, the chapter sets a framework for what follows in *Part II*. However, before considering the potential for community involvement within restorative justice, an introduction to its core values is required.

An Understanding of Restorative Justice

Despite the expansion of practices which draw on the concept of restorative justice, there is no generally agreed definition. A frequently cited definition is that offered by Marshall, which emphasises the *process* of restorative justice: 'Restorative justice is a process whereby parties with a stake in a specific offence collectively resolve how to deal with the aftermath of the offence and its implications for the future.'[12] While this definition captures some of the

---

12. *Restorative Justice: An Overview* (1999), Marshall T, London: Home Office, 5.

key elements of restorative justice—the importance of a decision-making process, the notion of stakeholders, a collective resolution, a forward-looking approach—it is not clear enough about the outcomes to be sought. He makes no mention in the definition of the need to work towards restoration for stakeholders or repairing the harm or about the values that should guide the resolution made by the parties. Without this, the process is vulnerable to diversion towards non-restorative ends.

A preferred definition of restorative justice is one that also emphasises the *outcome* to be sought. Bazemore and Walgrave define restorative justice as 'every action that is primarily oriented toward doing justice by repairing the harm that has been caused by a crime'.[13] Walgrave has since proposed a more inclusive and detailed definition of restorative justice as 'an option for doing justice after the occurrence of an offence that is primarily oriented towards repairing the individual, relational and social harm caused by that offence'.[14] Both of these conceptions of restorative justice prioritise what should be its primary aim—reparation and restoration.[15]

While a generally agreed definition of restorative justice seems difficult to achieve (perhaps this is inevitable and not of consequence), there is more consensus among proponents about its core values. Restorative justice is about viewing crime in its social context as interpersonal conflict, prioritising harm by the offender against the victim and community rather than harm being seen as primarily against the state.[16] Harm tends to be defined in broad terms, including material losses, physical and psychological injuries,

---

13. 'Restorative Juvenile Justice: In Search of Fundamentals and an Outline for Systemic Reform' (1999), Bazemore G and Walgrave L, in Bazemore G and Walgrave L (eds), *Restorative Juvenile Justice: Repairing the Harm of Youth Crime*, Monsey, New York: Criminal Justice Press, 48.
14. *Restorative Justice, Self Interest and Responsible Citizenship* (2008), Walgrave L, Cullompton: Willan Publishing, 21.
15. 'But What Does It Mean? Seeking Definitional Clarity in Restorative Justice' (2007), Doolin K, 71(5) *Journal of Criminal Law*, 427 at 429; and 'Restorative Justice and the Law: the Case for an Integrated, Systemic Approach' (2002), Walgrave L, in Walgrave L (ed.) *Restorative Justice and the Law*, Cullompton: Willan Publishing, 194.
16. *Changing Lenses: A New Focus for Crime and Justice* (1990), Zehr H, Scottdale, Pennsylvania: Herald Press.

relational problems, social dysfunctions,[17] and the rupture of social bonds and relationships between victim, offender and community.[18]

The needs of the victim should be central to restorative processes, which should seek to repair the specific harm done to the victim. Reparation of the harm is recognised as going beyond physical and material losses to encompass emotional aspects, involving attempts to restore victims' self-respect, dignity, feeling of safety, and empowerment.[19] Drawing particular attention to victims' loss of participation in their own cases, Christie suggests that conflicts have been taken away from the parties directly involved, by the state and by the professionals who represent them. He argues that the victim,

> ... is a sort of double loser; first, *vis-`a-vis* the offender, but secondly and often in a more crippling manner by being denied rights to full participation in what might have been one of the more important ritual encounters in life. The victim has lost the case to the state.[20]

Thus, a restorative process should provide the opportunity for victims to ask questions about the offence and express their feelings about its impact on them, including anger, fear, hurt, and to receive information and support.[21] Attempts should also be made to empower victims, to help them regain a sense of control, and this includes having the chance to be involved in discussions about how the reparation can be made to them. As Pranis points out, empowerment comes through not only having the right to speak but includes the right to be heard.[22]

---

17. 'Restorative Juvenile Justice: In Search of Fundamentals and an Outline for Systemic Reform' (1999), Bazemore G and Walgrave L, in Bazemore G and Walgrave L (eds), *Restorative Juvenile Justice: Repairing the Harm of Youth Crime*, Monsey, New York: Criminal Justice Press, 49.
18. 'The Past, Present, and Future of Restorative Justice: Some Critical Reflections' (1998), Daly K and Immarigeon R, 1(1), *Contemporary Justice Review*, 21 at 22.
19. 'Critiquing the Critics: A Brief Response to Critics of Restorative Justice' (2002), Morris A, 42, *British Journal of Criminology*, 596 at 604.
20. 'Conflicts as Property' (1977), Christie N, 17(1), *British Journal of Criminology*, 1 at 3.
21. *Changing Lenses: A New Focus for Crime and Justice* (1990), Zehr H, Scottdale, Pennsylvania: Herald Press, 26-27.
22. 'Restorative Values and Confronting Family Violence' (2002), Pranis K, in Strang H and Braithwaite J (eds), *Restorative Justice and Family Violence*, Cambridge: Cambridge University Press, 23.

Restorative justice is about encouraging offenders to accept responsibility and to take active steps to repair the harm caused, both materially and symbolically. It is also about requiring offenders to participate in the process that decides how to deal with their offending behaviour. In so doing, the aim is to try and make offenders aware of the consequences of their actions and how the harm they have done affects others and themselves. In restorative processes, offenders are actively encouraged to speak about their offending and listen to how victims have been affected. The presence of victims means that it is harder for offenders to insulate themselves from the victim, and rationalisations for their offending can be challenged more directly than what happens in the conventional criminal justice system.[23]

While reparation of the harm done to the victim should be prioritised, a restorative process should also try to restore offenders' sense of belonging and support attempts to reintegrate them into their community. However, there are challenges in trying to achieve offender reintegration through community involvement, many of which will be discussed in the final section of this chapter.

Fundamental to a restorative justice approach is the notion of inclusion; providing the opportunity for those most affected by crime to participate in a process that seeks to collectively work out how to deal with the aftermath of offending. As Van Ness explains:

> Inclusion is the way we make sure that whatever the legitimate interests the State may have in the crime, and it does have some, these do not become the only focus of the processes established.[24]

This bottom-up approach to justice is based on the inclusion of, encounter between, and consequent empowerment of the key stakeholders — the victim,

---

23. 'Reforming Criminal Justice: The Potential of Restorative Justice' (2000), Morris A and Young W, in Strang H and Braithwaite J (eds), *Restorative Justice: Philosophy to practice*, Aldershot: Ashgate/Dartmouth. See also, *Changing Lenses: A New Focus for Crime and Justice* (1990), Zehr H, Scottdale, Pennsylvania: Herald Press:, 40-41.
24. 'The shape of things to come: a framework for thinking about a restorative justice system' (2002), Van Ness D, in Weitekamp E and Kerner H-J (eds), *Restorative Justice: Theoretical foundations*, Cullompton: Willan Publishing, 6.

the offender, and the community. A restorative process strives to maximise the participation of these stakeholders by providing opportunities for dialogue (direct and indirect) between them as they seek to reach agreement about a desirable restorative outcome.

Strengthening and Empowering Communities through Restorative Justice

The widening of the scope of victimisation, in which the state is no longer considered to be the primary stakeholder of an offence, is an important part of what restorative justice entails. As Umbreit explains:

> The basic principles of restorative justice require a fundamental shift in the power related to who controls and owns crime in society—a shift from the state to the individual citizen and local communities.[25]

With this in mind, some proponents conceive restorative justice as a bottom-up rather than top-down, state dominated, approach to dealing with the aftermath of offending, emphasising that 'the justice process belongs to the community.'[26]

In restorative justice literature there are often diverse definitions given to the meaning of community. They range from emphasising geographical links (such as places of work or neighbourhoods), 'communities of place',[27] to a 'non-geographic perspective' where community is defined as a sense of belonging, 'a feeling, a perception of connectedness'.[28] Some proponents define community narrowly in terms of a 'micro-community',[29] 'commu-

---

25. *Victim Meets Offender: The Impact of Restorative Justice and Mediation* (1994), Umbreit M, Monsey, New York: Criminal Justice Press, 162.
26. 'Fundamental Concepts of Restorative Justice' (1998), Zehr H and Mika H, 1(1) *Contemporary Justice Review*, 47 at 53.
27. *The Little Book of Restorative Justice* (2002), Zehr H, Intercourse, PA: Good Books, 27.
28. 'Community is not a Place: A New Look at Community Justice Initiatives' (1998), McCold P and Wachtel B, 1(1) *Contemporary Justice Review*, 71 at 72.
29. 'What is the Role of Community in Restorative Justice Theory and Practice?' (2004), McCold P, in Zehr H and Toews B (eds), *Critical Issues in Restorative Justice*, Monsey, New York:

nity of care',[30] 'personal community'[31] or 'primary stakeholders'[32] comprising of the victim, offender and their family and friends–people who know and care about them. Some advocate that the involvement of community should only be in this narrow, more restrictive, sense to provide support during a restorative process and reinforce the offender's acceptance of his or her wrongdoing.[33] Other proponents also emphasise that notions of community go beyond just those directly affected by the offence. There are the interests and concerns of a macro-community ('secondary stakeholders', 'indirect stakeholders')[34] those not directly affected by an offence, for example, the local community.[35] These wider concerns derive from the macro-community's interest in the resolution of offences— concern for public safety, human rights and the general well-being of community members.[36] In all definitions of community it should be emphasised that what is important to achieving restoration is that whoever cares about and supports the victim and the offender needs to be present in the restorative process. This could include their families, friends, supporters, church leaders and, for young offenders, their sports coaches and school teachers.

As a result of the breadth, and often abstract nature, in the way community is defined by restorative justice proponents, it is perhaps of more

---

Criminal Justice Press, 161.
30. *The Little Book of Restorative Justice* (2002), Zehr H, Intercourse, PA: Good Books, 27.
31. 'Restorative justice theory validation' (2002), McCold P and Wachtel T, in Weitekamp E and Kerner H-J (eds), *Restorative Justice: Theoretical foundations*, Cullompton: Willan Publishing, 114.
32. *Ibid*, 114.
33. 'The Practice of Family Group Conferences in New Zealand: Assessing the Place, Potential and Pitfalls of Restorative Justice' (2000), Morris A and Maxwell G, in Crawford A and Goodey J (eds), *Integrating a Victim Perspective within Criminal Justice: International debates*, Aldershot:Ashgate/Dartmouth, 216.
34. 'What is the Role of Community in Restorative Justice Theory and Practice?' (2004), McCold P, in Zehr H and Toews B (eds), *Critical Issues in Restorative Justice*, Monsey, New York: Criminal Justice Press, 161; and 'Restorative justice theory validation' (2002), McCold P and Wachtel T, in Weitekamp E and Kerner H-J (eds), *Restorative Justice: Theoretical foundations*, Cullompton: Willan Publishing, 114.
35. 'Restorative Justice and the Role of Community' (1996), McCold P, in Galaway B and Hudson J (eds), *Restorative Justice: International Perspectives*, Monsey, New York: Criminal Justice Press, 85.
36. *The Little Book of Restorative Justice* (2002), Zehr H, Intercourse, PA: Good Books, 28.

use to work out who should represent the community (however conceived). Johnstone notes that:

> For the purposes of restorative justice, the relevant community does not exist independently of the conflict, it is brought into being by the conflict.[37]

Thus, the definition of community will depend on the nature of the conflict, the level of harm inflicted, the relationship between victim and offender, and the consequent aggregation of interests represented. Where it is a minor offence involving people who know each other, the community involvement is likely to be restricted to victims' and offenders' own communities of care. However, if the offence involves the victim as a stranger and is serious enough to raise general public concern, the wider community interest will need to be represented.[38] As will be discussed later, this latter situation could lead to the community interest being represented by someone acting in an official public capacity.

While representation is likely to be more straightforward when dealing with a micro community—the communities of care of both victim and offender—working out who should represent the macro community—the wider community interest—could still pose difficulties. Deciding who has a stake in an offence and whether his or her interest should be represented may often be difficult to determine; 'the issue seems inherently contestable'.[39] This has led some to consider that the question of who makes up the community should be secondary to working out what are the roles and responsibilities of the community.[40]

Within restorative justice, the community is considered to have a dual role both as a victim of crime with needs to be met and also as a participant with responsibilities to victims, offenders and its other members. Processes

---

37. *Restorative Justice: Ideas, Values, Debates* (2002), Johnstone G, Cullompton: Willan Publishing, 154.
38. 'Restorative Justice and the Role of Community' (1996), McCold P, in Galaway B and Hudson J (eds), *Restorative Justice: International Perspectives,* Monsey, New York: Criminal Justice Press, 91.
39. *Restorative Justice: Ideas, Values, Debates* (2002), Johnstone G, Cullompton: Willan Publishing, 155
40. *Ibid*, 155.

underpinned by restorative values are seen as having the potential to fulfil a community's need for empowerment in conflict resolution. The community may be a primary stakeholder as a direct victim of crime, such as vandalism, or act as a surrogate victim where the actual victim does not wish to take part in a restorative process. Moreover, involving communities in the process that works out how to deal with the aftermath of crime may be a way of strengthening communities at a local level. It is argued that communities need a sense of justice to be demonstrated, to be a part of determining concrete actions to help prevent offences reoccurring, bringing feelings of reassurance and safety, which should ultimately lead to more peaceful community relationships.[41]

Communities are also a key resource in supporting and helping to deliver processes based on restorative justice values. At a micro level, involving the offenders' communities of care may help to influence them to repair the harm they have caused, refrain from reoffending, and offer the support they often need.[42] While at a macro level the local community may be involved in providing financial resources, lay volunteers to take part in restorative processes, and fostering efforts to raise public awareness about restorative justice. The state also has a vital role to play in providing the resources to support restorative practices, as will be discussed later.

The Challenge of Empowering Communities through Restorative Justice

The recognition of *giving justice back to the community* raises a number of challenges to the achievement of community empowerment, some of which will be discussed below. Some commentators assert that little sense of community actually exists in modern, urbanised society. For them, the irony is that this renewed emphasis on community comes at a time when there is a

---

41. 'Restorative Justice and the Role of Community' (1996), McCold P, in Galaway B and Hudson J (eds), *Restorative Justice: International Perspectives,* Monsey, New York: Criminal Justice Press, 96.
42. *Restorative Justice: Ideas, Values, Debates* (2002), Johnstone G, Cullompton: Willan Publishing, 151-152.

declining sense of community identity.[43] For others, getting the local community involved means persuading members to participate and in modern societies, where people have busy lives and little time left for civic duty, it can be difficult to get a representative range of people involved.[44] However, restorative justice processes are founded on values of inclusion and collective responsibility and, as such, could play an important role in redeveloping a sense of local community. Any perceived absence of community is, as Christie argues, a reason for adopting restorative processes and strengthening and revitalising communities by directly involving them in the justice process.[45]

As noted above, an important part of a restorative process should seek to reintegrate offenders into their communities–restoration through reintegration. Of course, reintegration is premised on the willingness of the community of care and, in some situations, the local community to accept the offender back. Successful reintegration relies on the strength of interdependent relationships and common values that evoke personal obligations to others within a community of concern. Moreover, reintegration of offenders into their communities can only deliver a successful outcome if their support network recognise and acknowledge that the offender has caused harm. Further, it is essential that these supporters share society's views of right and wrongful behaviour and are capable of providing beneficial law-abiding support.

It is also important that offenders' communities be of a type that they would benefit from being part of again. Despite the notion of community often being portrayed in restorative justice literature in positive terms, the experiences of communities for many offenders can in fact be authoritarian, repressive, intolerant, coercive, anti-liberal and exclusionary.[46] Crawford warns us against romanticising about the notion of community:

---

43. *Age of Extremes: The Short Twentieth Century, 1914-1991* (1994), Hobsbawn E, London: Abacus, 428 (quoted in 'The state, community and restorative justice: heresy, nostalgia and butterfly collecting' (2002), Crawford A, in Walgrave L (ed.), *Restorative Justice and the Law*, Cullompton: Willan Publishing, 114).
44. *Restorative Justice: Ideas, Values, Debates* (2002), Johnstone G, Cullompton: Willan Publishing, 152.
45. 'Conflicts as Property' (1977), Christie N, 17(1), *British Journal of Criminology*, 1 at 12.
46. *Understanding victims and restorative justice* (2005), Dignan J, Maidenhead: Open University Press, 102.

Communities are not the havens of reciprocity and mutuality, nor are they the utopias of egalitarianism, that some might wish. Rather, they are hierarchical foundations, structured upon lines of differential power relations ... upon lines of gender, but also upon lines of ethnicity, age, class (if these social categories are not in themselves grounds for exclusion) and other personal attributes. Thus, the 'moral voice of a community' and the interests and values for which it speaks, are often not only exclusive and parochial, but also dominated and controlled by powerful elites.[47]

Problems may arise in practice where the interests of the community being represented compete with the interests of the other stakeholders—the victim and the offender—making it necessary to work out whose interests should be prioritised.[48] Further, where community members 'stand for the wider public interest'[49] they may have a decision-making role and the authority to propose or veto outcomes of a restorative process. This raises the question of their ability and willingness to apply the essential legal restraints of fairness, consistency and proportionality.[50] In practice the problem is often addressed by involving state representatives, for example, police officers, youth offending team workers, to help guard against problems relating to due process.

Where state representatives are involved in restorative processes there is a need to make sure that they do not move beyond their role in ensuring fair outcomes by becoming the dominant party in making decisions about how to repair the harm caused and deal with the aftermath of the offending behaviour. It is essential to protect the inclusive, deliberative ethos of a restorative justice process in order that it is not undermined by a top-down approach, which disempowers the primary stakeholders and reinforces the power imbalance between the offender and state representatives.

Taking into account the importance of involving victims and communities in restorative justice, consideration must be given to the legitimate interests of the state and how to ensure these do not become the primary focus when responding to crime. The role of the state should be defined in a

---

47. 'The state, community and restorative justice: heresy, nostalgia and butterfly collecting' (2002), Crawford A, in Walgrave L (ed.), *Restorative Justice and the Law*, Cullompton: Willan Publishing, 110.
48. *Understanding victims and restorative justice* (2005), Dignan J, Maidenhead: Open University Press, 99.
49. *Ibid*, 101.
50. 'Responsibilities, Rights and Restorative Justice' (2002), Ashworth A, 42 *British Journal of Criminology*, 578 at 585.

way that does not intrude or take away from restorative values and the presence of a state party should not markedly affect the collaborative process. Nevertheless, it must also be remembered that the state has an important function in any justice process. The state as an indirect, or secondary, stakeholder has a continuing and necessary role in enforcing legal safeguards and due process guarantees of victims and offenders. The state also has a vital role in providing the resources to support restorative practices and helping to create the conditions whereby victims, offenders and their communities, in appropriate situations, can be involved in the decision-making about how to repair the harm caused and deal with offending behaviour.[51]

Conclusion

Many restorative justice processes have the potential to engage and empower victims' and offenders' communities of care and local communities by giving them the opportunity to take part in working out how to deal with the offending behaviour and repair the harm caused. Additionally, communities may be called upon to encourage and help offenders to make reparation and refrain from reoffending, and attempt to support and reintegrate them into the community. Thus, while the nature of the community representatives deemed to be stakeholders will vary, these should include those who are able and willing to support the restoration of the victim and the reintegration of the offender.

However, there are challenges with attempting to involve communities in restorative responses to crime such as a declining sense of community, competing interests with other stakeholders, and an unwillingness of community members to take part in the process or attempt to reintegrate offenders. Nevertheless, these difficulties should not prevent efforts being made to secure community involvement if to do so is judged to be beneficial to victim, offender and community, and legal guarantees are upheld.

---

51. 'Restorative justice theory validation' (2002), McCold and Wachtel T, in Weitekamp E and Kerner H-J (eds), *Restorative Justice: Theoretical foundations*, Cullompton: Willan Publishing, 114.

As Prior (*Chapter 9*) and Raine (*Chapter 10*) suggest, the emphasis on involving communities in responding to crime and disorder seems set to remain on the political agenda. As noted in the introduction to this chapter, this would accord with Cameron's vision of a 'Big Society' and the mention given to restorative justice in the Coalition government's 'Programme for Government' document. The priority given to strengthening, engaging and empowering communities needs to be met with an equally strong commitment to ensuring that communities have the resources available to take on this responsibility. It is hoped that restorative justice is recognised for its effectiveness as an alternative approach for dealing with crime, at least in relation to certain categories of offending, rather than simply as a cheaper option in response to the need to reduce public spending.[52]

---

52. For discussion of this see, 'Criminals Should Say Sorry' (2010) *Guardian*, available at www.guardian.co.uk/society/2010/jul/25/criminals-should-say-sorry.

CHAPTER 9

SAFER COMMUNITIES AND COMMUNITY JUSTICE

DAVID PRIOR

The emergence of community-based strategies and initiatives as a response to local problems of crime and disorder is a relatively recent phenomenon.[1] Historically, in Britain, responsibility for crime control in specific localities has rested with the public police service; indeed, maintaining order on the streets and in public places, and ensuring the safety and security of people in the areas where they live and work, has been a core function of policing since the foundation of the modern police force in the first part of the nineteenth century. This only began to change in the 1970s and 1980s when, in response to a continually rising crime rate and a growing lack of confidence in the police, the first initiatives in developing a new kind of approach to local crime control were taken. This process of change culminated in the Crime and Disorder Act 1998 which, for the first time, created a statutory basis for local strategies of crime prevention and reduction that gave legal responsibilities to agencies other than the police, in particular local authorities. The new approach also laid strong emphasis on the role of local communities in identifying problems of crime and disorder that affected them and in developing solutions to them.

The policies, institutions and practices that constitute this community-based, multi-agency response to local crime issues have been both expanded and consolidated in the years since the 1998 Act was passed. While phrases

---

1. See, *inter alia*, 'Community crime prevention' (1995), Hope T, in Tonry M and Farrington D (eds) *Building a Safer Society*, Chicago: University of Chicago Press; *Crime Prevention and Community Safety: Politics, Policies and Practices* (1998), Crawford, A, Harlow: Longman; *Crime Reduction and Community Safety: Labour and the politics of local crime control* (2007), Gilling D, Cullompton: Willan.

such as 'community safety', 'crime reduction' and 'community crime prevention' are all used at different times to denote this policy response, it is the aspirational title 'Safer Communities' that runs through both political discourse and a series of policy initiatives[2] that seems to best capture the spirit of the approach. My aim in this chapter is to explore the meaning and significance of 'Safer Communities' with particular reference to:

- the specific notion of 'justice' embodied in the approach and how this relates to conventional notions of criminal justice;
- the distinctive kinds of concerns that are addressed by 'Safer Communities', and how they are addressed; and
- the relationship between processes of 'state regulation', on the one hand, and 'community empowerment', on the other.

Crime, Disorder and Community Justice

Various commentators have pointed to the influence of communitarian philosophy on the policies of the New Labour government (1997-2010), in response to social issues generally and crime and disorder in particular.[3] The communitarian claim is that 'community' is the primary source of reciprocal bonds of support and responsibility between individuals and the locus of social identity for individuals; citizenship, in this view, is principally concerned with the active and responsible membership of a community.[4] This has important implications for ideas of justice. The liberal approach to

---

2. See, for example, *The Safer Communities Initiative. Circular 14/2002* (2002) Home Office, London: Home Office; *Building Safer Communities Together* (2003), Home Office, London: Home Office and *The Way Ahead for Safer Communities: Government Response to Casey Review* (2008), Home Office, available at http://www.egovmonitor.com/node/19493/print.
3. 'New Labour's communitarianisms' (1997), Driver S and Martell L, *Critical Social Policy*, 17 (3): 27-46; *The Inclusive Society?* (2005), Levitas R, Second Edition, Basingstoke: Palgrave Macmillan; *The Politics of Crime and Community* (2007), Hughes G, Basingstoke: Palgrave Macmillan and 'Community cohesion and the politics of communitarianism' (2008), Robinson D, in Flint J and Robinson D (eds) *Community Cohesion in Crisis?* Bristol: Policy Press: 15-34.
4. *Citizenship: Rights, community and participation* (1995), Prior D, Stewart J and Walsh K, London: Pitman.

crime and justice is based on the relationship between the individual and the state, where the former has offended against the state's laws and the state represents the substantive victim in the pursuit of justice. Communitarianism, however, introduces the idea of the community as itself a moral subject that can be offended against and that can claim protection against harm.[5] Crime is seen as an infringement of the moral and social code that binds the community together and, therefore, as detrimental to the quality of community life. The offender, in turn, is seen as breaking the relationship of mutuality and obligation on which the status of citizen rests; as, in effect, excluding themselves by their criminal act from the benefits of citizenship. Justice — 'community justice' — therefore involves a multi-dimensional response: the improvement of the quality of life of the community, attention to the needs of the specific victim and the restoration of the offender's status as a community member.[6] My focus in this chapter is on the first of these dimensions, but we can note in passing the increasing policy attention paid to means of providing reparation to victims and to 'restorative justice' initiatives aimed at the reintegration of offenders (see Doolin, *Chapter 8*).

Community justice thus expands conventional ideas about justice by introducing a new subject, the community, as an entity with legitimate interests in and entitlements to just outcomes from the processes of controlling crime. However, the communitarian influence on strategies of crime control expands the scope of justice in a further way. This arises from the view, noted above, that claims on behalf of communities are justified by their status as moral beings with rights to a quality of life that is measured by the community's own standards. The community can then be held to suffer harms when people's behaviour infringes those standards, even if no individual is directly harmed or no criminal act is committed. Such behaviours are identified as deserving of censure 'because they are contrary to a community's idea of itself and because they offend against the sense that individuals owe responsibilities to their communities'.[7] Thus, community justice signals an

---

5. *Justice in the Risk Society* (2003), Hudson B, London: Sage, 82-3.
6. 'Risk and Community Practice' (2001), Clear T and Cadora E, in Stenson K and Sullivan R R (eds) *Crime, Risk and Justice: the Politics of Crime Control in Liberal Democracies*, Cullompton: Willan.
7. *Justice in the Risk Society* (2003), Hudson B, London: Sage, 83.

expansion of ideas of criminal justice into concerns with behaviours that do not in themselves constitute an infringement of the criminal law. Moreover, the concern is not just with behaviours that have disturbed or harmed community norms and detracted from the quality of life in the community, but also with behaviours that are perceived as posing a risk to the community — as *likely* to lead to a negative impact on the quality of community life. The continued prioritisation by successive New Labour governments of legislative and policy responses to these concerns has been identified by many commentators as the emergence and consolidation of a 'politics of behaviour' underpinning contemporary strategies of crime control.[8]

The paramount example of such responses is the rapid development and expansion of policy aimed at tackling anti-social behaviour (ASB) (see Lynch in *Chapter 5* of this volume). In a period of what has been described as 'hyper-innovation',[9] starting with the Crime and Disorder Act 1998, a series of new powers were created enabling legal action to be taken by a growing range of agencies against individuals (including children and young people), parents, families and social groups. The powers extend from the infamous and generic anti-social behaviour order (ASBO), through the more specifically targeted parenting order and child curfew order, to the dispersal order which is aimed at groups of two or more people gathering in a public place. Alongside these, many other legally enforceable interventions have been established to address specific, but non-criminal, issues such as alcohol consumption on the streets and the presence in a community of persistent 'nuisance neighbours', while policy guidance in addition promotes a number of officially sanctioned informal or 'voluntary' actions.[10] While the precise nature and extent of the problem which this substantial array of legal and official powers is intended to resolve remains unknown,[11] a more general

---

8. *Neighbours from hell: the politics of behaviour* (2003), Field F, London: Politico's; 'The Responsible Tenant: Housing Governance and the Politics of Behaviour' (2004), Flint J, *Housing Studies*, 19(6), 893-909 and 'Respect and the politics of behaviour' (2009), Burney E, in Millie A (ed) *Securing Respect: Behavioural Expectations and Anti-social Behaviour in the UK*, Bristol: Policy Press, 23-40.
9. 'Governing through anti-social behaviour: regulatory challenges to criminal justice' (2009), Crawford A, *British Journal of Criminology*, 49(6), 817.
10. *Ibid.*
11. 'The "problem" of anti-social behaviour and the policy knowledge base: analyzing the power/

driver of its development is concern about the impact of anti-social behaviour and low-level disorder on the quality of community life:

> The behaviour of a persistent minority can sometimes ruin whole communities. No one should have to put up with behaviour that causes misery and distress ... Tackling anti-social behaviour is central to improving people's quality of life.[12]

Importantly, in seeking to protect communities from ASB, the powers are concerned not just with actual harms caused but with the potential risk posed to the quality of community life by certain behaviours, that is, the policy is characterised by a future orientation.[13] This is clear from the statutory definition of ASB in the Crime and Disorder Act 1998, which refers to behaviour that is 'likely to cause' alarm, harassment and distress to others. The politics of behaviour thus signals a distinct break with the conventional 'post-crime' criminal justice focus on offences actually committed; community justice is as much concerned with 'pre-crime', with risks and their possible consequences, as with actual effects.[14]

Regulating Safer Communities

The Safer Communities initiative displays all the characteristics of contemporary governance arrangements.[15] Achievement of its national policy objectives requires the articulation of complex relationships between different central government departments and a range of local agencies, between those local agencies themselves (which are likely to include public, private and voluntary sector organizations) and between the local agencies and members of the public who may, in turn, be acting on behalf of specific individual or group interests or as more general community representatives. Networked forms

---

knowledge relationship' (2009), Prior D, *Critical Social Policy*, 29 (1), 5-23.
12. *Respect and Responsibility* (2002), Home Office, London: Home Office, 14.
13. 'Governing through anti-social behaviour: regulatory challenges to criminal justice' (2009), Crawford A, *British Journal of Criminology*, 49 (6).
14. 'Pre-crime and post-criminology?' (2007), Zedner L, *Theoretical Criminology*, 11(2), 1362-1386.
15. *Modernizing Governance: New Labour, policy and society* (2001), Newman J, London, Sage.

of coordination, involving 'partnerships' or other varieties of inter-agency collaboration, are the dominant means of directing action, drawing on a potential pool of financial resources that is split between the mainstream service budgets of the various partner agencies and a range of 'special' and usually temporary funds to support certain kinds of initiative. The response of the New Labour government when faced with such complex and inherently unstable arrangements for the realisation of its policy ambitions was to introduce elaborate systems of performance management and regulation.

The management and regulation of Safer Communities, as with other areas of public service where local delivery arrangements were involved, centred on the system of Public Service Agreements (PSAs) and Local Area Agreements (LAAs). Linked to the Treasury's system of three-year budget planning periods, which set overall public spending plans, PSAs spelled out the 'key priority outcomes' for the government over the period ahead.[16] They were intended to bind relevant government service departments and their various partners into a common framework of objectives and priorities for service delivery.

At the time or writing there were thirty PSAs in all, grouped under five broad headings. The heading 'Stronger Communities' itself covered the following five individual PSAs:

- PSA 21 Build more cohesive, empowered and active communities;
- PSA 23 Make communities safer;
- PSA 24 Deliver a more effective, transparent and responsive criminal justice system for victims and the public;
- PSA 25 Reduce the harm caused by alcohol and drugs; and
- PSA 26 Reduce the risk to the UK and its interests overseas from international terrorism.

However, the Safer Communities agenda extends beyond those particular PSAs. A key document in setting out the previous government's approach

---

16. *Public Service Agreements* (2007), HM Treasury, www.hm-treasury.gov.uk/pbr_csr07_psaindex.htm (accessed 13 January 2010).

was the National Community Safety Plan 2008-11 (NCSP),[17] whose purpose was 'to describe a shared endeavour to deliver safer communities'[18] and which was aimed at 'all local partnerships with a role in delivering community safety'.[19] In so doing the plan drew together not just the PSAs referred to above, but a number of others that were regarded as relevant to the delivery of safer communities. These were:

- PSA 17 (Indicator 4) Increase the proportion of people over 65 who are satisfied with their home and their neighbourhood;
- PSA 14 Increase the number of children and young people on the path to success;[20]
- PSA 13 Improve children and young people's safety; and
- PSA 16 Increase the proportion of socially excluded adults in settled accommodation and employment, education or training.

The effect of including these PSAs in the National Plan for Safer Communities was to extend the potential remit of local partnerships beyond narrowly conceived 'crime control' concerns, into broader 'quality of life' issues.

Local Area Agreements derived from the separate national performance framework for local authorities.[21] This framework contained 198 national indicators (NIs) covering most of the main areas of local authority activities and services. These indicators were linked to the national PSAs; thus a subset of the local authority indicators was headed 'Safer Communities', and comprised 34 individual indicators reflecting aspects of the five PSAs listed above. For example, NI 17 'Perceptions of anti-social behaviour' linked to PSA 23; and NI 38 'Drug-related (Class A) offending rate' linked to PSA 25. The composition of an individual LAA was negotiated between each

---

17. *National Community Safety Plan 2008-11* (2007), Home Office, London: Home Office.
18. *Ibid*, 3.
19. *Ibid.*
20. This PSA is concerned with helping children and young people achieve positive outcomes, such as good health and involvement in education, training or employment, and avoiding negative outcomes such as involvement in crime or drugs.
21. *The New Performance Framework for Local Authorities and Local Authority Partnerships: Single Set of National Indicators* (2007), DCLG, London: Department for Communities and Local Government.

local authority and its Regional Government Office, and consisted of up to 35 indicators chosen from the national indicator set (plus some required indicators relating to educational performance) according to the particular priority needs and problems of the local authority area. The performance of local authorities was then monitored against their LAA indicators, resulting in possible rewards or sanctions. LAAs could thus be seen as a devolved mechanism for supporting the delivery of PSA outcomes.

Whilst the system of PSAs and LAAs, with their large number of prescribed indicators, appears as a very strong top-down 'micro-management' approach to regulation, the official documentation was at pains to stress that the priorities and activities actually pursued at the local level should reflect local needs and circumstances and not involve a slavish following of national priorities. Thus PSA 23 ('Make communities safer') emphasised the importance of local flexibility so that local agencies and partnerships 'respond to the issues that matter most in each locality'.[22] Moreover, in order to establish the issues that mattered most, local communities were to be involved and engaged in the business of identifying needs and determining priorities. This community engagement was 'fundamental to the success of the strategy behind this PSA'[23] and was, in turn, the subject of another of the 'Stronger Communities' family of PSAs: PSA 21, which aimed to 'build more cohesive, empowered and active communities'.

PSA 21 set out a number of actions that 'are key to ensuring empowered communities'[24] and these included:

- building the confidence, ability and interest of citizens and communities of all ages to understand public policy issues and influence the governance of public institutions and services;
- enabling citizens to play a successful part in guiding, directing and supporting the effective deployment of resources and delivery of services in their local communities;

---

22. *PSA Delivery Agreement 23: Make communities safer* (2009), HMG, London: HM Government, 16.
23. *Ibid*, 20.
24. *PSA Delivery Agreement 21: Build more cohesive, empowered and active communities* (2007), HMG, London: HM Government, 7.

- involving local people effectively in addressing their concerns about crime, drugs and anti-social behaviour; and
- giving communities more understanding of and influence over the activities of the criminal justice system (CJS) and enabling them to work with CJS agencies in reducing re-offending.[25]

We thus find that measures to promote community empowerment are integral to the regulation of the safer communities policy.

Safer Communities in Practice

An examination of the National Community Safety Plan, its component PSAs and the linked LAA indicators should provide a sense of what the risks are that communities need to be safer from, the meaning that we can ascribe to community empowerment in the safer communities context and the significance of all this for the idea of community justice. Inevitably, given the need to restrain the length of this chapter, this examination will be selective and I will focus on those elements that seem most relevant to the community empowerment theme. This is important, since much of what appears in the plan and in the national and local indicators can be read as 'mainstream' crime control concerns: priorities are spelled out with regard to reducing serious violent crime, reducing serious acquisitive crime, reducing reoffending, tackling drug misuse and responding to terrorist threats. Thus a large part of what 'Safer Communities' is about is reducing the risk of serious criminal activity impacting on 'ordinary' citizens, which is what one might expect any national crime policy to be concerned with. Yet even within these priorities, considerable emphasis is given to what can be done by local agencies working in partnership with local people and communities.

The NCSP, for example, highlights the potential for local multi-agency working to develop arrangements for the early identification of and intervention with individuals who are judged to be at risk of involvement in serious

---

25. *PSA Delivery Agreement 21: Build more cohesive, empowered and active communities* (2007), HMG, London: HM Government, 7-8.

violence, either as victim or perpetrator. This includes specific arrangements to address domestic violence, sexual offences, gang-based violence including gun and knife crime, and hate crime such as homophobic or racially motivated violence. Interestingly, also identified as a possible local focus for action are serious casualties resulting from traffic incidents. The NCSP provides illustrative case studies of local community-based action to tackle different priorities. One of these involves a project led by a previously violent offender, which 'goes into schools and community centres, targeting children with bad behaviour and high levels of absenteeism ... challenging how teenagers within the borough perceive knife, gun and drug culture'. In another project, developed in partnership with a local gay activist group, a new remote electronic system for reporting homophobic crime was established in a local gay venue. Substantial success is claimed for both projects, not just in terms of their impact on crime rates but in increasing the confidence of particular groups of local people in the criminal justice system.[26]

While considerable importance is attached to these issues of 'serious crime', and the involvement of local communities in addressing them, arguably the core of the safer communities approach is priority action 3 of PSA 23: 'Tackle the crime, disorder and anti-social behaviour issues of greatest importance in each locality, increasing public confidence in the local agencies involved in dealing with these issues'.[27] This harks back to the concern with 'low-level' issues of criminal and disorderly behaviour and their impact on the quality of life of local communities that marked the distinctiveness of New Labour's 'third way' approach to the politics of law and order and which were the focus of the Crime and Disorder Act 1998.[28] As the NCSP makes clear, the local determination of the needs to be addressed and the methods to be used is of paramount significance here:

---

26. *National Community Safety Plan 2008-11* (2007), Home Office, London: Home Office, 8-9.
27. *PSA Delivery Agreement 23: Make communities safer* (2009), HMG, London: HM Government, 12.
28. *Crime Reduction and Community Safety: Labour and the politics of local crime control* (2007), Gilling D, Cullompton: Willan.

... the Government wants to give local agencies and partnerships the freedom to tackle the anti-social behaviour and other crime and disorder issues that are of greatest importance to their local communities.[29]

This 'local freedom' is a key reason why the definition of 'anti-social behaviour' continues to be left open at a national policy level and to acquire different meanings in different localities.[30] Community justice, then, in contrast to classical understandings of criminal justice, with its principles of transparency and consistency, would seem to allow for a degree of variation and unpredictability in what may be perceived as behaviour harmful to the community and to warrant legal intervention.

However, despite this emphasis on localisation, PSA 23 highlighted two *national* strategies as key sources of 'support' to local areas: neighbourhood policing, including the deployment of police community support officers, which was to be 'rolled out' nationally and 'embedded into core policing'[31]; and the then government's anti-social behaviour strategy, in which the Home Office promised to work to increase the use of the legal powers available to tackle ASB by issuing guidance and by 'supporting improvement where tackling ASB is below par';[32] in other words, by intervening to raise the performance of local agencies whose response to ASB was judged to be inadequate. Moreover, 'other government departments also contribute to advancing ASB policy',[33] for instance in relation to social housing management and the improvement of parenting skills. This suggests that the 'freedom' accorded to localities in setting priorities and deciding on the best ways of addressing local problems of crime and ASB was, in practice, a freedom to act within the frameworks and imperatives of certain major national strategies. The limits on local discretion were in fact acknowledged in PSA 23 itself. Tackling ASB is 'a nationwide priority',[34] and the performance of local areas in addressing this priority was to be measured through

---

29. *National Community Safety Plan 2008-11* (2007), Home Office, London: Home Office, 11.
30. 'The "problem" of anti-social behaviour and the policy knowledge base: analyzing the power/knowledge relationship' (2009), Prior D, *Critical Social Policy*, 29(1), 5-23.
31. *PSA Delivery Agreement 23: Make communities safer* (2009), HMG, London: HM Government, 12.
32. *Ibid*, 13.
33. *Ibid*.
34. *Ibid*, 13.

two linked indicators, whereby measurement of the confidence that local communities feel in their local service providers is related to a measurement of success in reducing community perceptions of ASB. 'Progress against these two indicators will demonstrate whether local flexibility and national programmes of support are delivering what local people want'.[35] Local communities were thus given a clear voice in national systems for assessing the effectiveness of local action in response to a national priority.

Conclusion

The central argument of this chapter is that within the policy of 'Safer Communities', as developed by New Labour, the relationship between community empowerment and state regulation was not one of opposing forces or divergent tendencies. Rather, my analysis suggests that ideas and practices of community empowerment were integral to the framework of state regulation; that, in other words, the regulatory processes used by central government to ensure the delivery of the safer communities priority incorporated, and were indeed dependent on, processes of localisation and community empowerment.

Thus, the regulatory apparatus of national plan, public service agreements and formalised local priorities and indicators, actively promotes the development of ways of involving local communities in the shaping and delivery of policy. This involves, on the one hand, the engagement of local people in the identification of particular local problems of crime and disorder, the development of local strategies for addressing them and the holding of formal agencies to account for their performance in implementing such strategies. On the other hand, it involves communities themselves being encouraged and enabled to take responsibility for dealing directly with the potential risks and actual problems that arise in their midst. It is explicit within the regulatory policy framework that the promotion of community action in this way has a dual purpose: to deal with particular issues of crime and disorder *and* to revitalise and strengthen the 'community' itself. Hence

---

35. *PSA Delivery Agreement 23: Make communities safer* (2009), HMG, London: HM Government.

the bringing together in one set of priorities of PSA 21, with its objective of 'more cohesive, empowered and active communities', and PSA 23, with its intention to 'make communities safer'.[36]

One way of interpreting this dual aspect to the regulatory framework is to see it as the point where, expressed through a specific set of governmental practices, the 'politics of behaviour' and the 'politics of community' meet and are combined in a mutually supportive relationship. That is, it is in the objectives and priorities that constitute the Safer Communities policy that certain forms of individual and collective behaviour are problematised as threatening the viability and stability of community life and that community-based values and actions are themselves promoted as the means of controlling those behaviours. This bears out Hudson's observation that, in the communitarian thinking that underpinned so much of New Labour policy, community figures as both means and end; both as a resource for strategies for dealing with certain kinds of problem and as the desired outcome of those strategies. 'Communities are what control strategies are intended to restore, and community is simultaneously the resource by which control is to be effected'.[37] The recruitment of communities to the task of making themselves safer becomes a key mechanism for the advancement of more effective governmental regulation.

Community justice, as embodied in the policy of Safer Communities, is thus revealed as a set of values and practices whose principal motivation is not the liberty and security of individuals or society, but the legitimation of a particular mode of governing in which responsibility for the control of local crime and disorder shifts from the central state to local agencies and communities.[38] That mode of governing seems likely to be sustained under the Conservative-Liberal Democrat Coalition government, albeit with changes of emphasis. David Cameron's 'Big Society' imagery promotes individual citizens, communities and local organizations as the crucial driving-force in improving the quality of life in Britain, and promises new initiatives to

---

36. *PSA Delivery Agreement 21: Build more cohesive, empowered and active communities* (2007), HMG, London: HM Government.
37. *Justice in the Risk Society* (2003), Hudson B, London: Sage Publications, 85.
38. *Powers of Freedom* (1999), Rose N, Cambridge: Cambridge University Press.

push power downwards.[39] At a philosophical level, there appear to be strong continuities here with New Labour's communitarianism. At the same time, the weight and complexity of the central regulatory apparatus described in this chapter is being reduced,[40] while new mechanisms such as the 'Total Place' initiative[41] (inherited from Labour) and the proposal for elected local police and crime commissioners suggest a move in which 'state regulation' gives way to 'local accountability'.[42] If the task of keeping communities safer is being placed even more firmly in the hands of communities themselves, one likely consequence is that the significance of 'community justice' as a response to issues of crime and disorder will be enhanced and its distinctiveness from conventional values and principles of criminal justice will become more marked.

---

39. www.number10.gov.uk/news/speeches-and-transcripts/2010/07/big-society-speech-53572 (accessed 21 July 2010).
40. Comprehensive Area Assessments were abolished on 25 June 2010 and other elements of the performance system for local agencies placed under review. See www.communities.gov.uk/localgovernment/performanceframeworkpartnerships/inspectioncomprehensive/ (accessed 21 July 2010).
41. *Total place: a whole area approach to public services* (2010), HM Treasury and Department of Communities and Local Government
42. 'More Accountability—Less Regulation? Coalition Plans for Policing', (2010) Savage S, *British Society of Criminology Newsletter*, no.66, 10-12.

CHAPTER 10

COMMUNITY JUSTICE AND THE COURTS: A STEP FORWARDS, BACKWARDS OR SIDEWAYS?

JOHN RAINE

Introduction

In recent years in Britain, as in an increasing number of other countries, the concept and ideology of *community* has taken on a new prominence in the context of criminal justice, as indeed it has in relation to public services more generally. No doubt to some extent this reflects a certain nostalgia for an illusory *golden age* and an almost inevitable pendulum swing away from the centralisation that has characterised the past three decades at least in the world of public services, including within the field of justice. As was argued in *Chapter 1*, in part also, it could be understood as a response to the growing disappointment with the outcomes of those years of increasing centralisation—and realisation that, for all the well-intentioned initiatives to create more effective and efficient public services, and to address the key problems of our time, the difference made in practice was in many instances felt to have been marginal. Crime is an obvious example and, as we saw earlier, for all the reforms, reorganisations and initiatives—most of which have tended to shift more control towards the centre—the impact in terms of reduced levels of offending and re-offending had been distinctly underwhelming and public confidence in the agencies largely unmoved.

Another interpretation altogether, however, would be that attraction to the concept of community was less a reaction to the centralising tendency but instead more a purposeful tactic through which the centre could increasingly take the initiative for policy formulation while delegating the responsibility for implementation (and any blame for failure) to localities. In this context, for example, Crawford, has highlighted the central promotion and funding of crime prevention and yet the significant local dimension to such activity (through initiatives such as Neighbourhood Watch, Priority Estates and Safer Cities), as a 'decentring/re-centring dialectic'.[1] The work of Victim Support can perhaps also be seen in this light; with the Ministry of Justice (and previously the Home Office) keen to support the work as part of the core policy concerning the treatment of victims within the criminal justice system, yet also content to leave responsibility for devising and providing the services to individual communities and those who volunteer in this context.

The Roots of Community Justice

Whatever the explanations, in Britain at least, throughout the post-war period during which the trend of centralisation has held sway, the fascination with and attachment to the concept of community seems to have been a consistent counter-theme, with the 'small in beautiful' mantra having been regularly chanted in response to any proposals that suggested some centralising tendency. As Lacey and Zedner have commented, ideas of community have been 'invoked for both "diagnostic" and "therapeutic" purposes; as explanations for, and as a means of curing, social disorder'.[2] They point to the cluster of values that the term community tends to suggest — 'solidarity, reciprocity, mutuality, connection, care, and sharing'.[3] As Bell and Newby wryly observed some forty years ago, 'everyone — even sociologists — has wanted to live in a community'.[4]

---

1. See, for example, 'Citizenship, Community and the Management of Crime' (1987), Clarke M, *British Journal of Criminology*, 27, 387; 'The Partnership Approach to Community Crime Prevention; Corporatism at the Local Level?' (1994), Crawford A, *Social and Legal Studies*, 3, 497-518; 'Appeals to Community and Crime Prevention' (1995), Crawford A, *Crime, Law and Social Change*, 22, 97-126.
2. 'Discourses on Community in Criminal Justice' (1995), Lacey N and Zedner L, *Journal of Law and Society*, 22, 3, 301-325.
3. *Ibid*, 302.
4. *Community Studies* (1971), Bell C and Newby H, London: Unwin, 21.

Referring specifically to the criminal justice context, Lacey and Zedner have posed two leading questions: first, what explains the apparent power of the idea of community to render policies attractive, given that it is the very breakdown of community to which many crime problems are attributed? And second, why is it that the rhetorical figure of community is so regularly invoked notwithstanding criticism of its conceptual and political vagueness?[5]

In addressing these questions, they have highlighted two rather divergent post-war histories of community. On the one hand, we have that of welfarism and the development of 'community studies' in the 1950s and 1960s. On the other, there was the appeal to community in the Conservative politics of the 1980s when the need for response to an earlier fiscal crisis (and world recession) invoked moves towards deinstitutionalising initiatives such as 'care in the community', decarceration of patients with learning difficulties and, for the courts, an equivalent policy shift towards the use of 'community service orders' and reparation and mediation services wherever possible as alternatives to custody. In this latter context, community approaches could be seen as cheap, though also potentially effective, alternatives to state responsibility.

For most people, the notion of community immediately sounds socially comforting and inclusive. The notion responds positively to the anxieties people have in an increasingly hectic and transient world about the atomisation and disconnection of society and perceived vulnerabilities to crime and victimisation. However, at the same time some important questions about community also arise, both about access to and the distribution of power and resources between and within communities, and about processes of exclusion which may be especially significant in relation to criminal justice. Moreover, as Cohen has pointed out, the focus on communities in criminal justice, notably in relation to crime prevention, surveillance and punishment, has invoked a significant increase in social control throughout society, not least through CCTV and civil penalties as well as criminal sanctions.[6]

A key part of the community narrative in criminal justice has been around engaging local people in taking responsibility for addressing the crime prob-

---

5. 'Discourses on Community in Criminal Justice' (1995), Lacey N and Zedner L, *Journal of Law and Society*, 22, 3, 301-325.
6. 'The Punitive City: Notes on the Dispersal of Social Control' (1979), Cohen S, *Contemporary Crises*, 3, 339-364.

lem and at the same time reducing dependency on the official agencies. The advocacy of Neighbourhood Watch schemes is perhaps among the most direct and obvious examples of this. But in the same way so too has been the promotion of 'private' parental control responsibilities. More recently, as again discussed in *Chapter 1*, we have also seen the introduction of police community support officers (PCSOs), in addition to the more longstanding tradition of special constables, as quasi-professional police patrolling and addressing a range of crime and anti-social behaviour issues in their own neighbourhoods.[7] There has also been much promotion of the idea that responses to crime should ideally be community-based, and this has been reflected in the development of mediation between victims and offenders, in the focus on developing a wider range of community penalties and, as indicated, by encouragement and funding for community-based Victim Support work. Co-opting the community into the challenge of combating crime, encouraging self-help, and enlisting the co-operation of citizens—whether as reporters of crime, as special constables, or as volunteer magistrates, probation or victim support workers—has been a key plank of recent policy from Whitehall and Westminster, and not least because it would help to dispel the idea that crime is somehow the problem of government.

The connection in this way between the concept of *community* and criminal justice has, however, been further cemented by the emerging notion of 'community justice'—a phrase that, although with a long tradition of academic interest, particularly in the US,[8] has more recently slipped easily into the vocabulary of practitioners on this side of the Atlantic and which has now developed quite specific connotations in relation to the courts and the judicial process. In particular here has been the interest in developing more locally responsive courts—community justice centres, as they tend now to be

---

7. See, for example, 'Issues concerning visibility and reassurance provided by the new "policing family"' (2005), Cooke C, *Journal of Community & Applied Social Psychology*, 15, 229-240; 'Diversifying Police Recruitment? The Deployment of Police Community Support Officers in London' (2006), Johnston L, *Howard Journal of Criminal Justice*, 45, 4, 388-402.
8. See for example, *Community Justice: An Emerging Field* (1998), Karp D (ed), Rowman & Littlefield Publishers, 327; 'Neighbourhood Justice at the Midtown Community Court, in Crime and Place: Plenary Papers of the 1997' (1998), Feinblatt J *et al*, *Conference on Criminal Justice Research and Evaluation*, 81, National Institute of Justice.

called—which, as Fagan and Malkin have described, do three things.[9] First, they suggest, the centres bring 'citizens and defendants closer in a jurisprudential process that is both therapeutic and accountable'. Second, they link providers of specialist support and other relevant services to the court, and so to the individuals and their families caught up in criminal justice cases. In this way, they claim to be more responsive to their needs. Third, they bring the court and the associated services into a local area—usually one that has particular problems for residents—for example, of poor public and private service provision, and a poor quality of life in general.

Community Justice in Practice: from Red Hook to North Liverpool

The pioneering development in community justice centres took place at the turn of the 21st century with the opening of a community justice centre in the relatively deprived neighbourhood of Red Hook in Brooklyn, New York. The simple idea was for a court that, in being physically closer to its community, would be able to be more responsive to local problems that gave rise to crime and would also be more accountable to the community for its contribution to crime reduction and for 'problem-solving'. The concept was in stark contrast to the context at the main court centre previously serving the area where issues of size, management and bureaucracy had steadily created inefficiency, inflexibility and unresponsiveness. Crucially, the change to community justice that Red Hook Community Justice Centre invoked was from the court as an 'impartial arbiter of state power' to one which would 'serve a victimised community…in need of repair'.[10]

The key mechanisms for making a difference were to place the mobilisation of social services under the auspices of the court (community justice centre) and to promote a more open, democratic and engaging relationship with local citizens. As a result, the court and the individuals who appeared before

---

9. 'Theorizing Community Justice Through Community Courts' (2002), Fagan J and Malkin V, *Fordham Urban Law Journal*, 897- 953.
10. *Ibid*, 902.

it would no longer act alone but in conjunction with a third party—the community—whose perspectives and daily activities, so the argument went, had been shaped by crime, both real and perceived. That said, the centre would focus strongly on the problems encountered by individuals, such as low levels of social capital, problems of addiction, insecure or lacking employment, mental health issues, poor housing and so on, and would link the sanctions it imposed to services addressing such problems, in this way seeking to reduce the motivation or propensity for criminality. At the same time, emphasis would be placed on restorative justice principles and practices, again with sanctions and processes being applied that would aim to help the individual victim or the collective community as a victim. Thus, community service teams would undertake renewal projects in Red Hook, clearing scrubland, removing graffiti, collecting litter etc., and in turn, the visibility of such work would, it was felt, send powerful signals to other offenders and the community at large about the unacceptability of anti-social behaviour and of the law's commitment to prevention.

Another key element of the approach at Red Hook was the leadership provided by a particular judge—the comparatively small geographical area which the community justice centre served, meaning that almost all the caseload could go before a single member of the judiciary, who would become familiar with the local issues, with the persistent offenders and their problems, including their excuses and promises made at previous hearings. The single judge would, therefore, be able to challenge any inconsistencies and make more informed assessments of the likelihood of compliance with particular court orders. In this way, the argument was that the court could dispense a form of justice with greater prospect of solving the problems.

Working in conjunction with different agencies and groups—social services, support agencies, community associations, churches and other local bodies—the community justice centre itself would seek to strengthen the sense of community and, by having the specialist support agencies sharing space in the same building as the court, would be able to address the problems at the time that justice was being dispensed rather than, as more usually, by a recommendation for referral and by adjourning the hearings.

The messages about Red Hook quickly spread across the Atlantic, and various delegations, including the Lord Chief Justice and the Home Secretary, visited in 2003 to learn about the approach, its impact and the potential which a community justice centre approach might offer. Within a short time commitment was made to establish a similar pilot in England and Wales.[11] A neighbourhood in North Liverpool was selected, a disused school building there was chosen for conversion into the court centre, and a judge was appointed to lead the initiative. The North Liverpool Community Justice Centre (NLCJC) eventually opened in September 2005.

Unlike traditional magistrates' courts, a set of specific objectives were set for NLCJC, all much in line with what had been seen as the key aims at Red Hook. These were as follows:

- to reduce low level offending and anti-social behaviour;
- to reduce fear of crime and increase public confidence in criminal justice;
- to increase compliance with community sentences;
- to increase victims' and witnesses' satisfaction with criminal justice;
- to increase the involvement of the community in criminal justice; and
- to reduce the time from arrest to sentence.

Other key features of the NLCJC pilot, which again borrowed heavily from Red Hook, were:

- The running of the court by a single judge[12] to ensure consistency in decision-making and enhanced accountability through continuity. The judge pursues close links with the community, where he has a high profile, to reassure local people that strong action is being taken against offenders in the community;
- Multi-agency working—with co-location at the centre of the local authority anti-social behaviour team, a housing association, and a range of other service providers to enable speedier inter-agency working to process the cases and tackle offending;

---

11. *Respect and Responsibility—Taking a Stand Against Anti-Social Behaviour* (2003), Home Office, White Paper, Cm 5778, London Home Office.
12. The judge hears all non-trial summary cases and most either-way offences committed within the designated catchment area, and he is also able to sit as a Crown Court judge for sentencing purposes. A team of magistrates hear summary trials.

- A one-stop shop approach on-site, including support for victims and witnesses, housing advice, drugs and alcohol counselling, mediation, education and vocational advice, debt counselling and mentoring, to enable underlying causes of offending to be holistically addressed;
- A focus on socially harmful behaviour as well as criminal offences, with the centre hearing ASB applications, enforcement of confiscation orders, education welfare cases, local authority prosecutions for non-school attendance, and environmental offences;
- A problem-solving approach which underpins the way the court operates—seeking to identify and tackle the causes of offending behaviour and thus lowering the risk of re-offending, while at the same time seeking to address fear of crime and public confidence;
- Involving the local community through an extensive programme of activities so that they can learn more about the court, identify local issues and projects which offenders might undertake as unpaid work as part of their sentences, and increase participation in criminal justice generally;
- Establishing Community Reference Groups—of local residents and businesses—to provide feedback to, and liaise with, the centre; and
- Providing a resource for the community so that local people on a 'drop-in' basis and for community projects and diversionary activities.

Evaluating the Community Justice Centre Concept

In 2007, an evaluation was undertaken of the impact of the NLCJC which painted a generally positive picture from the first two years of operation.[13] In particular, the court was found to be working efficiently in addressing robustly any causes of delay and ensuring speedier justice overall. The strong judicial leadership afforded by the single judge model was considered to be a key factor here, with an average of 2.2 hearings per case to completion compared with a regional average of some 2.8. One factor here appeared to be the reduced tendency of defendants to plead 'not guilty' (guilty pleas were

---

13. *Evaluation of the North Liverpool Community Justice Centre* (2007), Ministry of Justice, Ministry of Justice Research Series 12/07, London: Ministry of Justice.

found to be running at 82% of all cases compared with a national average of just 68%) suggesting that the firm approach of the judge was causing defendants to think twice about not-guilty pleas as a delaying tactic.

More than managerial performance though, the evaluation highlighted the positive impacts of the 'problem-solving approach', and particularly the effects of the meetings held prior to sentencing in cases where underlying problems were identified as causing or exacerbating offending, such as drug addiction, debt or housing problems. Interviews with offenders confirmed that such sessions were indeed proving helpful in finding solutions to contributory problems. Also significant in the evaluation was the finding that the practice at the NLCJC of regularly calling offenders back to court for reviews of their progress on community orders (a mechanism specially enacted on a pilot basis for the NLCJC from the Criminal Justice Act 2003) was effective in reducing the likelihood of non-compliance or highlighting and addressing any other emerging problems that might be resolved before matters got out of hand. Clear perceived benefits were also noted for victims and witnesses because the centre offered a full-time on-site service of Victim Support personnel, which meant a higher proportion received support of one form or another and were, as a result, proportionately more satisfied with their experience than among equivalent groups of witnesses and victims nationally.

On the other hand, the impact of the efforts at community engagement was found to be much less impressive; although in the first two years of the NLCJC some 2,904 people attended the 100 community engagement events that had been organised, and although awareness about the centre was found to be increasing, the surveys concluded that the difference was only from 1 in 5 (20% of the local community) to around 1 in 3 (32%). The evaluation also noted that community involvement in Community Reference Groups was largely restricted to those community members who were already active in some other way. Perhaps the most disappointing finding was that, for all the community engagement activity, the initiative had not yet led to any discernible increase in public confidence in criminal justice in the area—indeed the surveys revealed a slight decrease over the two year period—much in line with the wider regional and national picture. This suggested that the impact of national media and other factors outside the control of the NLCJC were proving more influential on public perceptions than any local efforts.[14]

Enthusiasm in government about the community justice concept was such that it did not wait for the evaluation of NLCJC before announcing a second pilot (at Salford Magistrates' Courts) and then a further 12 around the country, again each based at an existing magistrates' court. To be fair, the Government quickly recognised that, because of the high costs involved, any wider roll-out of the concept could not be on the basis of North Liverpool, of a new/refurbished court building and with all the ancilliary services provided on site. Instead, implementation would have to be focused more around the 'processes of justice' that had been piloted at North Liverpool rather than the physical infrastructure. In particular, the principle of the 'problem-solving approach' and its associated inter-agency working arrangements were perceived as being the vital elements to replicate more widely.

Community Justice and Community Engagement

It was also very clear by this time that the new mood for localism and for the challenges of community engagement had indeed become strongly established in public administrative thinking more generally, including within criminal justice. This was most notably apparent in the advent of neighbourhood policing and the associated recruitment of many thousands of police community support officers across the country.[15] More ambitious aims were also strongly evident in the publication in 2009 of the Green Paper 'Engaging Communities in Criminal Justice'[16] which appeared to prescribe a new vision and culture for the justice sector based on a 'localising, democratising

---

14. *Evaluation of the North Liverpool Community Justice Centre* (2007), Ministry of Justice, Ministry of Justice Research Series 12/07, London: Ministry of Justice.
15. See, for example, *Building Communities, Beating Crime*, (2004) White Paper, Cm 6360, London: Home Office; *From the Neighbourhood to the National: Policing our Communities Together* (2008), Green Paper, Cm 7448, London: Home Office.
16. *Engaging Communities in Criminal Justice* (2009), Office for Criminal Justice Reform, Green Paper, Cm 7583, London: Home Office.

and participative' public service model.[17] More specifically, the Green Paper offered a range of policy proposals including:

- Establishment of 'Community Prosecutors' as named officials for each local area 'to strengthen the contribution of the Crown Prosecution Service (CPS) to community engagement activity alongside the police, courts and other partners' and to encourage prosecutors to engage much more with their local communities and so become more informed about local concerns, involved with local organisations and generally to make the CPS become a more visible outward-facing organisation;
- Introduction of 'Community Impact Statements' in all courts (these having been piloted in some areas) as a means to make the views of the community as a whole on particular crime and anti-social behaviour problems better understood by the courts and other criminal justice agencies (for example, to assist the police and CPS in deciding whether or not to charge someone; to assist probation officers in making pre-sentence recommendations, and to assist the court in deciding sentence);
- Rolling out the 'Problem-Solving Approach' piloted in the community justice initiatives in magistrates' courts across England and Wales to strengthen the connection between justice and communities (with a tailored more intensive approach in areas of most need);
- Expanding use of the principles and practices of multi-agency working as also pioneered in the community justice projects—especially in areas of high deprivation–where possible through co-location of the relevant agencies and elsewhere through other means (e.g. *virtual courts* to allow agencies to make their inputs by video-link technology);
- Inviting local people to nominate projects in their local areas which might be the subject for offenders undertaking unpaid work as part of the 'Community Payback' scheme, and also to suggest how any assets seized from offenders might be used in the local area;
- Advocating more extensive use of restorative justice principles and practices, with a key priority being to raise awareness of the benefits to victims

---

17. 'Engaging Communities in Criminal Justice: An Appraisal' (2009), Raine J, *EuroVista*, 1, 26-31.

of restorative justice approaches and to encourage more provision for and participation in offender-victim reparations work;
- Making more information on crime and justice more readily available to local communities, and following the path taken in policing, of arranging regular meetings, agreeing local priorities, providing monthly updates on crime and progress in addressing problems, and detailing what actions are being taken to make neighbourhoods safer; and
- Promoting more volunteering within criminal justice (for example, as police special constables, members of independent advisory groups; members of Police Authorities, Probation Boards/Trusts or Courts Boards; as magistrates; as members of Youth Offender Panels; as appropriate adults for young people being interviewed by the police and so on).

Conclusion: Community Justice Centres as a Step Forwards, Backwards or Sideways?

As things turned out, the process of finalising and implementing such proposals in a formal manner (i.e. through a White Paper) was somewhat disrupted by the general election in Spring 2010 and the subsequent formation of a Coalition government which quickly set to work on an agenda dominated by public sector financial restraint and reducing the size of public debt grown in the preceding months of economic recession and banking crisis. As indicated, this largely dictated that there could be no more high profile and prestige community justice centre projects of the North Liverpool type for the foreseeable future. Furthermore, rather than a move towards more *justice within communities* it seemed far more likely that that the public finance problems would force a raft of closures of the lesser used court houses and therefore a distancing of courts from many local residents. However, there seemed no sign of retreat at least from the key notions in community justice of a *problem-solving* approach and of engagement with, and accountability to, local people. Indeed, that idea seemed to resonate quite as well with the rhetoric of the new administration of Conservatives (with the ambitions for 'a Big Society rather than for Big Government') and the Liberal Democrats (with theirs for constitutional reform) as with the values of Labour and its concern with citizen and community engagement as part of democratic renewal).

But it is also important to recognise the controversial nature of such community justice ideas, particularly because of the implication that the values of *localism* and *democracy* would be placed ahead of those more traditionally associated with justice — of *consistency* and of *professionalism*. For some, indeed, the shift in these directions would perhaps even seem to challenge the constitutional imperative of judicial independence because of the closer linkages that the community justice approach demanded between judicial decision-making and the local polity. At the same time, it needs to be recognised that, while decentralisation, responsivity, openness, inclusivity and community engagement are, to many minds, welcome hallmarks of a modern democratic state, so too is the reputation for independence of the judiciary.

Most especially in the context of the overarching theme of this book, however, it is pertinent to highlight the apparent paradox of the advent and development of community justice centres in England and Wales as having been largely inspired and driven by central government — and, as such, essentially by the executive arm of the state rather than by the judicial branch too. And herein lies a potential problem, particularly in an era of constrained public financial resources, that, unless there was strong *ownership* and commitment from within the judicial branch itself, and unless the concept of community justice were to be formulated and implemented by the judges and magistrates in their own way, and as they felt to be most appropriate to their perspectives on the interests of justice, there would be risk of community justice being little more than a new fad with its own constraints and bureaucracy and something that would perhaps make little difference to people's lives in practice.

CHAPTER 11

INTOLERANT OR INTOLERABLE?: ANTI-SOCIAL YOUTH IN ASOCIAL COMMUNITIES

NATHAN HUGHES

This chapter will explore the apparent alienation of *youth* from the communities they live in. It begins with an examination of accusations of increasing intolerance amongst young people, as voiced by the media, politicians and the public. With reference to concepts of ontological insecurity and moral panic, an apparent parallel intolerance amongst adults will then be explored, plotting a growing concern with what might be considered normality in young people's behaviour. In doing so, I consider Stuart Waiton's assertion that 'the "anti-social offender" and the "easily offended" should be understood as two sides of the same asocial coin'.[1]

Through an examination of policies and practices in tackling anti-social behaviour, I conclude by questioning whether approaches to *empowering* communities are in danger of disempowering or even victimising young people. Ultimately, therefore, the chapter seeks to question whether the problematic relationship between young people and adults in many communities is the result of anti-social youth or asocial communities: are our youth intolerant or intolerable? In doing so it furthers a number of the themes of this book. In particular, it questions the efficacy of engaging communities in constructing and tackling the local crime agenda, given an apparent imbalance and rupture in the relationship between adults and youth within local communities; or rather it warns of the challenges inherent in understand-

---

1. 'Asocial not anti-social: the 'Respect Agenda' and the 'therapeutic me'" (2008), Waiton S, in Squires P (ed) *ASBO Nation: The criminalisation of nuisance,* Bristol: Policy Press.

ing and addressing community relationships, dialogue and conflict so as to ensure *community justice* becomes possible.

'The Kids of Today': Images of 'Problem Youth'

At present in the UK, we are surrounded by images that portray the unacceptable and intolerable behaviours and attitudes of a whole generation of young people. Various forms of media regularly depict young people to be increasingly violent and disrespectful. Negative and highly emotive newspaper headlines appear to be the norm, for example:

- 'Out of control' British Teens Worst in Europe;[2]
- Hoodie hell on streets every 8 secs;[3] and
- Today's youth: anxious, depressed, anti-social.[4]

Leading the way has been *The Sun* which has described a 'scourge of feral youngsters' as being 'the most important issue now facing Britain'.[5]

Other forms of media also contribute to this popular perception. The lyrical content of 'R&B' and rap music (popular with the younger generation, yet frowned upon by their elders) is frequently criticised for endorsing violence and glorifying the use of guns, whilst representations of anti-social teenagers such as *Little Britain*'s Vicky Pollard and Catherine Tate's Lauren provide pervasive images of a generation of thoughtless, uncouth, obnoxious teens. Such imagery has, itself, fuelled numerous newspaper headlines purporting to have identified 'real life Vicky Pollards',[6] demonstrating the clear and ready transfer of fiction to reality.

---

2. '"Out of control" British Teens Worst in Europe' (2007), Clark L, *Daily Mail*, 26th July, 2007.
3. 'Hoodie hell on streets every 8 secs' (2009), Lyons J, *Daily Mirror*, 4th February, 2009.
4. 'Today's youth: anxious, depressed, anti-social' (2004), Bunting, M, *Guardian*, 13 September, 2004.
5. 'Britain's Mean Streets' (2008), Mayer C, *Time magazine*, March 26th 2008, www.time.com/time/magazine/article/0,9171,1725547,00.html.
6. For example, see Judge bans real-life Vicky Pollard from her own home', (2005), Wainwright M, *Guardian*, 10 May 2005 www.guardian.co.uk/uk/2005/may/10/ukcrime.prisonsandprobation; 'Yeah, but no, but they're the real Vicky Pollards' (2006), Newling D and Alison C,

Our political leaders seem happy to reflect such media portrayals. Upon winning the 2005 General Election, Tony Blair promised to tackle what he presented as an escalation of inappropriate and unacceptable behaviour amongst young people: 'there is a disrespect that people don't like… whether it's in the classroom, or on the street, or on town centres on a Friday or Saturday night'.[7] After becoming Prime Minister, Gordon Brown voiced similar concerns that 'Kids are out of control… roaming the streets… out late at night'.[8] Our present Prime Minister, David Cameron, has also joined the chorus. Despite encouraging us all to 'hug a hoodie' and show 'more love' to adolescents in recognising the challenges of youth,[9] more recent portrayals of a 'Broken Society'[10] have been criticised for politicising the recent attempted murder carried out by two young people in Doncaster, exaggerating the relevance of a horrific (yet isolated) incident, and in doing so fuelling 'populist paranoia' regarding youth behaviour.[11]

Of course, such representations are not without a basis in reality. The most recent analysis of youth crime statistics carried out by Nacro (www.

The Daily Mail, 3rd January 2006, www.dailymail.co.uk/news/article-373096/Yeah-theyre-real-Vicky-Pollards.html and 'Nursery assistants 'creating a generation of Vicky Pollards', teachers warn' Paton, (2008), Daily G, *Telegraph*, 30th July 2008 www.telegraph.co.uk/news/uknews/2474823/Nursery-assistants-creating-a-generation-of-Vicky-Pollards-teachers-warn.html.

7. *PM's speech on returning to 10 Downing Street on 6 May 2005* (2005), Blair T, www.number10.gov.uk/Page7459 (last accessed July 2010).
8. See, 'Britain's Mean Streets' (2008), Mayer C, *Time magazine*, March 26th 2008, www.time.com/time/magazine/article/0,9171,1725547,00.html and 'Brown: Kid gangs 'out of control" (2008) Roberts B, *Daily Mirror*, 9th January 2008, www.mirror.co.uk/news/top-stories/2008/01/09/brown-kid-gangs-out-of-control-115875-20279567/.
9. 'Cameron softens crime image in 'hug a hoodie' call' (2006), Hinsliff G, *The Observer*, 9 July 2006, www.guardian.co.uk/politics/2006/jul/09/conservatives.ukcrime.
10. *Speech: Mending our Broken Society* (2010), Cameron D, 22nd January 2010 www.conservatives.com/News/Speeches/2010/01/David_Cameron_Mending_our_Broken_Society.aspx (last accessed July 2010).
11. 'Cameron feeds populist paranoia over British youth' (2009), Cecil N, *London Evening Standard*, 6th October 2009. www.thisislondon.co.uk/standard/article-23752971-cameron-feeds-populist-paranoia-over-british-youth.do and 'David Cameron sparks fury by using the Doncaster child torture case for "point-scoring"' (2010), Lyons J, *Daily Mirror*, 23rd January 2010, www.mirror.co.uk/news/top-stories/2010/01/23/david-cameron-sparks-fury-by-using-the-doncaster-child-torture-case-for-point-scoring-115875-21989241/.

nacro.co.uk) suggests a continual rise in youth crime since 2003, reversing more than a decade of declining offending rates.

> During 2007, 126,000 children and young people aged 10-17 received a reprimand, final warning or conviction for an indictable offence and this, while still some 12% lower than the equivalent figure for 1992, represents an increase of 20% since 2003.[12]

A rise in the frequency of some serious crimes by young people is also apparent. The Youth Justice Board (YJB) suggests violent crime against the person by those under 18 to have risen 39% between 2005 and 2008, whilst, in the same period, robberies committed by young people increased by around 45%.[13] The picture is not straightforward, however, with the YJB[14] reporting 'a 7.5% fall in the number of re-offences committed by children and young people from 2005 to 2007', as well as 'a 21.6% drop in the numbers of young people receiving a reprimand, warning or conviction for the first time in England' in 2008-09.[15]

It is of little surprise that the perceptions of the public appear to resemble those presented by the media and politicians. Rather than the official crime figures, it is the stereotyping and emotive headlines that seem to have the greatest influence, with perception of the extent of youth crime far out of kilter with reality. In an Ipsos MORI survey of 1001 adults, over a third of respondents suggested that young people were responsible for over half of reported crimes, with 14% suggesting the proportion was 70% or more.[16] Taking a mean average across all responses, young people were seen as being responsible for 47% of crime. Such a perception is drastically different to the

---

12. *Some facts about children and young people who offend — 2007* (2009), Nacro, Youth Crime briefing, March 2009, London: Nacro, 2.
13. *Youth Justice Annual Workload Data 2006/07*, (2008), Youth Justice Board, London: Youth Justice Board.
14. *Reoffending figures for young people drop* (2009), Youth Justice Board www.yjb.gov.uk/en-gb/News/ReoffendingFiguresForYoungPeopleDrop.htm?area=MediaCentre (last accessed July 2010).
15. *Fewer young people entered the criminal justice system last year* (2009), Youth Justice Board, 20,448 www.yjb.gov.uk/en-gb/News/20448feweryoungpeopleenteredthecriminaljusticesysteml astyear.htm?area=MediaCentre (last accessed July 2010).
16. *Attitudes Towards Teenagers and Crime,* (2006), Ipsos MORI, London: Ipsos MORI, www.ipsos-mori.com/researchpublications/researcharchive/poll.aspx.

official figures in that same year, which suggested that young people committed 12.6% of all detected offences.[17] The accuracy of crime statistics is, of course, much debated.[18] Notwithstanding a healthy scepticism, the disparity between perception and reality appears profound.

Of further concern is the lack of an apparent distinction in popular perception between an offending minority of young people and the law-abiding majority. The Barnardos' campaign, *Children in Trouble*[19] sought to identify and challenge negative views regarding young people. Drawing on a poll of 2021 adults conducted by YouGov, the campaign argues that a large proportion of the adult population hold a negative view of *all* children. For example, 49% of those surveyed believed 'that children are increasingly a danger to each other and adults', and 43% agreed that 'something has to be done to protect us from children'. A review of readers' comments made to local and national newspapers revealed the frequency of powerfully emotive language and phraseology, such as: 'Shoot a few and if that doesn't work shoot a few more'; 'To hell with their human rights' and 'Let's sort these parasites out'.

Recent research suggests such opinions to be widespread—if less dramatically expressed. A report published by the Institute for Public Policy Research presents a society gripped by 'paedophobia'—a fear of its children and young people.[20] Symptoms of this phobia are seen to include a reluctance to intervene when young people might be behaving in an anti-social manner compared with adults in other European countries, yet a growing likelihood to perceive young people 'hanging around' as a problem. The survey suggests that:

- 1.7 million British adults admitted avoiding going out of doors after dark for fear of conflict with young people; and

---

17. *Some facts about children and young people who offend—2006* (2008), Nacro, Youth Crime briefing, March 2009, London: Nacro, 2.
18. See, for example, 'Crime Data and Statistics' (2006), Maguire M, in M. Maguire R, Morgan and Reiner R (eds) *The Oxford Handbook of Criminology*, Fourth Edition. Oxford: Oxford University Press.
19. See www.barnardos.org.uk/what_we_do/children_in_trouble_campaign.htm.
20. *Freedom's orphans: Raising youth in a changing world* (2006), Margo J and Dixon M, London: Institute for Public Policy Research.

- 1.5 million Britons considered moving away from their local area in the last twelve months as a result of young people 'hanging around'.

The report offers a detailed analysis of the complex influences on this seemingly growing divide between adults and children, emphasising not the behaviour of young people but the day-to-day interactions and relationships between young people and adults. It is this interaction within local communities that I seek to explore in the remainder of this chapter; firstly in considering the causes of the apparent divide, and subsequently in examining the efficacy of the associated policy and practice response.

A Moral Panic over Youth Misbehaviour?

Jock Young traces 'the transition between the Golden Age of the post-War period within the First World to the crisis years of the late-1960s onwards.'[21] Labelling the latter as 'late modernity', he describes a diversification of behaviour and culture that has 'challenged our notions of material certainty and uncontested values, replacing them with a world of risk and uncertainty, of individual choice and pluralism, and of a deep-seated precariousness both economic and ontological'.[22] Young cites Giddens' analysis of 'late modern life', characterised by 'heightened choice' and 'a constant questioning of established beliefs and certainties'.[23] This has given rise to an 'ontological insecurity' throughout the population, causing the dominant majority to try to impose their own values on wider society in an attempt to 'create a secure base'.-

> That is to reassert one's values as moral absolutes, to declare other groups as lacking in value, to draw distinct lines of virtue and vice, to be rigid rather than flexible in one's judgement, to be punitive and excluding rather than permeable and assimilative.[24]

---

21. 'From inclusive to exclusive society: nightmares in the European dream' (1998), Young J, in Ruggerio V, South N and Taylor I (eds) *The New European Criminology: Crime and social order in Europe*, London: Routledge, 64.
22. *Ibid* 64.
23. *Modernity and Self-Identity* (1991), Giddens A, Cambridge: Polity, 70-88.
24. 'From inclusive to exclusive society: nightmares in the European dream' (1998), Young J, in

Such an analysis leads Stuart Waiton to argue that 'the problem we face is ultimately not one of an anti-social society but of an asocial society.'[25] Waiton cites Truss who describes an introverted society of fragmented communities and social networks.[26] This has given rise to a 'my bubble, my rules' mentality, through which a self-defined 'elite' perceive others as breaking these rules and attempt to address this; for example, by limiting the wearing of 'hoodies' or drinking on street corners. Certain sections of society are therefore cast as 'folk devils' and made the subject of what Stan Cohen defined as a 'moral panic', whereby:

> A condition, episode, person or group of persons emerges to become defined as a threat to societal values and interests.... The moral barricades are manned by editors, bishops, politicians and other right-thinking people; socially accredited experts pronounce their diagnoses and solutions; ways of coping are evolved or resorted to; the condition then disappears, submerges or deteriorates and becomes more visible.[27]

It appears that young people are particularly prone to being cast in such a way. Cohen's original analysis emerged from a consideration of public concern with the Mods and Rockers. A parallel analysis is equally possible in relation to punks, raves, or many other youth cultures that have developed since.

Whether the label of a 'moral panic' can be applied to the current concern with youth anti-social behaviour is debatable. Whilst it lacks the singular, high profile event, such as the violence of the Mods and Rockers on Clacton Sands or the death of Leah Betts after taking ecstasy, youth anti-social behaviour is certainly portrayed as a 'threat to societal values and interests' and is seemingly prone to the exaggeration by the mass media that Cohen sees as a significant characteristic of a moral panic. As discussed above, emotive headlines and stereotypical portrayals feed perceptions of ubiquitous

---

Ruggerio V, South N and Taylor I (eds) *The New European Criminology: Crime and social order in Europe*, London: Routledge,73.

25. 'Asocial not anti-social: the 'Respect Agenda' and the 'therapeutic me'" (2008), Waiton S, in Squires P (ed) *ASBO Nation: The criminalisation of nuisance*, Bristol: Policy Press, 337.
26. *Ibid*, 345, citing *Talk to the hand: The utter bloody rudeness of everyday life* (2005), Truss L, London: Profile Books.
27. *Folk Devils and Moral Panics: The Creation of the Mods and Rockers* (1980), Cohen S, Oxford: Martin Robertson, 9.

'problem youth', whilst the 'hoodie' has provided a symbolic focus of the concern here.

Perceptions of vulnerability are increased through isolation, with people feeling more exposed to incidents of crime and anti-social behaviour, and less able to react. Over recent decades we have become an increasingly private society. We no longer know our neighbours, and readily erect physical and emotional barriers between them and ourselves. Paradoxically, Donnison argues that this makes us feel even more exposed.[28] 'Fear then becomes cumulative: if others fear us, they are more likely to behave in ways which make us fear them'. The lack of a personal network of family, friends and 'good neighbours' in close proximity, who can be relied on at times of difficulty, might accentuate a sense of vulnerability, particularly where there is a specific cause of fear or concern. This is effectively articulated by Nils Christie:

> If I am acquainted with my neighbours and have some sort of network close to me, I have an easy time if some youngsters misbehave in my hallway. I can call for someone who might know some of them, or I can turn to the athletic neighbour one floor up—or perhaps better still—I can ask for help from the little lady I know as particularly good at handling local conflicts. But without a network, and with all the information on the increase in crime in mind, I would have locked the door and called the police. I would therefore have created conditions for encouraging unwanted behaviour, and for giving unwanted behaviour the meaning of crime.[29]

Isolation from our neighbours leads to a lack of collective community capacity to deal with problems or concerns, or to provide a sense of security should such problems arise. Denied the informal means to tackle such problems, we have instead become increasingly reliant on formal intervention through state authorities in the form of heightened policing and the development of a range of new legislative powers to tackle what has now become commonly and officially labelled as 'anti-social behaviour'.

---

28. 'Creating a safer society' (1998), Donnison D, in Jones, Finer C and Nellis M (eds) *Crime and Social Exclusion*, Oxford: Blackwell, 8.
29. *A Suitable Amount of Crime* (2004), Christie N, London: Routledge, 69-70.

Empowering the Law-abiding (Adult) Majority

The statutory definition of 'anti-social behaviour' is provided by the Crime and Disorder Act 1998. The Act defines behaviour as 'anti-social' if it 'caused or was likely to cause harassment, alarm or distress to one or more persons not of the same household' as the alleged perpetrator. The significant difficulties that have emerged in attempts to apply this definition are well documented.[30] This definition is deliberately 'subjective', allowing the alleged victim to determine that a particular behaviour caused 'harm', and was therefore, by implication, anti-social. A Home Office review provides a list of the sorts of behaviour that it considers likely to be experienced as anti-social.[31] However, this list merely adds to the breadth of the definition, with a number of the behaviours listed remaining undefined, including 'noise', and 'intimidation'. In addition, the inclusion of a number of criminal offences (such as 'criminal damage', 'arson', 'shoplifting' and 'prostitution') exemplifies the overlap between concepts of 'anti-social behaviour' and 'crime'.[32]

This subjectivity in definition means that its application varies from context to context. As Millie suggests, 'the subjectivity and context specificity of anti-social behaviour means some behaviours will be unacceptable in one situation, but accepted, or even celebrated, in another context'.[33] Millie offers several examples, particularly highlighting the markedly different reactions to graffiti, with the work of Banksy being considered as 'street art' by some, yet as vandalism by others. It is similarly clear that variation is likely in considering whether 'noise' is 'harmful' or 'distressing'. For example, what is considered to be excessive noise within a rural neighbourhood may go unno-

---

30. 'Anti-Social Behaviour, Crime Control and Social Control' (2004), Brown A, *Howard Journal of Criminal Justice*, 43, 203-11; *Making People Behave: Anti-Social Behaviour, Politics and Policy* (2005), Burney E, Cullompton: Willan Publishing; *Anti-Social Behaviour Strategies: Finding a Balance* (2005), Millie A, Jacobson J, McDonald E and Hough M, Bristol: Policy Press and 'Anti-Social Behaviour, Behavioural Expectations and an Urban Aesthetic' (2008), Millie A, *British Journal of Criminology*. 48, 379-394.
31. *Defining and Measuring Anti-Social Behaviour* (2004), Home Office, Development and Practice Report 26, London: Home Office.
32. The difficulties associated with 'A Broad Statutory Definition of Anti-Social Behaviour' are further explored by Lynch in *Chapter 5* of this volume.
33. 'Anti-Social Behaviour, Behavioural Expectations and an Urban Aesthetic' (2008), Millie A, *British Journal of Criminology*. 48, 384.

ticed within an urban area. In combination, the flexibility and subjectivity of the statutory definition of anti-social behaviour therefore ensures that:

> ... virtually any activity can be anti-social depending on a range of background factors, such as the context in which it occurs, the location, people's tolerance levels and expectations about the quality of life in the area.[34]

This is, of course, deliberate, supporting one of the primary objectives of this policy strand: to protect the law-abiding majority from the minority in their neighbourhoods who are making their lives a misery. This is reflected in key policy documents. The stated aim of the White Paper *Respect and Responsibility—Taking a Stand Against Anti-Social Behaviour* is to create:

> ... a "something for something" society where we treat one another with respect and where we all share responsibility for taking a stand against what is unacceptable. But some people and some families undermine this. The anti-social behaviour of a few, damages the lives of many.[35]

Similarly the *Respect Action Plan* seeks 'to empower individuals and communities, enabling them not just to feel secure but to be more able to act together to make their neighbourhoods safer and better'.[36] Whether an exaggerated moral panic or a justified public concern, recent policy therefore seeks to enable the law-abiding majority to define what is unacceptable in their local area, and then empower state authorities to tackle this.

---

34. *The Economic and Social Costs of Anti-Social Behaviour* (2003), Whitehead C, Stockdale J and Razzu G, London: London School of Economics 4-5, cited in *Tackling Anti-Social Behaviour: A Critical Review* (2005), Jacobsen J, Millie A, and Hough M, London: King's College.
35. *Respect and Responsibility—Taking a Stand Against Anti-Social Behaviour* (2003), Home Office, London: HMSO, 3.
36. *Respect Action Plan* (2006), Respect Task Force, London: Home Office, 5.

Disempowering 'Problem Youth'?

The *Respect Action Plan* clearly and repeatedly highlights the importance of shared community values in successfully tackling anti-social behaviour. Respect relies on a shared understanding and clear rules and is strengthened by people acting together to tackle problems and improve their lives.'[37] Thus, 'The conditions for respect ... depend ultimately on a shared commitment to a common set of values expressed through behaviour that is considerate of others.'[38]

The notion that a community can define 'clear standards of behaviour' is, however, problematic. The idea that there might be a community consensus, or even majority view regarding what is unacceptable behaviour appears flawed. Whilst there may be certain behaviours that are universally considered unacceptable in a 'modern', 'civilised' society, this does not readily extend to the range of behaviour listed by the Home Office as 'anti-social', nor is it likely to capture the broad subjectivity of the statutory definition.[39] Instead, ideas of what constitutes 'acceptable' behaviour are likely to vary widely within a community, particularly between different age and cultural groups. Graffiti and noise again offer clear examples of behaviours where different perspectives might be apparent.

If we accept this variation, it is important to consider whose perspectives are dominant. If particular perspectives are able to define what is and is not acceptable behaviour, this allows certain sections of a community to label the behaviour of others as problematic. There is therefore a danger that the labelling of behaviour as 'anti-social' may not reflect its distressing or harmful effect, but instead emerge from the particular concerns of more vocal and dominant sections of society. The apparent growing intolerance of young people's 'misbehaviour' within many communities in the UK means that young people are therefore particularly vulnerable to having this legislation used against them. The political focus on anti-social behaviour is almost synonymous with youth, indelibly linked to an imagery of 'hoodies',

---

37. *Respect Action Plan* (2006), Respect Task Force, London: Home Office, 7.
38. *Ibid*, 5.
39. *Defining and Measuring Anti-Social Behaviour* (2004), Home Office, Development and Practice Report 26, London: Home Office.

intimidating street corner 'gangs', and a lack of 'respect'. Given its intention to empower potential victims against the risk of distress and harm, the extensive use of such anti-social behaviour legislation against young people is therefore unsurprising. The statutory definition and the associated legislative framework provides a terminology for, and therefore a legitimation of this fear, anxiety and mistrust, as well as the means to address it.

The disproportionate use of legislation against young people is repeatedly identified in recent research. Squires and Stephen found that the behaviour of young people was consistently identified as the major concern in local communities.[40] Reporting on the management of anti-social behaviour in one social housing estate, Goldsmith presents a dominance of adult definitions of 'anti-social' that often leave 'children and young people exposed to intervention for a range of behaviours not necessarily identified by them as "anti-social"'.[41] As a result, forms of behaviour that might be perceived as 'normal' by young people become the target for intervention. Playing football in the streets, 'hanging around' in groups in public places and on street corners, and talking loudly after dark might all now be labelled as 'anti-social'. Unsurprisingly, young people reported confusion in their understandings of exactly what is 'anti-social behaviour' and therefore how to avoid it.[42]

Tackling Anti-social Behaviour Amongst Young People

The new legislative framework provides significant new powers to tackle anti-social behaviour, as well as a statutory duty to do so. A series of Parliamentary Acts, including the Crime and Disorder Act 1998, the Police Reform Act 2002 and the Anti-Social Behaviour Act 2003, have established an array of new sanctions and orders. Whilst many of these powers are designed to be used against adults and young people, some are disproportionately used against

---

40. *Rougher Justice: Anti-social behaviour and young people* (2005), Squires P and Stephen D, Cullompton: Willan Publishing.
41. 'Cameras, cops and contracts: what anti-social behaviour management feels like to young people' (2008), Goldsmith C in Squires P (ed) *ASBO Nation: The criminalisation of nuisance*, Bristol: Policy Press, 223.
42. *Ibid*, 228 and 235.

under 18s, and others appear to be designed specifically to deal with behaviours particular to young people. In addition, as well as measures that seek to tackle the behaviour of individuals (such as the anti-social behaviour order), sanctions able to curtail potential anti-social behaviour amongst groups and even populations of young people are also prominent (including the dispersal order, and the banning of the 'hoodie' in Bluewater shopping centre).

Anti-Social Behaviour Orders

By far the highest profile measure, an anti-social behaviour order (or ASBO) is a court order which prohibits specifically-named threatening, intimidating or disruptive actions. An ASBO serves as a contract, the breaching of which is a criminal offence, even if the behaviour that results in this breach is not in itself a criminal act. Conditions might include curfews, not associating with named persons, or not going to certain places.[43] Such conditions can only ever be prohibitive; recipients cannot, for example, be required to engage in particular activities or interventions.

Whilst the ASBO was not originally designed with the intention of use with young people,[44] data recently released by the Ministry of Justice reveals that just over 40% of people made subject to an ASBO between June 2000 and December 2007 were under 18.[45] Of 14,668 ASBOs in which the age of the recipient is known, 6,028 were imposed on young people.

Dispersal Orders

As well as individual contractual approaches such as the ASBO, recent legislation has also provided powers to deal with the behaviour of whole communities. This is exemplified by the dispersal order which enables the police to disperse groups of two or more people from areas where it is designated that their presence or behaviour might be experienced as harmful or distressing. Whilst again such powers are used 'in a wide range of areas to address a diversity of social problems', a review of the implementation

---

43. For a more detailed discussion of the development and application of the ASBO, see the *Chapter 5* of this volume by Lynch.
44. 'Talking tough, acting coy: whatever happened to the Anti-Social Behaviour Order?' (2002) Burney E, *Howard Journal*, 41(5): 469-84.
45. Available to download at www.crimereduction.homeoffice.gov.uk/asbos/asbos2.htm.

and impact of dispersal orders suggests that they 'are most commonly used in relation to perceived problems with groups of young people'.[46]

Crawford and Lister suggest that a disproportionate targeting of young people can 'antagonise' and 'alienate' recipients, leading to feelings of stigmatisation and subsequent resentment towards the police and communities imposing these constraints. Of particular concern to those young people interviewed were feelings that all young people were perceived as problematic 'regardless of their actual behaviour', as illustrated by one 15 year-old female:

> Some of the powers like being able to take us home after nine or disperse us, they make it out that we're all doing something wrong. It puts across the message that every young person is delinquent. We're always portrayed for the bad things that some of us do, it's never the good things.[47]

By applying dispersal orders to entire populations within an area, the measure is seen to criminalise all young people by assuming their presence to be problematic, as much as their behaviour.

Particular concerns are also voiced over the implications of dispersal orders for the use of public spaces by young people. The importance of public space in the lives of young people is emphasised by Crawford and Lister.[48] Young people seek to live their lives in public places, away from the watchful eye of their parents. This need for independence from adults is arguably a necessary and healthy aspect of a young person's maturation, with Crawford and Lister suggesting that it 'constitutes a fundamental aspect of developing their own sense of identity, and provides space in which to forge their independent capacity to manage risk and danger'.[49]

Targeting the 'Hoodie'
Similar criticisms have been raised in relation to the banning of the wearing of 'hoodies' in Bluewater Shopping Centre in May 2005. Again the ban is

---

46. *The Use and Impact of Dispersal Orders: Sticking plasters and wake up calls* (2007), Crawford A and Lister S, York: Joseph Rowntree Foundation, xi, www.jrf.org.uk/sites/files/jrf/2133-dispersal-orders.pdf.
47. *Ibid*, 69.
48. *Ibid*.
49. *Ibid*, 70.

universal (leading to numerous cartoons in newspapers demonstrating its application to monks and babies), yet is clearly intended to target young people, and is experienced as such. It also demarcates particular public spaces where a young person can expect to be heavily monitored and treated with suspicion.

More pertinently, the targeting of an item of clothing represents the clearest attempt to pander to fears and anxieties within society, without regard to the impact of the specific behaviours that are being addressed. It is difficult to perceive how the wearing of a 'hoodie' is in itself harmful. Instead it appears to be merely a symbol of the distrust of youth, and a willingness to transpose a concern with the inappropriate behaviour of a minority of young people to any young person who might choose to follow this mainstream fashion.

Conclusion

The current emphasis on youth in political and media discussions of anti-social behaviour presents images of a generation out of control, increasingly violent and lacking the morals of previous generations. However, an analysis of communities might instead suggest a growing intolerance of 'normal' behaviour, deriving from an increasing isolation from our immediate neighbours, and associated perceptions of insecurity and vulnerability. Whilst this is not to deny or excuse the negative behaviour of some young people, such an analysis suggests that, through the current policy agenda, the 'demonisation of children and young people'[50] is given fresh impetus, with Burney arguing that 'Anti-social behaviour has become a convenient peg on which to hang general prejudices about young people and their activities'.[51]

In understanding anti-social behaviour as a community issue, it is axiomatic that community relationships, dialogue and conflict gain increasing relevance. In seeking 'community justice', how 'community' is understood, configured, and engaged with will have a clear impact on how 'justice'

---

50. 'Crisis: the demonisation of children and young people' (1997), Davis H and Bourhill M in Scraton, P (ed) *Childhood in Crisis?*, London: UCL Press, 28–57.
51. *Making People Behave: Anti-Social Behaviour, Politics and Policy* (2005), Burney E, Cullompton: Willan Publishing, 67.

is understood, configured and experienced. Power differentials within communities ensure that young people are readily defined as the problem, but far less often engaged in the solution. Young people interviewed by Goldsmith were left 'feeling vulnerable, angry and frustrated at their perceived inability to influence these developments'.[52] This reflects an apparent lack of dialogue between young people and adults in relation to issues of anti-social behaviour. In some communities, young people appear to lack the voice to influence definitions as to what behaviour is or is not acceptable in their locality. As such, approaches to 'empowering' communities are in danger of disempowering or even victimising young people.

To successfully tackle this, a dialogue between accuser and accused must be established.

> The people (children and adults) whose behaviour needs controlling are equally part of the syndrome and part of the community. Policies that fail to recognise these connections cannot provide any long-term answers.[53]

There is therefore a need to consider approaches that engage with anti-social behaviour as a *whole community* issue, including young people in understanding and responding to concerns with their behaviour.

---

52. 'Cameras, cops and contracts: what anti-social behaviour management feels like to young people' (2008), Goldsmith C in Squires P (ed) *ASBO Nation: The criminalisation of nuisance*, Bristol: Policy Press, 223.
53. *Making People Behave: Anti-Social Behaviour, Politics and Policy* (2005), Burney E, Cullompton: Willan Publishing, 170.

CHAPTER 12

POLICING SEXUAL OFFENDERS IN THE COMMUNITY: IS IT TIME TO MOVE FROM THE INVISIBLE TO THE VISIBLE?

MARK BLANDFORD AND ANTHONY BEECH

Introduction

We propose that there is an increasing public appetite for a range of social issues, including crime and anti-social behaviour, to be owned and managed at a more localised level. This continues to be underlined by the police in their endeavours to foster stronger local partnership working and community resilience in making local neighbourhoods and our wider communities safer.[1] It introduces a backdrop against which we can explore the option of expanding these neighbourhood-policing arrangements into tackling some of the more challenging aspects of public protection and has particular relevance for how we continue to develop effective strategies for the management of sexual offenders in the community. Here we argue that the arrangements for this are currently at a crossroads. What was once a priority for government—managing the risk posed by these individuals—is now being overshadowed and challenged by a new frontier of risk management and arguably the most significant threat to face our communities in recent times, that of terrorism and domestic extremism.[2] As these new threats emerge to alter the landscape of risk within our communities, other competing areas of business and the dramatic shift in economic climates add to the strain on our public serv-

---
1. *The Review of Policing 2008: Delivering in Partnership* (2008), Flanagan R, ch. 6.
2. See *Chapter 7* of this volume.

ices and their service level agreements with the public. What was once an unimaginable situation has now become a reality, the level of resources committed to protecting the public from sexual offenders in the community is at risk of being reduced or at the very least is unlikely to escape the on-going review of public sector spending. With each police area wrestling to meet the challenge posed by significant budget reductions, their commitment to the management of sexual offenders in the community will come under scrutiny. We argue, therefore, that our proposal of integrating existing risk management strategies within a local neighbourhood-based approach, one embraced by the public, will not only be timely but we propose will balance the provision of resources more effectively without reducing the high standards in public protection that have already been set.

We recognise the need for the state to continue to drive the management of the risk agenda, however, in this chapter we review the background to the current arrangements for managing the risk posed by sexual offenders in the community and propose a more viable, locally co-ordinated approach that could pave the way for greater reintegration of sexual offenders into the community. As we ease our way from a state controlled and regulated approach to risk management, towards a more local community ownership of such problems, we hope to create the environment that may be more accepting of the idea of a restorative justice response to dealing with some sexual offenders. The argument for the notion of a restorative justice approach in dealing with sexual offenders has become polarised,[3] opponents of restorative justice argue that its use with sexual offenders is particularly inappropriate given the serious nature of the crime and its harmful impact. Contrary arguments will suggest that the punitive nature of managing sexual offenders has been less than successful. However, as it is being increasingly realised that traditional methods of disposal via the criminal justice system are failing to rehabilitate offenders, the suggestion of a restorative justice philosophy being included within a range of risk management options has appeal in addressing the needs of both offenders and victims. This has particular relevance for young offenders where the notion of restorative justice is already evident through

---

3. 'Restorative Justice as a Response to Sexual Offending—Addressing the Failings of Current Punitive Approaches' (2008), McAlinden A, *Sexual Offender Treatment*, Vol. 3(1).

the development of referral orders and youth offender panels.[4] Such initiatives warrant further investigation, particularly in relation to sexual offenders.

The progress made over the last decade in managing sexual offenders in the community should not be underestimated. Our practice and learning has undoubtedly forged and shaped the government's approach to managing individuals responsible for acts of violent extremism and in supporting those vulnerable to radicalisation. The language of the government's PREVENT strategy,[5] part of its CONTEST programme, talks of encouraging community resilience and cohesion in challenging the radicalisation of vulnerable individuals, and in its wider ambitions mirrors much of the good practice in what works in ensuring robust public protection. Whilst the police will continue to pursue and investigate sexual offending there is now more than ever the need to focus on encouraging the public acceptance of their own role in managing risk within our communities.

Even the most empowered of communities will never be completely immune to sexual offending. But continued positive integration of public services by building upon existing partnership foundations will remain the key to delivering effective public protection arrangements. We encourage local services to work more directly in assisting in a strengths-based approach in managing risk by supporting the provision of accommodation, healthcare, education and employment considered to be critical elements to rehabilitating offenders.[6]

However, if we are to make progress then several factors will need to be overcome in the process first. These being:

1. The need to address continued public tension regarding sexual offenders which continues to resonate with anger and resentment;
2. Balancing the negative and sometimes distorted portrayal of sexual offenders within the media;
3. Distorted public perceptions on the risk posed by sexual offenders;

---

[4]. *The Introduction of Referral Orders Into the Youth Justice System: Final Report* (2002), Newman,T Crawford A, Earle R, et al, London: Home Office.
[5]. *Delivering the Prevent Strategy: An updated guide for Local Partners 2009* (2009), Home Office, Office of Security and Counter-Terrorism.
[6]. *Reducing re-offending by ex-prisoners* (2002), Social Exclusion Unit, HMG Cabinet Office.

4. Gaps in consistent risk assessment; and
5. The development of a wider range of management strategies.

Once achieved, we will have made a significant but cautious step towards a more localised integrated community risk management framework.

Background to Current Arrangements

It can be argued that the introduction of the Sex Offenders Act 1997 was one of the most significant legislative events in the history of the modern criminal justice system. Its impact was not just the beginning of a range of statutory requirements for sexual offenders to register personal information with the police, but it also provided a catalyst for further incremental legislation aimed at controlling sexual offenders in the community. High profile cases highlighting the abduction, sexual abuse and murder of children (Sara Payne, Holly Wells and Jessica Chapman) had created in the public a climate of fear and hysteria regarding sexual offenders. This had a cumulative effect of reducing public confidence in the authorities' ability to protect us from such offenders. Such was this increasing public concern and preoccupation, fuelled by emerging media campaigns and a sustained focus on this area of criminality, that the *sex offender* and particularly media-profiled *paedophiles* had become household names (e.g. Ian Huntley, Roy Whiting). The management of such individuals became a political issue on which the government was quick to act by delivering a programme of legislation and a centralised system of reform to ensure that the management of risk posed by sexual offenders would not only become a statutory requirement but also a priority for a range of statutory agencies.

This reform emerged against a backdrop of local risk management that was at the very best uncoordinated, and the primary responsibility of a limited number of agencies such as the probation service and youth offending services. Few other agencies felt any statutory responsibility for work in the management of risk posed by such individuals in the community.

The isolation of these services was exacerbated by the lack of any statutory gateway to allow for the effective information exchange with other agencies and developments were hampered by an atmosphere of underlying mistrust and suspicion which frustrated attempts to seek or share information.

The police would be key to the success of reforming arrangements for offender management and this was confirmed by ministerial comment of the time,[7] which ensured that the now commonly referred to Sex Offender Register introduced by the Sex Offenders Act 1997 was to be more than an administrative process for the police but rather the beginning of a more co-ordinated multi-agency approach to the management of risk posed by sexual and violent offenders. It was evident that the police, with their role in protecting life and enforcement, would be critical in ensuring safer communities and this was made into a statutory requirement with the introduction of the Criminal Justice and Court Services Act 2000. This Act followed on from the introduction of the Crime and Disorder Act 1998 (section 115 now provided a statutory platform on which agencies could share information with each other) and introduced a requirement for each area to have in place a 'responsible authority' made up of the police and probation services whose chief officers now had a legislative requirement to have in place arrangements for the management of risk posed by sexual and violent offenders. It also began one of the most significant shifts in modern policing culture and introduced offender management into the heart of policing.

Home Office guidance evolved from this legislation and the concept of Multi Agency Public Protection Arrangements (MAPPA) was born.[8] MAPPA is now recognised as one of the most advanced frameworks of offender management currently available in the UK, or indeed elsewhere. They seek to structure the way risk is to be assessed and managed through the effective identification, information exchange, risk assessment and management of offenders.

There was much for the police to learn. Whilst risk management and planning were the cornerstones of policing, this required specialist insight. How were sexual offenders to be assessed, and what would an effective risk management plan contain? These were the early challenges that in many

---

7. *MAPPA Guidance* (2003), National Probation Directorate, Version 1.
8. 'Community strategies for managing high-risk offenders: The contribution of multi-agency public protection arrangements' (2009), Kemshall H and Wood J, in Beech A, Craig L and Browne K, *Assessment and Treatment of Sex Offenders: A Handbook,* Chichester: Wiley.

ways remain unresolved. The media, sensing the negative mood of the public, began to shape government policy strengthening state ownership and accountability.

This was not a time for local criminal justice ownership; it was a period of central government driving local enforcement, restrictions and monitoring of offenders through further legislation and brought about the position of the state now fully regulating work in this area.

It was important that the public could see the progress being made and the introduction of a legislative requirement for each responsible authority to produce an annual report on how they were engaging with this lawful requirement provided the public with a local transparency to these arrangements. It was also a way in which the government could evaluate the performance of each area, and the requirements for each area to provide ongoing qualitative and quantitative data would also follow. More legislation emerged and the Criminal Justice Act 2003 saw the introduction of the prison service as part of the responsible authority and further strengthened the arrangements for public protection by placing a statutory responsibility on a range of other agencies to co-operate with the responsible authority in the assessment and management of risk. These agencies include:

- social care services;
- Jobcentre Plus;
- youth offending teams; local education authorities;
- local housing authorities or social care service authorities; registered social landlords;
- health authorities or strategic health authorities; primary care trusts or local health boards;
- National Health Service trusts;
- and electronic monitoring service providers.

Their involvement would be critical in ensuring a robust multi-agency approach in the assessment and management of risk. The 2003 Act also further established the type of offender required to be assessed and managed under these arrangements To summarise, these are commonly referred to as:

- the Category 1 offender who is the registered sexual offender, an individual convicted of a sexual offence listed under Schedule 3 of the Act and whose sentence meets the qualifying threshold;
- Category 2 offenders who are those other sexual offenders and violent offenders sentenced to 12 months or more and this includes those sentenced to hospital orders; and
- Category 3 offenders who, not being either a Category 1 or 2 offender, have been convicted of an offence that indicates they pose a risk of harm to the public and are presenting such a risk as can only be managed through an active multi-agency approach.

This definition of a Category 3 offender, unlike Category 1 and 2, required practitioners to make a subjective assessment that led to inconsistency in appropriate labelling of such relevant offenders. Later the requirement on the police to identify 'potentially dangerous offenders' spoke to the need for more effective risk assessment methods.

The Sexual Offences Act 2003 revised and strengthened the requirements for Category 1 offenders to register with the police and also introduced a suite of 'civil orders',[9] which in effect ensured that the police could conduct pre-emptive strikes on offenders. Such qualifying offenders could be placed before the courts where it was felt that their behaviour indicated an unacceptable level of risk. Available to the courts is a range of prohibitive orders, the most significant of these being the sexual offences prevention order (SOPO). There are some 1,512 SOPOs currently in force.[10] These orders contain a wide range of prohibitions that principally place restrictions on the movement, contact and activities of on the offender and rightfully the very nature of such orders requires police resources to monitor and enforce them. Whilst the introduction of these preventative court orders was a welcome addition to risk management options, it is to be questioned whether the negative framing of such prohibitions add real value in all cases.

---

9. The Sexual Offences Act 2003, Part 2.
10. *National Statistics: Data collected from 42 areas of England and Wales 2008-09*, (2009) MAPPA Annual Reports.

Despite the multi-agency dimension to these arrangements it is the police that retain accountability for all Category 1 offenders for the duration of the notification period whilst they are in the community and these numbers are growing. The principal reason why this should be the case is that the probation, prison and youth offending services have a time restricted statutory involvement in the management of offenders dependent upon sentence and not the length of an offender's notification requirements. With the majority of registered sexual offenders having a statutory requirement to register with the police for life, this would inevitably place increasing demand on police resources, but, arguably, its real purpose was to underline the government's commitment to send out a strong message on the control of sexual offenders in the community. With so many offenders likely to have a lifetime obligation to notify the police of their address and travel it was possible to make some early predictions for the level of growth in sex offender numbers. Such predictions arrived at some concerning figures and indicated that it was likely to reach some 120,000 over the next 20 years.[11] There are too many factors requiring consideration to have real confidence in such predictions but we can be confident that the numbers are growing. Ministry of Justice figures reveal that there are some 32,336 sexual offenders with a statutory requirement to register with the police with a trend developing which confirms a year-on year-growth of 3%.[12]

One of the most significant developments that will have to be considered in predicting future growth in numbers is the human rights challenge proffered by the High Court and subsequent Court of Appeal ruling that:

> ... the indefinite nature of the notification requirements of Part 2 of the Sexual Offences Act 2003 [the Sex Offender Register] is a disproportionate breach of Article 8: there is no opportunity for review of the necessity of the requirements, and the case is stronger in the case of young offenders.[13]

---

11. *Public Protection Conference* (2004), ACPO.
12. *National Statistics: Data collected from 42 areas of England and Wales 2008-09*, (2009) MAPPA Annual Reports.
13. *R (TF and Thompson) v SSHD* Court of Appeal July 2009, *R (TF and Thompson) v SSHD* Supreme Court April 2010.

A further appeal to the Supreme Court by the Secretary of State for the Home Department was also dismissed by that court. The Supreme Court repeated the lower court's decision in that the current notification requirement on some sexual offenders to register for life was incompatible with Article 8 of the European Convention on Human Rights (ECHR). It introduced a notion of a tribunal determining the risk of an individual committing a further sexual offence allowing for some offenders to de-register, placing greater emphasis on effective risk assessment procedures.

Whilst the result of this legal challenge could significantly alter these early predictions, welcomed advances in DNA-profiling, greater support for victims and improved investigative training is likely to ensure an increase in the detection of sexual offenders and add to the numbers on the register. But can the suggested continued growth in sexual offenders requiring police management be sustained? And how do these numbers add to the operational pressures on the police? The answer lies not only in legislation but in national guidance that established the policing obligations in managing sexual offenders in the community. Association of Chief Officers of Police (ACPO) Guidance on Public Protection sets out how this should be delivered.[14] For example, each registered sexual offender must be visited by the police 'to check out their domestic circumstances and residence'[15] in line with national minimum standards. What was initially designed to establish the offender was residing at the address provided on registration became an opportunity to conduct regular risk assessments. Further legislation ensured that the police would not be frustrated in conducting these checks by providing powers of entry to sexual offender's homes in certain circumstances where previous attempts have been frustrated.[16]

Guidance has established the purpose of such visits as being to:

- check compliance with legislation and court orders;
- confirm the offender resides or frequents his registered address;

---

14. 2007. ACPO Guidance 2010 (in press).
15. *Managing Sexual Offenders and Violent offenders 2007* (2007) ACPO (Association of Chief Police Officers) Guidance: Protecting the Public, 102.
16. *Power of Search and Entry to Risk Assess Sex Offenders Subject to Notification Requirements* (2007) Home Office Circular 17/2007.

- fulfil a 'duty of care' to protect the public;
- monitor the risk posed by the offender;
- gather information;
- detect offences; and
- fulfil a 'duty of care' to the offender.

However, the previous lack of a national consistent and co-ordinated training of police officers in conducting structured risk assessments and risk management plans led to inconsistency in practice and expertise. This had the effect of making it difficult for police officers to measure responsivity in the offender, leaving areas to rely on an investigative method of offender management. There is no doubt that there will remain a strong need for the police to continue with such a theme. However the development of a national police training programme[17] has begun to train specialist officers, front line staff and senior management to recognise a wider range of options in risk management rather than the often singular approach of restrictions. It is known that the research does not support the popular perception that all sexual offenders inevitably re-offend,[18] indeed 75% of sexual offenders monitored over a 21 year period were not reconvicted,[19] yet enforcement, prohibitions and monitoring had become the only tools of the trade, often leading to defensive risk assessments and the development of a risk averse culture rather than one that is risk conscious.

Towards More Dynamically-based Assessment and Management of Risk

It is surprising that currently there still remains no national consistency within the police services in the use of an effective dynamic risk assessment

---

17. *Public Protection and Learning Development Programme 2009* (2009) National Policing Improvement Agency (NPIA).
18. 'What we know and what we need to know' (2006), Hanson, Harris and Morton, *Sexual Offender Recidivism Risk*.
19. Evidence introduced by Secretary of State in *R (TF and Thompson) v SSHD* Supreme Court April 2010.

tool.[20] It is accepted that risk assessment is the central feature that influences all aspects of sexual offender management.[21] Although that is not to say the police lack consistency, since the introduction of the Sex Offenders Act 1997, the police have applied what has now become the industry standard across all the responsible authorities for the risk assessment of sexual offenders, using Risk Matrix 2000.[22]

Much has been written regarding the role of static or historical risk assessment methods; their main operational value for the police lies in relative ease of use, consistency and the recognition that they outperformed clinical judgement[23] which made it particularly appealing for an agency that prided itself on its 'gut feeling'. It was also a cost effective proposition.[24] However, one of the clear disadvantages of using such static tools in isolation is their limited benefit in the construction of an informed and bespoke risk management plan. Other weaknesses have been found in identifying treatment and management needs and in particular measuring change, which is unfortunate given the challenge posed to the police in ensuring resources are used effectively. There is now undoubted recognition by the police that the current approach to risk assessment lacks an effective relationship with the development of risk management plans and work is underway to combine the current actuarial approach with a more dynamically driven approach in addressing a range of risk factors associated with sexual offenders.

The police were, therefore, keen to take part in piloting of the 'Stable and Acute 2007' risk assessment tool and this was conducted across a number of areas in England and Wales in 2008-2009.[25] Scotland and Ireland had already adopted the tool in full so that the tool therefore had considerable

---

20. Even though such systems do exist e.g. STABLE/ACUTE 2007 (*Stable and Acute* (2007), Hanson & Harris), Structured Risk Assessment (SRA; Thornton), SVR-20, RSVP (Hart, Laws & Kropp).
21. *The Psychology of Criminal Conduct* (2003), Andrews D A and Bonta J (3rd ed.).
22. *Distinguishing and Combining Risks for Sexual and Violent Recidivism* (2003), Thornton D, Mann R, Webster S, Blud L, Travers R, Friendship C and Erickson M.
23. *The Characteristics of Persistent Sexual Offenders: A meta-analysis of recidivism studies* (2005), Hanson and Morton-Bourgon.
24. *Professional Psychology, Research and Practice* (2003), Beech, Fisher and Thornton, Risk Assessment of Sex Offenders.
25. *Stable and Acute* (2007), Hanson & Harris.

appeal particularly as it would ensure consistency across the UK. However, the subsequent review of the pilot findings in England and Wales[26] revealed a number of critical issues with its application, not least the length of time practitioners invested in identifying the level of a range of stable factors. Typically this would take some one and a half hours and this was felt not conducive to operational realities and the time spent would prove difficult to digest particularly given the need to maximise resources more effectively. It could also be argued that the stable nature of the first part of the tool does not in itself inform the risk management strategy. The pilot did find that there remained an appetite within the police for the development of an assessment process that looked at dynamic factors as their value was recognised. It was therefore clear that another option would have to be considered and work has already begun on identifying a more appropriate dynamic risk assessment with more relation to those factors that measure acute indicators of risk. To maximise the potential of the tool it would have to work in convergence with the RM 2000[27] and the probation service risk assessment tool OASys.[28] Professionals will require ongoing support and mentoring to ensure improved accuracy in coding and effective training will be crucial if the application of the tool is to inform and develop a risk management plan. With the current standards failing to inform the police management plan in any meaningful way and with the majority of sexual offenders eventually being managed by the police as a single agency this work will be critical in laying the foundations for future practice.

Encouraging Community Integration

Nervousness in relaxing what has become a covert culture of managing sexual offenders in the community and adopting a wider integrated

---

26. *Examining implementation of the Stable and Acute dynamic risk assessment tool pilot in England and Wales* (2010), Nichols C M, Callanan M, Legard R, Tomaszewski T, Purdon S and Webster S.
27. *Distinguishing and Combining Risks for Sexual and Violent Recidivism* (2003), Thornton D, Mann R, Webster S, Blud L, Travers R, Friendship C and Erickson M.
28. Offender Assessment System NOMS (2009).

community-based approach is understandable given the backdrop of media 'name and shame' campaigns. Such publicity has fuelled public outcry and led to vigilantism. The example of the Paulsgrove Estate riots,[29] where instances of mob mentality within the community catapulted the area into international notoriety, was sparked by the mere notion that a predatory paedophile was to be housed amongst it. The outbreak of public disorder still resonates with the authorities and questions the readiness of the community's ability to embrace such responsibilities.

Despite this, there are tempting reasons why the time is right to consider encouraging community involvement in the management of risk posed by sexual offenders. Two of the more compelling reasons is the success of the recent community disclosure pilot and an emerging police desire to share information on such offenders with the local community in a more structured way. Furthermore is the continued role of Circles UK, which promotes the Circles of Support and Accountability (CSAs) in the UK in managing the risk posed by high risk sexual offenders. Neither the role of the media be underestimated, which at one time appeared to promote and encourage the hysteria around sexual offenders, but may now be more consolatory in recognising a time for change. More notably, there is a hunger and desire by the police to balance resources more effectively with outcomes and for the first time there is consistent national training available for officers in public protection roles and this is being rolled out across the country. Through this new approach to training officers the notion has been introduced of balancing practice with a more positive approach to risk management, including training on understanding offending pathways, avoidant and approach driven offender strategies as proposed in the Self-Regulation Model[30] and the concept of offenders being goal driven organisms as proposed in the Good Lives Model[31] so as to make stronger links with assessment and risk management planning.

---

29. 'Vigilance or Vigilantes: The Paulsgrove Riots and Policing Paedophiles in the Community' (2004), Williams A and Thompson B, *Police Journal*, Part 1: The Long Slow Fuse, and, Part 2: The Lessons of Paulsgrove, 77, 99-119 and 193-206.
30. Ward, Hudson & Keenan 1998.
31. Ward & Stewart 2003.

It was in 2006 that the then Home Secretary commissioned a review of the measures in place to protect children from sex offenders leading to a number of recommendations.[32] One of the key recommendations was to improve the level of disclosure to the public on the risk posed by individual offenders and this led to the piloting of a disclosure scheme. Up until now the disclosure of information to members of the public on named individual sexual offenders has been tightly regulated and would usually only occur on the authority of an executive member of the police force (this would later be on the authority of a MAPPA panel).[33] However, these new recommendations were going to lead to something completely new and because of the perceived notions of the risks involved there were no obvious volunteers. The police were fearful that once announced and the scheme marketed, they would be met by queues of concerned parents demanding information at every police station and leading to sexual offenders becoming targets for the public. However, the reality was markedly different. The four pilot areas Cleveland, Warwickshire, Cambridgeshire and Hampshire ran the scheme for several months during 2008-2009 with the aim of measuring the effectiveness of giving parents, carers or guardians of children a more formal mechanism for requesting information about people who may become involved in their children's lives. It was to address the specific risk posed by sex offenders and many saw this as the first step towards introducing the much-promoted 'Sarah's Law'.[34] At this time the government and the police were been keen to avoid any inevitable comparison with either 'Sarah's Law' or the community disclosure obligations on sex offenders in the United States of America under 'Megan's Law' which lacks the strength of evidence to suggest the implementation here of similar community notification law.[35] Repeated evaluations of the American model led to a number of previous Home Secretaries refusing to implement a similar scheme in the

---

32. *Review of the Protection of Children from Sex Offenders* (2007), Home Office, Action 3.
33. The Criminal Justice and Immigration Act 2008, section 140 (amended by the Criminal Justice Act 2003, section 327).
34. See, for example, 'Sign here for Sarah' (2000), *News of the World* and 'Named, Shamed' (2001), *News of the World*.
35. *Megan's Law Does it Protect Children: An updated review of evidence on the impact of community notification as legislated for by Megan's Law in the United States* (2006), NSPCC Report (Fitch).

UK. Inconsistencies in how it is applied, low offender compliance rates and little evidence to indicate that it reduced levels of recidivism were just some of the reasons. No matter how the disclosure scheme was to be marketed it did herald a significant step in engaging the community in the management of risk and the subsequent review of the pilot findings was found to be encouraging.[36]

Surprisingly, across the four pilot areas only 315 enquiries were made with little evidence of any mischievous enquiries being received. Over 20 of these enquiries turned out to relate to convicted sex offenders and its role as a tool to underpin existing child protection arrangements was confirmed. This will now lead a national roll out of the scheme across the country and whilst the police will continue to avoid any comparison with Sarah's Law, it has for the first time introduced a legal framework through which the public are encouraged to seek information on persons coming into contact with their children and the association with Sarah's law will be difficult to resist. More significantly, it has introduced the sharing of confidential information with the public on a trust and confidence basis and supports further recommendations within the review of a need to create an atmosphere of greater transparency with the public. This will lead to closer ties with the community and a more community-focused management of risk.

This notion of a more community cohesive approach has been epitomised in the Circles of Support scheme, a community justice initiative using this philosophy of restorative justice, where volunteers provide a 'circle of support' to sexual offenders in the community. The idea of a circle of support was developed in Canada and provides support for sexual offenders being released from prison into the community.[37] It quickly spread through North America and was introduced into the UK in 2002. Today Circles UK contributes to the scope of public protection by working towards a substantial reduction in sexual offending through the provision of a range of services to local CSA projects. Further, it aims to develop a greater public understanding of community approaches to public protection. The voluntary nature of

---

36. *Child Sex Offender Review (CSOR) Public Disclosure Pilots: A process evaluation* (2010), Kemshall H et al.
37. *Releasing Sex Offenders into the Community 'Through Circles of Support'* (2001), Cesaroni C.

the scheme has some appeal and a circle usually includes family, friends and other community members having contact with the offender (and who are unpaid). A circle, properly facilitated, is empowering to all of the individuals involved and unlike many service systems avoids encouraging dependence. The circle meets together on a regular basis to help somebody accomplish his or her personal goals in life. The circle acts as a community around the offender who, for one reason or another, is unable to achieve what they want in life and which without skills and support in such circumstances could lead to relapse and further offending. The take up in the UK can be best described as patchy; one of the main reasons for this may be the level of resources required to manage the circle, funding limitations and the cost of training and supporting volunteers. Encouragingly, a review of CSA[38] in Canada showed that only 5% of those in the scheme went on to re-offend compared to 17% in the non-attendance group and has been shown to reduce the predicted rate of reoffending by more than 70%,[39] so there is much to learn from this type of restorative engagement.

Conclusion

To begin, we propose that if we are to harmonise what has become a framework of state regulatory control through enforcement, surveillance and prohibition with a holistic package that considers strength-based options delivered and supported locally, then the police will have to develop as a priority a more dynamically driven risk assessment methodology that supports a professional approach to producing a structured risk management plan.

It is recognised and generally accepted that sexual offenders are not a homogenous group,[40] therefore further development in the police risk assessment methods is to be encouraged and will assist in improving the approach

---

38. *An Evaluation of the Pilot Project in South-Central Ontario* (2005), Wilson R J, Picheca J E and Prinzo M, Circles of Support and Accountability.
39. 'Quality Time with Paedophiles' (2004), Wilson D, *Guardian*.
40. 'Paraphilias and sexual offending' (in press) Harkins L and Beech A, in Sturmey P and Hersen M (eds.) *Handbook of evidence-based practice in clinical psychology*, volume 2, adults, Hoboken, NJ: Wiley USA.

to risk management planning where the assessment has a direct relationship with the risk management strategy. We suggest integrating a more realistic scenario based approach[41] to assist the risk management planning process, which arrives at a better identification of priority and encourages the development and application of wider risk management strategies, ultimately leading to the right plan being identified for the right offender at the right time. We encourage continuing work towards enhancing the current model of static risk assessment that at the moment places individual offenders into rigid silos of categorisation, that is to say, Very High, High, Medium and Low risk, by converging it with a more dynamic approach. We believe that this will lead to a more workable and informative categorisation that identifies the level of priority to be attributed to each offender rather than arriving at a risk label.

Subsequent management planning should include realistic scenarios that will prioritise offenders for levels of intervention but at the same time recognise strengths in the offender that could be supported through community-based local services. These interventions will require co-ordination but not necessarily by specialist officers or the involvement of active MAPPA Level 2 or 3 panels.[42] For example, low priority offenders could be managed under local neighbourhood policing arrangements where the 'local officer' monitors the offender within the community without the need of engaging specialist officers. Higher priority individuals would be managed by local community police officers who would co-ordinate local services, assist reintegration into the community and engage the public to reduce tension and promote a balanced perception of risk. Those individuals considered to pose imminency of risk requiring high prioritisation would require management by specialist officers using specialist risk assessment tools to identify critical risk factors that could be addressed through a range of options both punitive and supportive, utilising community engagement through circles of support.

Offenders will inevitably become more visible and although we have been keen in the past not to mix 'high visibility' and sex offenders we suggest that

---

41. *Structured professional Guidelines for assessing risk of sexual violence* (2003), Hart S D, Laws D R, Kropp P R, Klaver J, Logan C and Watt K A, Risk of Sexual Violence Protocol.
42. Multi-agency panels to address the assessment and management needs of offenders.

the climate is right to relax the tradition of 'hiding' such individuals in society. Therefore effective communication with the community will be essential and we suggest that each responsible authority represented by a local Strategic Management Board should further evaluate and develop local initiatives aimed at creating greater transparency within the community. Lay Advisors to the board are encouraged to work more closely with the media in creating a greater understanding by the public of the risk posed by sexual offenders and to encourage a more positive style of community risk management.

By retaining the specialist officer but making greater use of local neighbourhood policing teams we have allowed the specialist officer to focus more upon the higher priority cases thereby making more effective use of resources in supporting the risk management plan. That is not to underestimate the role of neighbourhood teams, they provide the high visibility reassurance to the community and being in touch with local services they are able to act swiftly to respond to areas of concern. They are particularly well-placed to measure community tension and will be crucial in supporting a more localised risk management plan, particularly with regard to the inevitable increase in disclosure of information into the public domain.

Inevitably some offenders are so approach driven that nothing short of a range of proactive enforcement measures under the direction of specialist officers will be needed to manage their risk, whilst others will respond more effectively to strength-based work. Each offender therefore requires bespoke assessment and planning if we are to effectively manage risk in the community. Officers must continue to be trained to understand and recognise the varying pathways to offending and the nature of goals in relation to offending so as to encourage this assessment of the viability of strength-based work and recognise responsivity in offenders. We need to continue to review the Circles of Support scheme and look to each area to consider more local uptake of it. More locally funded, owned and managed schemes, supported by local neighbourhood policing teams and where necessary specialist officers, will help to integrate a more local cohesive approach to risk management and can provide that early alert to the escalation of risk. Crucial to the development of a more local harmonised approach will be the 'duty to co-operate' with and of agencies and community-based services who will be required to work more closely with sexual offenders in a more positive and supporting capacity, particularly in relation to accommodation housing, employment and educational training. Whilst the police will continue to be pivotal in co-ordinating this work, if it is to be integrated correctly and if the community is supportive, our existing arrangements will be enhanced without the need to increase resources at this difficult time.

CHAPTER 13

TOWARDS A COMMUNITY RESPONSE TO THE PERPETRATION OF DOMESTIC VIOLENCE

ZAHIRA LATIF

Introduction

In rural locations in countries such as India and Pakistan, local grievances between villagers are managed at a local community level through village councils. These resolutions to local problems present models of community justice where the 'first port of call' for the aggrieved is not criminal justice agencies. In these cases, family disputes are managed through local community conferences where resolutions to family problems are based on achieving collective harmony. The principle belief in these approaches is that the community has rights to intervene in family affairs to bring 'collective peace'. In India, special community conferences are arranged between the victim, perpetrators, their families and the local villagers to resolve domestic violence disputes.[1] There are two key factors in this approach to take into consideration: the role of the criminal justice system is not the primary source for the aggrieved, and the family is not socially recognised as private and personal space where there is minimal intervention from external parties.

This chapter argues that in the UK context, historically, the dominant social discourse of the ideology of the privacy of family-life has influenced criminal justice responses to domestic violence crimes. As a result, interventions in the 1970s adopted a minimalist approach to tackling domestic

---

1. *Community Justice: West Bengal's Women Draw on Village Tradition to Stop Domestic Violence*, (2000), Sadasivam B, Ford Foundation, 6-9.

violence. Socio-political perceptions of domestic violence have changed significantly since the 1970s; from a personal and family issue to a social and legal problem. The current day 'criminalisation' discourse of domestic violence, through the Domestic Violence and Victims Act 2004, largely offers victims' protection through legislation. Although legislation provides basic protection for victims, laws and the criminal justice system are not able to manage the everyday threats of violence and abuse that victims are constantly exposed to in the home. The chapter argues that an exclusively institutionalised approach to tackling domestic violence crimes may not be the most appropriate way forward. This chapter explores the benefits of a community-based approach where ultimately the responsibility for combating domestic violence shifts from the criminal justice system to a localised-community setting.

What is Domestic Violence?

Domestic violence has been used interchangeably with terms like 'wife-beating', 'wife abuse', 'intimate partner violence', 'family violence', 'violence against women', 'violence against women by known men' and 'inter-personal violence'.[2] In the UK there are various definitions of domestic violence according to the government or voluntary sector agency under consideration. Agencies have tended to use definitions that suit their particular needs and purposes.[3] In England and Wales, the government's national report on domestic violence[4] has recognised the need for a common definition and defines domestic violence as:

---

2. 'Domestic Violence and "Rough Music": A Case of Community-based Intervention' (2006), Owen JR and Owen S, *British Journal of Community Justice*, Vol 4, No 2, 18. *Domestic Violence; Action for Change* (2005), Hague G and Malos E, Cheltenham: New Clarion Press 3.
3. *Safety and Justice — The Government's Proposals on Domestic Violence* (2003), Secretary of State, HMSO.
4. *National Report on Domestic Violence* (2005), Home Office, HMSO, 7.

Any incident of threatening behaviour, violence or abuse (psychological, physical, sexual, financial or emotional) between adults who are or have been intimate partners or family members, regardless of gender or sexuality.[5]

This broad definition has not only recognised the existence of abuse amongst homosexual groups but is the first step in understanding the nature and dynamics of abuse. Abuse from family members may include collusion with perpetrators by in-laws[6], forced marriages[7] and honour-related violence[8]. Abuse need not necessarily involve physical violence but financial, sexual, emotional and psychological mistreatment. Conversely, legal definitions of domestic violence vary; there is no one definitive legal definition of domestic violence. Legal definitions of domestic violence 'are limited to specific acts recognised under legislation'[9], these include acts of harassment, and physical harm. They include 'psychological molestation that affects the well-being of the victim' even if there is no physical violence i.e. the use of 'physical force'.[10] The term 'psychological molestation' is open to interpretation by the courts.[11] The discussion in this chapter will focus on domestic violence in the context of intimate partner relationships; consequently the terms 'domestic violence' and 'intimate partner violence' are used interchangeably.

Feminist literature[12] argues that domestic violence is gendered in nature.[13] Where men face dangers in the public domain; women are more likely to face

---

5. An adult is defined as any person aged 18 or over. Family members are defined as mother, father, son, daughter, brother, sister, and grandparents, whether directly related, in laws or step family.
6. 'Domestic Violence by Extended Family Members in India', (1997) *Journal of Interpersonal Violence*, Vol. 12, 433.
7. 'Coercion, Consent and the Forced Marriage Debate in the UK' (2009), *Feminist Legal Studies*, Vol. 17, No 2, 165.
8. *Honour, Violence, Women and Islam* (2011), Mazher, I and Abbas, T, (eds.) Oxon: Routledge.
9. Domestic Violence and 'Rough Music': A Case of Community-based Intervention' (2006), Owen J R and Owen S, *British Journal of Community Justice*, Vol. 4, No 2, 18.
10. *Domestic Violence and Protection from Harassment*, (1997), Bird, R, Jordan Publishing; Bristol, 2.
11. *Ibid.*
12. *Domestic Violence; Action for Change* (2005), Hague G and Malos E, Cheltenham: New Clarion Press.
13. Although aware of academic literature which contests the gendered nature of domestic violence (see the work of Michael Johnson), the debate in this chapter will focus on women as principal victims and men as the perpetrators.

violence and abuse in the home from men that they know.[14] Crime figures demonstrate that there has been a consistent trend over time with women more likely to be victims of intimate partner violence.[15] The sensitivity and complexity surrounding domestic violence, particularly its hidden nature, and the subsequent under-reporting and under-recording of it make it a difficult problem to monitor[16]. Indeed, even data on domestic violence-related crimes from the British Crime Survey is most likely to be on the conservative side. Domestic violence is socially perceived as a hidden crime because there is an assumption that it is largely, though not exclusively, 'perpetuated within the home, in the private sphere and hidden from public gaze'.[17] Social perceptions of domestic violence as a private phenomenon, which occurs behind closed doors, is a common social misconception and undermines the complexity surrounding domestic violence-related crime. Violence and abuse between partners is not necessarily tied to conjugal spaces and often spills over into public realms and places of family interaction beyond the 'marital' home.

The problematising of domestic violence into a private matter has to a certain extent allowed minimalist state interventions into 'managing domestic violence'[18]. The extent to which legal intervention is perceived as appropriate may be affected by the fact that inter-personal violence may not readily be identified as a crime and may continue to be construed as a private and family matter. Responses by frontline police officers during the 1980s were atypical of this privacy notion. When called to respond to 'couple disputes' their

---

14. *Violence Against Wives* (1980), Dobash R and Dobash R, Somerset: Open Books; *Private Violence and Public Policy* (1985), Pahl J, London: Routledge; *'A Haven in a Heartless World? Women and Domestic Violence'*. Goldsack, (1999), in T. Chapman and J. Hockey (eds.), *Ideal Homes? Social Change and Domestic Life*, London: Routledge
15. *Statistics on Women and the Criminal Justice System: A Ministry of Justice Publications Under Section 95 of the Criminal Justice Act 1991* (2010), Ministry of Justice.
16. *Making it count: A practical guide to collecting and managing domestic violence data* (2003), Hall T and Wright S, Nacro, London.
17. 'The Domestic Violence, Crime and Victims Act 2004; Relevant or 'Removed Legislation" (2007), Musgrove A and Groves N, *Journal of Social Welfare and Family Law*, Vol. 29, No 3, 239.
18. *Domestic Violence: The Criminal Justice Response*, (2003), Buzawa, E S and Buzawa, C G, California: Sage Publications.

response was often 'it's *just* a domestic'.[19] A response that not only suggested that family was a private space but also the lack of seriousness associated with these types of crimes. There is no doubt that domestic violence presents deviant behaviour, however, developing appropriate responses has been more problematic. The extent of intervention is always certain to be subjected to arguments about how much 'policing' of 'family-life' is appropriate.[20] In the UK, until the 19th-century, socio-political discourses of the *private family* were dominant with minimal intervention from the state in family life.[21] Throughout the 20th and 21st-century, state involvement in family policy and family development has steadily increased.[22] As far as intimate relationships are concerned, any intervention is most likely to shape conjugal rights and responsibilities. On the other hand, *laissez-faire* approaches are not only morally inconceivable but as suggested by Hague and Malos, 'fail to punish deviant behaviour' and perhaps even 'legitimatize it'.[23]

Domestic Violence Legislation

In the UK, pre-1970s there was very little legislation to adequately protect women experiencing abuse by intimate partners. Although assault in intimate partner relationships is theoretically treated the same as any other violent crime, the reality is somewhat different. Women are less likely to report abuse within marriage particularly sexual violence and consequently are less likely to bring criminal charges against abusers.[24] As a result, in the early years the feminist movement was active in bringing changes to the civil legislation to help protect women. Civil legislation allowed women protection through injunction orders against the abuser[25] and in later legislation offered protec-

---

19. *Gender, Crime and Criminal Justice* (2001) Walklate, S, Devon: Willan Publishing.
20. *The Policing of Families* (1980), Donzelot J, London: Hutchinson.
21. 'Family change and family policies: Great Britain', (1997) Ringen S, in Kamerman S and Kahn A (eds.) *Family Change and Family Polices in the West*, Vol. 1, Oxford: Clarendon Press.
22. *Ibid.*
23. *Domestic Violence; Action for Change* (2005), Hague G and Malos E, Cheltenham: New Clarion Press.
24. *Ibid.*
25. The Domestic Violence and Matrimonial Proceedings Act 1976.

tion from family members or associated persons which include partners who stay away from the home.[26] However, despite these legislative changes, rights for women experiencing domestic violence were still limited.[27] Problems came in the form of the limited authority of the county court to protect women experiencing domestic violence. In the county courts, power of arrest was rarely attached to injunctions because of the reluctance by judges to interfere in the legal rights of men, particularly concerning rights to the home and exclusion from it.[28] Without powers of arrest, injunctions did not act as suitable deterrents for abusers.[29]

The move from civil to criminal legislation for protection of victims of domestic violence came inadvertently through the Protection from Harassment Act 1997. Initially, the 1997 Act was not intended to target domestic violence victims but was instead aimed at protecting victims from harassment, normally 'stalking' by strangers. However, the legislation came to be used by domestic violence victims who no longer lived with their abusers or had never lived with them,[30] thus, providing protection for women who could not seek protection under the Family Law Act 1996. The 1997 Act introduced two new criminal offences, which include criminal harassment[31] and offences relating to fear of violence.[32] The criminalisation of domestic violence is overtly clear through the newly introduced, Domestic Violence and Victims Act 2004 and a signal to society of a zero tolerance approach to intimate partner violence. The 2004 Act is the first piece of criminal domestic violence legislation which closes some of the loopholes in the existing law. The breach of certain types of injunctions (non-molestation orders[33]) is now

---

26. The Family Law Act 1996. For discussion, see, 'Relevant or "Removed Legislation"' (2007), Musgrove A and Groves N, *Journal of Social Welfare and Family Law*, Vol 29, No 3.
27. *Domestic Violence* (1997), Lockton D and Ward R, London: Cavendish.
28. *Domestic Violence; Action for Change* (2005), Hague G and Malos E, Cheltenham: New Clarion Press.
29. *Five Years On: A review of legal protection from domestic violence* (2004), Barron J, Women's Aid Federation of England.
30. *Domestic Violence and Protection from Harassment* (1997), Bird R, Bristol: Jordan.
31. Protection from Harassment Act 1997, section 2.
32. *Ibid*, section 4.
33. A court order which prevents a person from being violent, threatening or harassing towards another person.

a criminal offence, carrying a maximum prison sentence of five years.[34] Common assault is also now a statutory offence for which the police can arrest an individual on suspicion of assault without an arrest warrant,[35] whereas previously the requirement was that the courts must attach a power of arrest. Equal rights are now included for married and cohabiting partners[36] and assault on an intimate partner is now an arrestable offence.[37] The relative merit of using civil and criminal remedies for domestic violence incidents have been debated considerably[38] and an early evaluation of the current discourse that criminalises domestic violence has shown 'the impact by December 2007 [of the 2004 Act] has been limited and in some respects unclear'.[39] Although the evaluation notes some improvement and a positive impact of making common assault a statutory offence, the impact of breaching non-molestation orders is less clear. Legislation provides victims of domestic violence with a framework for protective measures. Nevertheless, legislation itself is not the complete answer because 'domestic violence is a major social issue which has policy implications far beyond purely legislative change'.[40]

Institutionalising Responses to Domestic Violence

Social responses in the UK have recognised that domestic violence is a major social issue and current intervention broadly includes: legislation, law enforcement, social services support and housing. Current domestic violence policy in England and Wales, is based on a strategic model for tackling violence against women which incorporates the three P's of prevention, provision

---

34. Domestic Violence and Victims Act 2004, s1.
35. *Ibid*, s10.
36. *Ibid*, s2.
37. The Domestic Violence, Crime and Victims Act 2004; Relevant or 'Removed Legislation" (2007), Musgrove A and Groves N, *Journal of Social Welfare and Family Law*, Vol 29, No 3.
38. *Domestic Violence; Action for Change* (2005), Hague G and Malos E, Cheltenham: New Clarion Press.
39. *Early Evaluation of the Domestic Violence, Crime and Victims Act 2004* (14/08/2008), Hester M et al, Ministry of Justice Research Series, 42.
40. 'Domestic Violence and Social Policy perspectives from Women's Aid' (2000), Harwin N and Barron J, in Hanmer J, *Home Truths About Domestic Violence: Feminist Influences on Policy and Practice—A Reader*, Oxford: Routledge, 233.

and protection. Preventing violent crimes against women is seen as 'tackling the causes as well as its effects'.[41] The provision of adequate support services for women, as well as children is also considered a priority. Protecting victims is left to the criminal justice system with four priorities: a 'pro-arrest approach by the police to domestic violence';[42] providing victim/witness support by the Crown Court; improving the quality of evidence collecting by police forces; and specialist domestic violence courts.[43] However, policy responses still rely extensively upon criminal justice responses as the primary mechanism to protect victims of domestic violence. There are still three key problems associated with domestic violence which the criminal justice system alone has been ineffective in tackling: victim retraction which may lead to non-conviction of perpetrators in court,[44] victim non-disclosure; and repeat offending in many cases by serial perpetrators with multiple partners.

The reason domestic violence victims retract criminal cases is complex, including a lack of victim support, fear of reprisal from the perpetrator and not wanting to terminate the relationship (which often may be perceived as the eventual outcome of legal action). Research in the US[45] noted that women involved the police as a mechanism to help them manage the abuse; after this objective was met they would drop the case against the offender. In cases where criminal action has been instigated, victims may face pressure to retract cases. These include facing pressure by family, kinship and community to reconcile with the perpetrators and drop charges against abusers. Pressure may come in different forms and includes: isolation and stigmatisation by family and kinship; institutional systemic racism and fear of the authorities.[46] Abuse in intimate relationships is open to repeat

---

41. *Living Without Fear* (1999), Cabinet/Home Office, Women's Unit of the Cabinet, London, 45.
42. *Ibid*, 46.
43. Refers to a partnership approach between the various agencies of the criminal justice to provide a system specialised way of dealing with domestic violence cases (*Specialist Domestic Violence Courts Review 2007- 2008: Justice with Safety* (2007), Crown Prosecution Service).
44. 'Understanding Victim Retraction in Cases of Domestic Violence: Specialist Courts, Government Policy and Victim-Centred Justice' (2006), Robinson A and Cook D, Contemporary Justice Review, Vol 9 Issue 2, 189–213.
45. See 'Prosecution as a victim power source: A note on empowering women in violent conjugal relationships' (1991), Ford DA, *Law and Society Review*, Vol 25, 313.
46. See, *The Hidden Struggle: Statutory and Voluntary Responses to Violence Against Black Women in the Home* (1989), Mama A, Race and Housing Research Unit, London, and *Silenced 'n Caught:*

offending or recidivism by offenders in their current relationships but also with any partners in the past and the future. As part of the rehabilitation of offenders, domestic violence offender treatment programmes have been used to change the behaviour of perpetrators. Such programmes can be difficult to evaluate particularly because of low completion and high drop-out rates. Although criminal justice intervention can increase attendance rates,[47] it is still unclear if programmes make any real short or long term changes amongst perpetrators.

Against the current policy background there are several questions raised. The most significant of these is the role of institutional structures in protecting victims and preventing domestic violence. In particular, is the role of the criminal justice system as the primary or sole mechanism by which protection is offered to victims. The main objective of the existing criminal justice system is to punish those who commit a crime and are found guilty. The criminal justice system provides a *top-down* approach to managing domestic violence where sole responsibility for making decisions lies with the system. In a top-down approach the centralised nature and inflexibility of the system restricts choice. For example, although research in the US by Erez and Belknap[48] has purported that survivors of domestic violence want to retain choice and importantly be treated as autonomous individuals, the complexity of the legal system combined with a lack of 'real power' means that opportunities for survivors to be involved in decision-making are most likely to be limited.

The criminal justice system is not in a position to adequately address the distinct nature of domestic violence. For example, although perpetrators of domestic violence do act alone, they are often supported knowingly or unknowingly by family, friends, cultural, social and economic forces.[49]

Unlocking the Barriers to Reporting Domestic Violence in an Asian Community (1998), Currell S and Gill A, Police Research Group, Home Office, London.

47. *Reducing Domestic Violence What Works? Perpetrator Programmes* (2000), Mullender A and Burton S, Policing and Reducing Crime Unit, Crime Reduction Research Series, Home Office, London.
48. 'In their own words: Battered women's assessment of the criminal processing system's responses, (1998), Erez E and Belknap J, *Violence and Victims*, Vol. 13, 252-268.
49. 'Enhancing autonomy for battered women: Lessons from Navajo peacemaking', (1999), Coker D, *UCLA Law Review*, 47,

Criminal justice agencies monitor and manage the violation of criminal laws and do not directly focus on these cultural, social and economic factors. There is also an additional factor to consider of whether the criminal justice system provides victims of domestic violence with substantive justice, where the penalties for committing are appropriate.[50] This might extend to prison sentences and/or offender rehabilitation, but considering that the consequences of domestic violence may include continuous threats to a victim's safety and considerable change to their personal life, in serious cases of domestic violence it is not uncommon for survivors to re-locate from their original homes to re-build new lives.[51] Under these circumstances exploring alternative solutions to domestic violence crimes is necessary in order to provide a holistic solution to what is a social problem.

Alternative Models to Tackle Domestic Violence

Alternative solutions are broadly based on restorative justice principles. Although there is no one conclusive definition of restorative justice,[52] the main focus of this type of justice is to involve the 'victim in the justice process and address the harm that they have sustained'.[53] Koss,[54] argues that restorative justice practices adopt 'communitarian approaches', which she purports are methods which bring perpetrators, victims and community together to 'help design perpetrator rehabilitation, victims restoration and social reintegration of both victims and perpetrator' and they include 'informal justice, peacemaking, positive justice, relational justice, family group conferencing, effective cautioning and community accountability conferencing'. The role

---

50. *Giving Desert its due: Social Justice and Legal Theory* (1985), Sadurski, W, Dordrecht: D Reidal Publishing Company.
51. 'Domestic violence and housing' (2000), Morley, *Home Truths About Domestic Violence: Feminist Influences on Policy and Practice—A Reader*, Oxford: Routledge.
52. See Doolin, *Chapter 8*. See also, 'Principles of restorative justice' (2003) Braithwaite J, in Hirsch A, Roberts J, Bottoms A, Roach K and Schiff M (eds), *Restorative Justice and Criminal Justice: Competing or Reconcilable Paradigms*, Oxford and Portland, Oregon: Hart Publishing.
53. 'Blame, Shame, and Community: Justice Responses to Violence Against Women' (2000). Koss P, *American Psychologist*, Nov, Vol. 55, No 11, 1332-43.
54. *Ibid*.

of the criminal justice system in communitarian approaches can range from a total non-interventionist approach to adopting a primary role with communitarian approaches becoming secondary. [55]

Communitarian approaches are not uncommon in rural areas of Pakistan and India. Local village grievances are dealt with through a *panchayat*—a village council made up of village elders; approaches involve community conferences which take place in local villages to solve local problems.[56] In these circumstances the criminal justice system is not necessarily the first port of call for the aggrieved. Although village councils are inherently patriarchal, caste and male dominant,[57] they nevertheless provide a mechanism by which solutions to social problems can be dealt with at a local level by local people instead of a criminal justice system consisting of abstract laws and complex legal systems. In the case of domestic violence examples of 'people's courts' include *saalishi*.[58] A *saalishi* is 'a traditional Indian village institution that brings together community members who have disputes before they go to the police and the courts'.[59] In a *saalishi* all parties have an opportunity to air their grievances and for 'community wisdom' to prevail and ensure 'public shaming of the guilt party'.[60] Although *saalishi* and *panchayat* models of justice make offenders accountable for their actions, the main purpose of both is to restore harmony, promote healing between parties and, most importantly as noted by Sadasivam,[61] to bring a collective notion of peace. Like Giustina I do not advocate directly translating *saalishi*

---

55. *Restorative Justice and Criminal Justice: Competing or Reconcilable Paradigms* (2003), Hirsch V, Roberts V, Bottoms A, Roach K and Schiff M, Oxford and Portland, Oregon: Hart Publishing.
56. *Functioning of Village Panchayats* (1970), Inamdar R, Bombay: Popular Prakashan.
57. *Panchayats Turn into Kangaroo Courts* (2007), Rohit M and Neelam R, The Times of India, Special Report, 9 September.
58. 'Violence against women in intimate partner relationships: Community responsibility, community justice' (2008), Giustina D, *Contemporary Justice Review*, Vol 11, No 4, 359.
59. *Ibid.*
60. 'Violence against women in intimate partner relationships: Community responsibility, community justice' (2008), Giustina D, *Contemporary Justice Review*, Vol 11, No 4, 359, citing '*Community justice: West Bengal's women Draw on Village Tradition to Stop Domestic Violence* (2000), Sadasivam B, Ford Foundation, 6-9.
61. '*Community justice: West Bengal's women draw on village tradition to stop domestic violence*, (2000), Sadasivam B, Ford Foundation, 6-9.

and/or *panchayat* schemes into the UK, particularly in domestic violence cases, where there is a possibility such schemes may compromise the safety and well-being of victims.[62] However, there is some merit in exploring communitarian approaches within local community settings because they can help to deconstruct the privacy of family.

The notion of family as a private space potentially acts as a mechanism to protect abusers. Abuse and violence within the realm of family involves the abuse of power, the 'most powerful abusing the least powerful'.[63] Power differentials have the potential to create secrecy surrounding abuse types, such as sexual abuse of children and intimate partner violence. Secrecy has a silencing effect upon victims and delays and/or prevents disclosure of the abuse. Social responses play an important role in 'policing' these power differentials, and even early disclosure by victims. In domestic violence cases communitarian approaches are based on the notion that it is the right of the community to intervene in family matters to bring harmony.[64] However, in domestic violence cases, communitarian approaches are best suited alongside existing criminal justice systems.[65] There are two key reasons for this: to prevent the offender using the community conference to psychologically abuse the victims through his comments;[66] and to monitor the community's management of the case.[67] The key factor in any communitarian approach is the level and type of interventions that are used. The most effective interventions are likely to be those where perpetrators are accountable for their actions and which do not undermine their responsibilities and duties to the victims.[68]

---

62. 'Panchayats turn into kangaroo courts' (2007), Rohit M and Neelam R, *The Times of India,– Special Report*, 9 September.
63. 'Common Features of Family Abuse' (1983), Finkelhor D, in Finkelor D et al, *The Dark Side of Families: Current Family Violence Research*, California: Sage Publications, 18.
64. '*Community justice: West Bengal's women draw on village tradition to stop domestic violence* (2000), Sadasivam B, Ford Foundation, 6-9
65. 'Blame, Shame, and Community: Justice Responses to Violence Against Women' (2000), Koss M, *American Psychologist*, Nov, Vol. 55, No 11, 1332-43.
66. *Ibid.*
67. 'Shame, defiance, and violence against women: A critical analysis of "communitarian" conferencing' (1997) Stubbs J, in Cook S and Bessant J (Eds.) *Women's encounters with violence: Australian experiences*, London: Sage.
68. 'Blame, Shame, and Community: Justice Responses to Violence Against Women', (2000), Koss M, *American Psychologist*, Nov, Vol. 55, No 11, 1332-43.

A theoretical model of a communitarian approach to tackle domestic violence is presented by Giustina.[69] Giustina considers some different approaches to domestic violence policy in the USA. The model is operationalised in a local community setting where Giustina presents some alternative forms of managing domestic violence. These include neighbourhood support groups, neighbourhood watch groups and residential shelters for perpetrators. Giustina's approach addresses the everyday threat of domestic violence experienced by victims rather than providing any outright resolution between aggrieved parties. In this case the model addresses a shortcoming of the criminal justice system. The criminal justice system does not have the resources to monitor the constant threat of violence from the abuser in and outside the home. However, local community members are in a position to address this threat. Giustina's model is by no means perfect, for example the role of state intervention is not clear, but it provides an initial framework for further debate.

A Communitarian Based Approach

Currently in the US and the UK, institutional efforts to deal with domestic violence include models of intervention which are termed 'community co-ordinated responses'. There are no formal definitions or singular type of community-coordinated model,[70] but they are largely though not exclusively influenced by the success of the US based Domestic Violence Intervention Project (DVIP).[71] The DVIP is based on developing a 'common philosophical approach', which co-ordinates the different efforts of the many voluntary/community and public sector agencies involved in supporting victims of domestic violence.[72] Community-coordinated responses prioritize coordination between agency-based intervention efforts at a local level. Yet, within

---

69. 'Violence against women in intimate partner relationships: Community responsibility, community justice' (2008), Giustina J.D, *Contemporary Justice Review*, Vol 11, No 4, 351.
70. 'Coordinated Community Responses to intimate partner violence in the 20th and 21st centuries', (2008), Garner, J.H and Maxwell, C.D, *American Society of Criminology: Criminology and Public Policy*, Vol. 7, No. 4, 525-535.
71. See *Domestic Violence: The Criminal Justice Response*, (2003), Buzawa, E S and Buzawa, C G, California: Sage for a discussion on impact of DVIP and community-coordinated responses.
72. 'Duluth: A Co-ordinated Community Response to Domestic Violence' (1999), Pence E and McMahon M, in Harwin N et al, *The Multi-Agency Approach to Domestic Violence: New Opportunities, Old Challenges?* London: Whiting and Birch, 150.

these models there are few mechanisms in place to involve non-agency based social actors, for example friends, family and neighbours. Research[73] has noted that victims of domestic violence will access a whole range of support structures which include: family, friends, other close kin, neighbours, voluntary sector organisations and public sector agencies for help. The role of community and kinship is paramount in reducing and preventing domestic violence. In societies where the community believe that it is their right to intervene (if they were aware of the abuse), the rates of domestic violence are lower than in societies where domestic violence is considered a private family matter.[74]

An approach which involves the 'community' in managing domestic violence entails going beyond institutional frameworks and needs to involve the family, faith groups, neighbours, other local residents and even employers, as well as local law enforcement and local voluntary and community organisations. Giustina in her model uses communitarian approaches in a local community setting and attempts to bridge the chasm between agency and non-agency-based responses, which subsequently provide victims with a wider support network. Her model is community integrated in nature where responses to domestic violence become the duty of the community. Although she offers no overt definition of 'community', Giustina offers an implicit definition through her discussions of the possible ways to operationalise the model and include the family, neighbours, other local residents and employers.

In Giustina's model, the first tier support for victims could potentially be provided by the immediate community. Again no formal definition exists of who this may be. However, each social actor(s) may perform several roles in the model. For example, neighbours may act as the initial point of contact during a violent domestic situation. Their role, depending on the severity of the incident, may include contacting appropriate community-based support groups to get further help and they may also provide support to the victim.

---

73. See 'The role of social support in the lives of women exiting domestic violence shelters: An experimental study', (1995), Tan, C, Basta, J, Sullivan, C M and Davidson W S, *Journal of Interpersonal Violence*, Vol. 10, No. 4, 437-451.
74. 'Violence Against Women: An Integrated Ecological Framework', (1998), Heise, L L, *Violence Against Women*, Vol.4, No.3, 262.

> An integrated ... community response would include general community education and awareness, community protection for battered women and their children, community sanctioning of batterers[75] and coordinated effort with the police for severe or persistent cases of intimate partner violence.[76]

The model would incorporate 'a community controlled violence centre' which would not only coordinate the community's response to domestic violence but would act as the first point of contact for women experiencing domestic violence. The centre would include 'a trained neighbourhood support group', 'a neighbourhood watch group' and a 'residential shelter for batterers'.[77] The roles of these groups are multi-faceted — they provide programmes to raise awareness of intimate partner violence in the community, awareness and support programmes for victims and accommodation facilities for batterers.

Giustina in her model does not provide a distinction between the roles of the 'neighbourhood support group' and the 'neighbourhood watch group'. Although, from her brief discussion, it is apparent that the role of the first group is to provide the initial intervention in less serious cases of violence. These are where abuse is 'not part of a power and control pattern and with no injuries'.[78] Intervention may range from neighbourhood support group members visiting the couple separately, and encouraging counselling and to get involved in delivering support services. Support services could include general support, as well as safety planning for the victim. The second group could provide 'protection' for the victim, 'escorting the [victim] to and from work, school, the store, or anywhere else she needs to go'. Giustina[79] makes a distinction between the delivery of services to more serious cases; in which case she suggests that the perpetrator 'could be escorted from the home and given the option to find his own alternative housing or go to the neighbourhood residential facility for batterers'. The role of the neighbour-

---

75. Domestic violence perpetrators are referred to as 'batters' in USA literature on domestic violence.
76. 'Violence against women in intimate partner relationships: Community responsibility, community justice' (2008), Giustina J D, *Contemporary Justice Review*, Vol 11, No 4, 357.
77. Ibid, 357.
78. Ibid, 357.
79. Ibid, 358.

hood watch group would then involve 'surveillance'.[80] If the victim 'sustained' any physical injuries, the role of the neighbourhood group would include involving the police and ambulance services. The role of state intervention in this scenario is that of providing emergency facilities, e.g. medical care and police protection.

Giustina suggests an alternative to prison for perpetrators: a community-based and managed residential facility for perpetrators. She purports that 'such a facility could combine the successful features of batterer intervention programs with housing detention, much like a therapeutic half-way house'.[81] Giustina continues to form various approaches as to when and how perpetrators could be placed in such a facility. She suggests that perpetrators could enter such a facility voluntarily after an arrest for domestic violence, or whilst awaiting a trial or even after a conviction. If a perpetrator is convicted, the residential shelter could assess whether they would be better-off in prison. The facility would provide the resources necessary to 'have limited freedom of movement'[82] for the perpetrator whilst maintaining his responsibility, such as continuing to work to support his family. Limiting freedom of movement would require close monitoring of the perpetrator, and here she suggests the use of electronic monitoring and other surveillance equipment. She continues to contend that involving the perpetrators employer would also be necessary for the system to run successfully.

Giustina argues that her communitarian-based approach has four distinct benefits: a shift in the responsibility for leaving the relationship from the woman to the perpetrator; provision of residential facility for the perpetrator while he makes 'important changes' to his life;[83] to involve the community in monitoring the abusive relationship; and to 'allow women to consider their options in a safe environment at home'[84] without any threats. Giustina's model is solution focused; it raises awareness of domestic violence in the community and prioritises solutions on the basis of meeting the imme-

---

80. 'Violence against women in intimate partner relationships: Community responsibility, community justice' (2008), Giustina J D, *Contemporary Justice Review*, Vol 11, No 4, 358.
81. *Ibid*, 358.
82. *Ibid*, 358.
83. *Ibid*, 358.
84. *Ibid*, 358.

diate needs of victims, for example their safety whilst they get on with their lives. Most importantly, the model provides substantive justice; it holds the perpetrator responsible for his actions and removes him from the home as opposed to the victim having to move, often into refuge accommodation.

Although, the approach attempts to deconstruct notions of 'privacy' surrounding family life and subsequently making domestic violence a social issue rather than a private matter, the extent to which community members, particularly neighbours, feel that it is their right and obligation to intervene is another matter. Quantitative research[85] on domestic violence intervention by local community members notes that members are less likely to intervene in incidents of intimate partner violence. The research suggests that possible factors for non-intervention may include fear and concerns about personal safety.

There are further 'grey' areas within Giustina's model, for example the role of the criminal justice system is not clear. There are elementary references to the criminal justice system dealing with more serious cases of domestic violence. However, there is little reference to what constitutes as a serious domestic violence case and who decides whether a case is serious or not? The answer seems obvious, the community of course. What is a matter of concern with community based communitarian approaches is whether the community is in a position to provide a fair system. There are possible scenarios where families and the community end up colluding with perpetrators and reinforcing patriarchal power structures and victim blaming.[86] Such approaches would need to be closely monitored to examine their effectiveness at providing a fair system where there are opportunities for victims who prefer to engage with authorities like the police. In communitarian approaches the role of the criminal justice system is to *police* the system. Communitarian-based approaches do not necessarily mean decriminalising domestic violence, but there is some merit in exploring approaches which

---

85. 'The Informal Social Control of Intimate Partner Violence against Women: Exploring Personal Attitudes and Perceived Neighbourhood Social Cohesion', (2007), Frye, V, *Journal of Community Psychology*, Vol. 35, No. 8, 1001-1018.
86. 'Blame, Shame, and Community: Justice Responses to Violence Against Women' (2000), Koss M, *American Psychologist*, Nov, Vol. 55, No 11, 1332-43 and 'Enhancing autonomy for battered women: Lessons from Navajo peacemaking', (1999), Coker D, *UCLA Law Review*, 47.

sanction community 'disapproval of domestic violence and implement interventions on this basis'.[87] Owen and Owen[88] note that during early-modern England, domestic violence interventions were decidedly community-based with perpetrators facing public humiliations for their actions.

Conclusion

In the UK, pre-1970s, the state adopted a minimalist approach towards preventing domestic violence and protecting women experiencing abuse in intimate partner relationships. Minimalist approaches largely supported social ideals which related to the privacy of the home and family life. In the post-1970s era, there have been important changes to domestic violence legislation. Today, domestic violence is taken more seriously by the criminal justice system than it has ever been on previous occasions. However, despite legislative changes, domestic violence is still a social problem, where agency-based solutions may not be providing appropriate long term solutions. Current problems associated with domestic violence crimes include: victims' being unable to disclose violence; the retraction of criminal cases against perpetrators by victims; and repeat violence by the same perpetrator towards current and future partners. Solutions to these problems may be sought using an alternative approach. The chapter explores one such approach put forward by Giustina.[89] In her model, domestic violence crimes are managed at a local community level. In such an approach there are considerable advantages. Agents outside of the criminal justice system are involved in decision-making and possibly provide solutions which may not be available through institutions. A decentralised and flexible approach also provides an opportunity for ownership and responsibilities for dealing with crime as community-centred experience. However, such an approach presents challenges too. Apart from the role of the victim, the roles of the various

---

87. 'Domestic Violence and "Rough Music": A Case of Community-based Intervention' (2006), Owen JR and Owen S, *British Journal of Community Justice*, Vol 4, No 2, 18.
88. *Ibid.*
89. 'Violence against women in intimate partner relationships: Community responsibility, community justice' (2008), Giustina J.D, *Contemporary Justice Review*, Vol 11, No 4, 351.

actors (i.e. state agencies, voluntary organisations and the community) in the community-based paradigm are likely to be fluid and not easily defined. In this complex scenario, allocating duties and managing responsibilities may potentially be challenging for all.

CHAPTER 14

CONCLUSIONS AND THE WAY FORWARD FOR CRIMINAL JUSTICE

ANTHONY BEECH, JOHN CHILD, KATHERINE DOOLIN AND JOHN RAINE

This volume has focused on the approaches and shifts identified in criminal justice over the past decade. More particularly, it has focused upon the twin dynamics of, on the one hand, a strong regulatory and risk reducing central state, and on the other, of more localism and a context in which communities are empowered to take more responsibility for addressing the problems of crime and anti-social behaviour in their neighbourhoods.

Seeking in this final chapter to draw the strands of the book together, it will be recalled that, in *Part I*, under the heading 'The Regulatory State and the Management of Risk', we began by examining the theoretical foundations of the criminal law. Here we raised questions about the justification for a number of the developments instituted in criminal justice by the New Labour government in the late-1990s and in the first decade of the 21st-century as it sought to combat and manage risk in society. We also considered the price that might be being paid here in terms of loss of freedom.

Successive chapters went on to consider aspects of those developments in more detail. They explored, in turn, the creation of new offences to address actions and intentions prior to occurrence of harm, and in so doing, raising further questions about the principles underlying such new offences. From here, the following two chapters examined the extending reach of the criminal law through case studies, respectively on liability in relation to the purchase of sexual services, and the introduction of the ASBO (through civil law and hybrid mechanisms) as a response to a new focus on 'anti-social' behaviour.

As well as focusing on the risks of those yet to commit offences (in the traditional sense), *Part I* of the book also considered responses to those deemed to be at risk of re-offending, and the gamut of standardising measures instituted by the central state under the new heading of 'offender management' (one pertinent example of the changing ethos here being the re-titling of probation officers as 'offender managers'). Finally in *Part I*, we reflected on the consequential feelings of (un)safety amongst Muslim minorities engendered by the state's 'war on terror', noting how counter-productive this had proved in terms of, first, giving rise to anxiety amongst Muslim groups and mistrust towards the police, second damaging community relations and social cohesion, and third stirring feelings of insecurity and isolation among Muslims within their local areas.

In *Part II*, under the heading 'Empowered Communities as Local Stakeholders in Criminal Justice', our attentions shifted to the 'new localism' and to the prospects for, and potential of, community-level responses to crime and disorder. We began by examining the potential of, and challenges to, involving communities in responses to crime through restorative justice processes. This was followed by a discussion of the evolution of the notion of 'safer communities' and 'community justice'. We also examined some of the community-level responses to anti-social behaviour and reflected on the challenges of implementing at the local level approaches to 'policing' sex offenders and responses to domestic violence. These two latter case studies highlighted not only the potential for change, but also the risks to be confronted and the attitudinal and behavioural changes required in communities for there to be more acceptance of responsibility at local level for the problem of crime and for the response to it.

Balancing the Roles of the State and the Community

So what overarching conclusions are to be drawn from these various analyses? The question posed on the cover of this volume 'Whose Criminal Justice?' perhaps suggested that we might come down firmly on one or other side and regard criminal justice as legitimately more the province of either the central state or local communities. However, the evidence we have examined within the various chapters leads to the rather less decisive, but probably more realistic, conclusion that they are both as vital as one another but that they need to play more complimentary and more mutually supporting roles than is currently the case. The key conclusion, then, is of the need to establish a better balance between the centre and locality in criminal justice and of the importance of realising a more effective contribution from each — contributions that better reflect their potential. Likewise, the challenge is to sustain the equilibrium of such contributions and to resist the tendency for criminal justice to be pulled and pushed by the pendulum swings of fashion in public policy between central control, as in recent years, and equally, of new localism, as now.

From our analyses, we are sure that there is a vital role for the central state in creating and keeping up-to-date the overarching framework of law and regulation to minimize the risks of insecurity and to provide reasonable protection for citizens. Indeed, reflecting the strongly embedded unitary state culture of this country, such a role would surely fit well with the established expectations of citizens about the legitimate purposes of national government and Parliament in relation to publicly-recognised problems. However, from here, our argument is two-fold: first, when Parliament legislates to prevent risk, it needs to do so with more careful regard to the implications for the freedom of citizens; and second, any such legislation needs to enable and promote, not overly constrain, the exercise of discretion by the practitioners in criminal justice. The framework of legislation, rules and guidelines, should therefore not be too prescriptive and should leave as much scope as possible for practitioners at local level — the police, the prosecutors, the judiciary in courts, the probation and prison officers — to determine the most appropriate responses for the particular cases with which they are confronted.

Conversely, at local level, we are sure that there needs to be a greater readiness among communities, and practitioners working on their behalf, to take ownership of the problems of crime and anti-social behaviour and to exercise with maturity the associated responsibilities. Local agencies need to learn to show less dependency towards the centre, how to address more of their problems for themselves and, most particularly, to become more directly accountable to local communities. Practitioners need to engage with their communities, listen more intensively to citizen perspectives and understand and appreciate better what matters to local people. They need to become more responsive within the limits of their authority. They also need to learn to explain better to communities what can reasonably be expected, what cannot and why, especially on issues where the decisions and actions may not be popular ones. The aim needs not only to be the building of more trust and confidence between communities and the criminal justice agencies at local level, but also the promotion of more active participation and volunteering, for example, as special constables, as magistrates, as providers of support to victims, as mentors for offenders and so on.

Learning from Experience

A rebalancing of powers to enable local communities to tailor their responses to crime and the practice of criminal justice within the bounds established by a well-defined, but essentially empowering, rather than restricting, national regulatory framework, is then, an overarching message from this volume and one which has been underlined and reinforced again and again, albeit in differing ways, in so many of the chapters presented here.

Andrew Sanders, for example, made the case in *Chapter 2* for a less prescriptive approach by the central state. However, in discussing the Freedom Perspective, he also emphasised the value to be attached, on the one hand, to the notion of consistency in responding to different forms of unacceptable behaviour and, on the other, to the importance of addressing less serious infringements in less serious ways (to maximise freedom). In this regard, for example, the same arguments suggest a strong case for using alternatives to prosecution through the courts because this would maximise freedom for most people. The same perspective also bolsters the case for the positive 'problem-solving' approaches discussed in several of the chapters and which seek to address the difficult personal circumstances that might likely underpin and foster criminal behaviour, notably unemployment, low educational attainment, difficulties in accessing skills training, boredom, drug and alcohol dependency, other health problems, inadequate housing and so on. It would also support the greater emphasis on restorative justice principles and on strengthening mentoring-type support arrangements to provide positive paths towards compliance for those at risk of slipping (back) into trouble — putting more emphasis on investment and intervention to prevent crime and thus needing to commit correspondingly less resources to responding to it.

Concerns particularly about the over-extending reach of the regulatory state in recent years, and the manner in which this has happened, were captured in *Chapters 3* and *4* by John Child and Adrian Hunt and by Jessica Elliott respectively. These two chapters warned of the need for vigilance and for a strongly principled approach in relation to further legislation designed at protecting people from the risk of harm, however well intentioned. While, as indicated, it would always be important to prevent criminal harms coming about, not just respond to them after the event, the authors here emphasised the need to be wary that the boundaries (and definitions) of criminality were not allowed to become so blurred and interventions so premature and anticipatory that the balance with the rights of defendant were to become distorted. The conclusion of both chapters was that this indeed had been happening and that it was now time to conduct 'a deeper and grander exploration'(Child and Hunt) of the conceptual basis of criminalisation and to scrutinise more rigorously and systematically the case for new criminal laws. In so doing, they argued, it would be important to recognise that often the existing laws would be adequate for the purposes (as for example, in relation to the problems of prostitution and pimping that Elliott discusses in *Chapter 4*).

Taken to its natural extreme in *Chapter 5*, Theresa Lynch discussed how the use of hybrid orders (and particularly the ASBO) had been employed by the state to extend the reach of the criminal law still further, whilst using the civil part of the order to avoid criminal procedural constraints. Tracing the breadth of use for which such orders had been employed, she concluded that, in the interests of fairness and (possibly) freedom, it might have been more appropriate to characterise anti-social behaviour as criminal rather than civil in regard to court processes.

The arguments for a less prescriptive regulatory approach from the central state were developed further, and particularly in conjunction with the downsides of the overly bureaucratic risk assessment processes, in *Chapter 6* by Kathryn Farrow, Gill Kelly and Bernadette Wilkinson. Focusing on post-conviction dangerousness, the authors considered the consequences of a preoccupation with technical detail and with managerialist values at the expense of attention to the community context of offenders. Their arguments were for the need to learn to avoid the tendency to over-protect people from risk and to recognise that risk-taking is essential in moving people and society forward. To this end, as they suggested, criminal justice agencies need to engage more with communities and to address constructively their anxieties about crime; albeit while also taking their insecurities seriously. They should also help communities to understand and appreciate the scope for rehabilitation and its potential in desistance. Likewise, in *Chapter 7* by Shamila Ahmed and Basia Spalek, a picture was painted of the negative local consequences of an overly-dominant centre-driven policy-making process in criminal justice. In this case, as indicated, the real concern was with the damaging impact on local community relations, on social cohesion and, rather ironically, on the sense of personal safety as well, of the state's resort to the extremes of risk management in pursuing a 'war on terror'.

However, at the same time, the evidence presented in *Part II* showed equally how much more needs to be done at the community level to achieve the appropriate sense of local responsibility in relation to problems of crime and anti-social behaviour and properly to complement the role of the centre in this regard. In *Chapter 8*, Katherine Doolin explored the under-realised potential of restorative justice at the local level and the prospects for such an approach becoming more mainstream in the response to crime and anti-social behaviour into the future. Similarly, *Chapters 9* and *10*, by David Prior and John Raine respectively, examined the prospects for a stronger framework of community justice, building upon the foundations laid by the New Labour government, promoting and fostering a proactive and problem-solving approach by the local courts. However, the argument made was that this now needs to be driven much more strongly from the bottom upwards with support from, and accountability to, local communities, rather than, as in recent years, with all the pressure coming top-down from national government. Indeed, we noted in *Chapter 10* the paradox of the advent and development of community justice centres in England and Wales as having been largely inspired and driven by central government.

In *Chapter 11*, Nathan Hughes developed still further the argument for communities taking greater responsibility for addressing their problems specifically in relation to youth and anti-social behaviour. Here he identified the core of the challenge as being the power differentials within communities and within community justice under which young people tended to be all too readily defined (by adults) as the problem but who were far less often given opportunities to contribute directly to the process of seeking resolution. Rather than disempowering or victimising young people, Hughes' call was for communities to empower them to take responsibility.

Then in a similar vein, in *Chapters 12* and *13*, by Mark Blandford and Anthony Beech and then by Zahira Latif, the focus moved to two other key challenges for local communities. First, Blandford and Beech examined the issue of communities accepting greater responsibility for managing the risks of sex offenders living within their midst. Their findings in relation to a particular pilot initiative, Circles of Support and Accountability, give grounds for some optimism as to the potential for increased community responsibility and confidence and without undue risk, especially if combined with strong support from neighbourhood policing teams. Then Latif considered the role of the community and multi-agency working in more co-ordinated responses to domestic violence, notably specialist domestic violence courts with their more flexible and more victim-centred approach. Her conclusions, too, were hopeful in that such community-based approaches did seem to offer much potential for increased recognition of the community-centredness of this (for too long hidden) form of crime and for greater collective ownership of, and responsibility for, addressing it.

Where Next for Criminal Justice?

Written at a time just towards the end of a 12 year period of New Labour government in the UK and in the first few months of the succeeding regime of the Coalition government (between the Conservatives and Liberal Democrats), it has inevitably been an opportune and intriguing time to take stock of what has been happening in criminal justice, as in public policy more generally, and to ponder on what should happen next. But here, of course, while it is one thing to seek (as we have in this book) to make sense of what is now the past and to assess the impacts of the various developments of recent years, it is quite another to give equivalent focus to the agenda for the future. And in part the problem here has been that the focus on policy development for the new government has, in the early years at least, been somewhat blurred by the priority accorded to the making of significant reductions in public spending to alleviate a record financial deficit.

That said, from the outset there was certainly a sense of potential sea-change for criminal justice, and with the possibility of significant dismantling of much of the New Labour reform agenda of the 1990s and the 2000s. A prime example of this would be the ASBO, as discussed at some length in each *Part* of this volume, introduced with considerable pride early on in the life of the previous government but now likely to be abolished under the new political administration. Conversely, restorative justice (as discussed by Katherine Doolin in *Chapter 8*) appears set to become more prominent as a form of response, at least in relation to certain categories of offending, in the future—hopefully for its recognised effectiveness as an alternative to prosecution through the courts rather than simply as a cheaper option in response to the need to reduce public spending.[1]

More generally, and particularly in the light of our argument for rebalancing responsibility between the central state and local communities, the priority for us, we suggest, should be less about 'dismantling' the infrastructure of criminal justice and rather more about developing it and making it work more effectively, particularly as a component of the broader social policy agenda. And here, the government's commitment to developing the notion of a 'Big Society' (and of a smaller state) could perhaps be seen as a real opportunity for such rebalancing and for more decentralisation and empowering of local communities in the manner advocated in a number of our chapters.

More than that, there have been other positive signs in the early months of the new Coalition government of shifting perspectives in relation to criminal justice that could similarly be seen as potential steps in that rebalancing

---

[1]. For discussion of this see, 'Criminals Should Say Sorry' (2010) *Guardian*, available at www.guardian.co.uk/society/2010/jul/25/criminals-should-say-sorry .

process. Notable in this context was the early commitment made to a review of sentencing and the expressions of concern by the Secretary of State for Justice, the Right Honourable Kenneth Clarke MP, at the record size of the prison population that he had inherited and about his desire to see this reduced. Although in this book we have not focused specifically in any one chapter on sentencing policy, the subject has inevitably been touched on at many points, and it would seem entirely consistent with our advocacy of a stronger community dimension to criminal justice to expect a shift towards community-based sentencing options from the relatively high rates of custodial sentencing that have characterised these past two decades. Indeed, in our view, we would argue that, in the 21st-century, custody should very definitely be a last resort sentencing option, and one to be reserved only for those from whom society needs very clearly to be protected (i.e. because of the risk of personal harm). And even then, prison provision within the community setting would seem to be the more appropriate option to enable prisoners to benefit from the ongoing support networks of family and friends through their time in custody so as to make rehabilitation into the community afterwards all the easier.

For the most part, however, we would favour much greater emphasis being placed on reparations to victims or to the community, for example, through unpaid work on projects of local value; this, we think, being most likely to represent an appropriate form of response for those convicted of criminal offences. At the same time, as indicated, we would also advocate the more extensive use of restorative justice as an alternative to prosecution in the courts.

Furthermore, we would particularly lend endorsement to three guiding principles enunciated around the time of the General Election in 2010 by an independent commission on youth crime and anti-social behaviour[2]—prevention, restoration and integration—since these seem so relevant to our conception of a more empowered community-level response to unacceptable behaviour (by those of any age). With regard to the first of these—prevention—the independent commission advocated much greater emphasis on

---

2. *Time for a Fresh Start: Report of the Independent Commission on Youth Crime and Anti-social Behaviour* (2010), The Police Foundation, London: The Police Foundation.

interventions in early years to raise the quality of upbringing, education and support for children to reduce the likelihood of young people becoming caught up in anti-social behaviour and crime. As the commission argued, although more needs to be learned about the causal pathways here, there is plenty of knowledge already of the risk factors appearing to associate with such behaviour, notably 'individual children, their families, friends and peers, their education and the neighbourhoods in which they live'. Similarly, the commission highlighted the range of preventative services capable of reducing persistent childhood behaviour problems, including,

> ...parenting support, pre-school education, school tutoring, behaviour and "life skills strategies, family therapy, treatment foster care, constructive leisure opportunities and mentoring programmes..."[3]

The second principle—restoration—replicates our own advocacy of both restorative justice and of a problem-solving approach, 'whereby parties with a stake in a specific offender resolve collectively how to deal with the aftermath of the offence and its implications for the future'.[4] Again, while the commission focused specifically on young people, we are sure that the principle applies equally well for adults and deserves to be more widely adopted by police forces and in community justice processes.

Finally, what of integration; the third such guiding principle? Here too, the commission's conclusions strongly underline and echo our own advocacy of restorative, rehabilitative and community-based sentencing as the appropriate response to the majority of instances of offending behaviour and as the kind of responses most likely to give communities a sense of having a stake in criminal justice. This, in turn, is likely to help build confidence in the local agencies and foster the stronger sense of empowerment and responsibility at the community level that we have contended throughout this book to be the deserving equal partner to the nation state. Together, as

---

3. *Time for a Fresh Start: Report of the Independent Commission on Youth Crime and Anti-social Behaviour* (2010), The Police Foundation, London: The Police Foundation.
4. *Ibid.*

part of a coherent whole, these two can provide a respected framework of law and criminal justice practice.

REFERENCES

Abbot, C. (2009). *Enforcing Pollution Control Regulation*, Oxford: Hart.

ACPO (Association of Chief Police Officers) (2007). *Guidance on Protecting the Public: Managing Sexual Offenders and Violent Offenders*. London: ACPO.

Afshar, H., Aitken, R., & Franks, M. (2005). Feminism, Islamophobia and Identities. *Political Studies*, 53, 262-283.

Andrews, D. A. (2006). Enhancing Adherence to Risk-Need-Responsivity: Making quality a matter of policy. *Criminology and Public Policy*, 5, 595–602.

Andrews, D. A., & Bonta, J. (2003). *The Psychology of Criminal Conduct*, 3rd Edition. Cincinatti, OH: Anderson.

Ansari, F. (2005). *British Anti-Terrorism: A Modern Day Witch-hunt*. London: Islamic Human Rights Commission. www.ihrc.org.uk/file/2005BritishAntiTerrorism.pdf

Ashworth, A. (2000). Is the criminal law a lost cause? *Law Quarterly Review*, 116, 225-256.

(2002) Responsibilities, Rights and Restorative Justice. *British Journal of Criminology*, 42, 578-595.

(2004) Social control and anti social behaviour: The subversion of human rights? *Law Quarterly Review*, 120, 263-291.

(2009) *Principles of Criminal Law*, 5th edition. Oxford: Oxford University Press.

Ashworth, A., Gardner, J., Morgan, R., Smith, A. T. H., von Hirsch, A., & Wasik, M. (1995). Overtaking on the right. *New Law Journal*, 145, 1501-1502.

(1998) Neighbouring on the Oppressive: the Government's Community Safety Order Proposals. *Criminal Justice*, 16, 7-14.

Ashworth, A., & Redmayne, M. (2005). *The Criminal Process*, 3rd edition. Oxford: Oxford University Press.

Ashworth, A., & Zedner, L. (2008). Defending the criminal law: Reflections on the changing character of crime, procedure, and sanctions. *Criminal Law and Philosophy*, 2, 21-51.

Ayres, R., & Braithwaite, J. (1992). *Responsive Regulation*. Oxford: Oxford University Press.

Bakalis, C. (2003). ASBOs: Criminal penalties or civil injunctions? *Cambridge Law Journal*, 62, 583-586.

(2007) ASBOs, Preventative orders and the European Court of Human Rights. *European Human Rights Law Review*, 4, 427-440.

Baker, K. (2007). Risk, uncertainty and public protection: Assessment of young people who offend. *British Journal of Social Work*, 8, 1463-1480.

Bakir, S., & Harburg, B. (2005). *Berlin German Anti Terror Law and Religious Extremism*. Berlin: HIA.

Bandura, A. (1997). *Self-Efficacy: The Exercise of Control*. New York: W.H. Freeman.

Barron, J. (2004). *Five Years On: A Review of Legal Protection from Domestic Violence*. London: Women's Aid Federation of England.

Bazemore, G., & Walgrave, L. (1999). Restorative juvenile justice: In search of fundamentals and an outline for systemic reform. In Bazemore, G., & Walgrave, L (eds.), *Restorative Juvenile Justice: Repairing the Harm of Youth Crime*. Monsey, New York: Criminal Justice Press.

Beck, U. (1992). *Risk Society: Towards a New Modernity*. London: Sage.

Beech, A., Fisher D., & Thornton, D. (2003). Risk assessment of sex offenders. *Professional Psychology, Research and Practice*, 34, 339-352.

Bell, C., & Newby, H. (1971). *Community Studies*. London: Unwin.

Bird, R. (1997). *Domestic Violence and Protection from Harassment*. Bristol: Jordan Publishing.

Blanchette, K., & Brown, S. L. (2006). *The Assessment and Treatment of Women Offenders: An Integrative Perspective*. Chichester: Wiley.

Blick, A., Choudhury, T., & Weir, S. (2006). *The Rules of the Game: Terrorism, Community and Human Rights*. York: Joseph Rowntree Foundation.

Body-Gendrot, S. (2008). Muslims: Citizenship, security and social justice in France. *International Journal of Law, Crime and Justice*, 36, 247-256.

Bonta, J., Rugge, T., Scott, T., Bourgon, G., & Yessine, A. K. (2008). Exploring the black box of community supervision. *Journal of Offender Rehabilitation*, 47, 248-270.

Bonta, J., & Wormith, S. J. (2008). Risk and Needs Assessment. In McIvor, G., & Raynor, P. (eds.), *Developments in Social Work with Offenders*. London: Jessica Kingsley Publishers.

Bosworth, M., Bowling, B., & Lee, M. (2008). Globalization, ethnicity and racism: An introduction. *Theoretical Criminology*, 12, 263-273.

Bowling, B., & Phillips, C. (2007). Disproportionate and Discriminatory: Reviewing the evidence on police stop and search. *Modern Law Review*, 70, 936-961.

Box, S., Hale, C., & Andrews, G. (1988) Explaining fear of crime. *British Journal of Criminology*, 28, 340-356.

Brah, A. (2009). *Identity, Ethnic Diversity and Community Cohesion*. London: Sage.

Braithwaite, J. (2002). *Restorative Justice and Responsive Regulation*. Oxford: Oxford University Press.

(2003) Principles of restorative justice. In von Hirsch, A., Roberts, J., Bottoms, A.E., Roach, K., & Schiff, M. (eds.), *Restorative Justice and Criminal Justice: Competing or Reconcilable Paradigms*. Oxford: Hart Publishing.

Bridges, A. (2009). *Public Protection and Safeguarding: An Inspectorate Perspective*. London: Her Majesty's Inspectorate of Probation.

Bridges, L., & Gilroy, P. (1982). Striking Back. *Marxism Today*, 34-35.

Brown, A. (2004). Social behaviour, crime control and social control. *Howard Journal of Criminal Justice*, 43, 203-211.

Burney, E. (2002). Talking tough, acting coy: Whatever happened to the Anti-Social Behaviour Order? *Howard Journal of Criminal Justice*, 41, 469-484.

(2005) *Making People Behave: Anti-Social Behaviour, Politics and Policy*. Cullompton: Willan.

(2009) Respect and the politics of behaviour. In Millie, A. (ed.), *Securing Respect: Behavioural Expectations and Anti-Social Behaviour in the UK*. Bristol: Policy Press.

Burton, J., & Van den Boeck, D. (2009). Accountable and countable: information management systems and the bureaucratization of social work. *British Journal of Social Work*, 39, 1326-1342.

Buzawa, E. S., & Buzawa, C. G. (2003). *Domestic Violence: The Criminal Justice Response*. Thousand Oaks, CA: Sage.

Cabinet Office, (1999). *Living Without Fear*. London: Women's Unit of the Cabinet, Office, London: HMSO.

Campbell, C., Devlin, R., O'Mahony, D., Doak, J., Jackson, J., Corrigan, T., & McEvoy, K. (2005). *Evaluation of the Northern Ireland Youth Conference Service*. Belfast: Northern Ireland Office.

Cao, L., Frank, J., & Cullen, F. (1996). Race, Community Context and Confidence in the Police. *American Journal of Police*, 15, 3-22.

Carson, D. (1996). Risking Legal Repercussions. In Kemshall, H., & Pritchard J. (eds.), *Good Practice in Risk Assessment and Risk Management*. London: Jessica Kingsley Publishers.

Cesaroni, C. (2001). Releasing sex offenders into the community through "Circles of Support": A means of reintegrating the "Worst of the Worst". *Journal of Offender Rehabilitation*, 34, 85-98.

Chakrabati, S., & Russell, J. (2008). ASBOmania, in Squires, P. (ed.), *ASBO Nation: The Criminalisation of Nuisance*. Bristol: Policy Press.

Christie, N. (1977). Conflicts as Property. *British Journal of Criminology*, 17, 1-15.

(2004) *A Suitable Amount of Crime*. London: Routledge.

Clarke, M. (1987). Citizenship, community and the management of crime. *British Journal of Criminology*, 27, 384-400.

Clear, T., & Cadora, E. (2001). Risk and community practice. In Stenson, K., & Sullivan, R.R. (eds.), *Crime, Risk and Justice: The Politics of Crime Control in Liberal Democracies*. Cullompton: Willan.

Cohen, S. (1979). The Punitive city: Notes on the dispersal of social control. *Contemporary Crises*, 3, 339-364.

(1980) *Folk Devils and Moral Panics: The Creation of the Mods and Rockers*. Oxford: Martin Robertson.

(1985) *Visions of Social Control*. Stafford, Australia: Polity.

Coker, D. (1999). Enhancing autonomy for battered women: Lessons from Navajo Peacemaking. *UCLA Law Review*, 47, 1-111.

Connelly, C., & Williamson, S. (2000). *A Review on the Research Literature on Serious Violent Sexual Offenders; Research Monograph*. Edinburgh: Scottish Executive Central Research Unit.

Consedine, J. (1999). *Restorative Justice: Healing the Effects of Crime*. Lyttelton, New Zealand: Ploughshares Publications.

Cooke, C. (2005). Issues concerning visibility and reassurance provided by the new policing family. *Journal of Community and Applied Social Psychology*, 15, 229-240.

Craissati, J., & Sindall, O. (2009). Serious further offences: An exploration of risk and typologies. *Probation Journal*, 56, 9-27.

Crawford, A. (1994). The Partnership Approach to Community Crime Prevention; Corporatism at the Local Level? *Social and Legal Studies*, 3, 497-518.

(1995) Appeals to community and crime prevention. *Crime, Law and Social Change*, 22, 97-126.

(1998) *Crime Prevention and Community Safety: Politics, Policies and Practices*. Harlow: Longman.

(2002) The state, community and restorative justice: Heresy, nostalgia and butterfly collecting. In Walgrave, L. (ed.), *Restorative Justice and the Law*. Cullompton: Willan.

(2009) Governing through anti-social behaviour: Regulatory challenges to criminal justice. *British Journal of Criminology*, 49, 810-831.

Crawford, A., & Lister, S. (2007). *The Use and Impact of Dispersal Orders: Sticking Plasters and Wake Up Calls*. York: Joseph Rowntree Foundation.

Crawford, A., & Newburn, T. (2003) *Youth Offending and Restorative Justice: Implementing Reform in Youth Justice*. Cullompton: Willan.

Currell, S., & Gill, A. (1998). *Silenced 'n Caught: Unlocking the barriers to reporting domestic violence in an Asian community*. London: Home Office.

Daly, K., & Immarigeon, R. (1998). The past, present, and future of restorative justice: Some critical reflections. *Contemporary Justice Review*, 1, 21-45.

Davis, H., & Bourhill, M. (1997). The demonisation of children and young people. In P. Scraton (ed.), *Childhood in Crisis?* London: UCL Press.

De Silva, N., Cowell, P., Chow, T., & Worthington, P. (2006). *Prison Populations Projections 2006-2013*. London: Home Office.

Dempsey, M. (2005). Rethinking Wolfenden: Prostitute-use, criminal law, and remote Harm. *Criminal Law Review*, 444–455.

Dignan, J. (2005). *Understanding Victims and Restorative Justice*. Maidenhead: Open University Press.

Dobash, R., & Dobash, R. (1980). *Violence Against Wives*. Shepton Mallett, Somerset: Open Books.

Donaghy, R. (2009). *One Death Too Many*, Department for Work and Pensions. Norwich: TSO.

Donnison, D. (1998). Creating a safer society. In Jones Finer, C., & Nellis, M. (eds.), *Crime and Social Exclusion*. Oxford: Blackwell.

Donzelot, J. (1980). *The Policing of Families*. London: Hutchinson.

Doolin, K. (2007). But what does it mean? Seeking definitional clarity in restorative justice. *Journal of Criminal Law*, 71, 427-440.

(2008) Translating restorative justice into practice: Lessons from New Zealand's Family Group Conferencing approach to youth offending. *International Journal of Restorative Justice*, 4, 1-24.

Driver, S., & Martell, L. (1997). New Labour's Communitarianism. *Critical Social Policy*, 17, 27-46.

Duff, R. A. (1996). *Criminal Attempts*. Oxford: Clarendon Press.

Eadie, T., & Canton, R. (2002). Practising in a context of ambivalence: The challenge for youth justice workers. *Youth Justice*, 2, 14-26.

Erez, E., & Belknap, J. (1998). In their own words: Battered women's assessment of the criminal processing system's responses. *Violence and Victims*, 13, 252-268.

Eriksson, A. (2009). *Justice in Transition: Community Restorative Justice in Northern Ireland*. Cullompton: Willan.

Fagan, J., & Malkin, V. (2003). Theorizing Community Justice through Community Courts. *Fordham Urban Law Journal*, 30, 897-953.

Farrall, S. (2004). Social capital and offender reintegration: Making probation desistance-focussed. In Maruna, S. & Immarigeon R. (eds.), *After Crime and Punishment*. Cullompton: Willan.

Farrington, D. (2003). Key results from the first forty years of the Cambridge Study in Delinquent Development. In Thornberry, T. P., & Krohn, M. D. (eds.), *Taking Stock of Delinquency and Overview of Findings from Contemporary Longitudinal Studies*. New York: Kluwer.

Farrington, D., Coid, J., Harnett, L., Jolliffe, D., Soteriou, N., Turner, R., & West, D. (2006) *Criminal careers and life success: New findings from the Cambridge study in delinquent development. Home Office Research Findings, 281*. London: Home Office. www.homeoffice.gov.uk/rds/pdfs06/r281.pdf

Farrow, K. (2004). Still committed after all these years? Morale in the modern-day Probation Service. *Probation Journal*, 51, 206-220.

Farrow, K., Kelly, G., & Wilkinson, B. (2007). *Offenders in Focus: Risk, Responsivity and Diversity*. Bristol: Policy Press.

Feinblatt, J. (1998). Neighbourhood Justice at the Midtown Community Court. In *Crime and Place*. Plenary Papers of the 1997, Conference on Criminal Justice Research and Evaluation, 81. New York: National Institute of Justice.

Fekete, L. (2004). Anti-Muslim racism and the European security state. *Race and Class*, 46, 3-29.

Field, F. (2003). *Neighbours from Hell: The Politics of Behaviour*. London: Politicos.

Findlay, M. (2007). Terrorism and relative justice. *Crime, Law and Social Change*, 47, 57-68.

Finkelhor, D. (1979). Common features of family abuse. In Finkelhor, D. *et al* (eds.), *The Dark Side of Families: Current Family Violence Research*. Thousand Oaks, CA: Sage.

Fitch K. (2006). *Megan's Law: Does it Protect Children: An Updated Review Of Evidence on the Impact Of Community Notification as Legislated for by Megan's Law in the United States*. London: NSPCC.

Flanagan, R. (2008). The review of policing 2008: Delivering in partnership. In

Flint, J. (ed.), *Housing Urban Governance and Anti-Social Behaviour: Perspectives, Policy and Practice*. Bristol: Policy Press.

Flint, J. (2004). The responsible tenant: housing governance and the politics of behaviour. *Housing Studies*, 19, 893-909.

Ford, D. A. (1991). Prosecution as a victim power source: A note on empowering women in violent conjugal relationships. *Law and Society Review*, 25, 313-334.

Frye, V. (2007). The informal social control of intimate partner violence against women: exploring personal attitudes and perceived neighbourhood social cohesion. *Journal of Community Psychology*, 35, 1001-1018.

Garner, J. H., & Maxwell, C. D. (2008). Coordinated community responses to intimate partner violence in the 20th & 21st centuries. American Society of Criminology. *Criminology and Public Policy*, 7, 525-535.

Garside, R. (2006). *Right for the Wrong Reasons: Making Sense of Criminal Justice Failure*. Crime and Society Foundation, Monograph No. 2. www.crimeandjustice.org.uk/opus293/RFWR.pdf

Gearty, C. (2006). *Can Human Rights Survive?* Cambridge: Cambridge University Press.

Giddens, A. (1991). *Modernity and Self-Identity*. Cambridge: Polity.

Gilling, D. (2007). *Crime Reduction and Community Safety: Labour and the Politics of Local Crime Control*. Cullompton: Willan.

Giustina, D. (2008). Violence against women in intimate partner relationships: Community responsibility, community justice. *Contemporary Justice Review*, 11, 351-361.

Goldsack, L. (1999). A haven in a heartless home? Women and domestic violence. In Chapman T. & Hockey, J. (eds.), *Ideal Homes, Social Change and Domestic Life*. London: Routledge.

Goldsmith, A. (2005). Police reform and the problem of trust. *Theoretical Criminology*, 9, 443-470.

Goldsmith, C. (2008). Cameras, cops and contracts: What anti-social behaviour management feels like to young people. In Squires, P. (ed.), *ASBO Nation: The Criminalisation of Nuisance*. Bristol: Policy Press.

Gregory, F. (2010). Policing the "new extremism" in 21st Century Britain. In Goodwin, R., & Eatwell, M. J. (eds.), *The "New" Extremism in 21st Century Britain*. London: Taylor & Francis.

Hague, G., & Malos, E. (2005). *Domestic Violence; Action for Change*. Cheltenham: New Clarion Press.

Hall, T., & Wright. S. (2003). *Making it Count: A Practical Guide To Collecting and Managing Domestic Violence Data*. London: NACRO.

Hammelmann, H. A. (1958). Committee on Homosexual Offences and Prostitution. *Modern Law Review*, 21, 68-73.

Hand, T., & Dodd, L. (2009). *Police Powers and Procedures England and Wales 2007/8*. Home Office Statistical Bulletin 07/09. London: Home Office.

Hanniman, W. (2008). Canadian Muslims, Islamophobia and National Security *International Journal of Law, Crime and Justice*, 36, 271-285.

Hanson, R.K., Bourgon, G., Helmus, L., & Hodgson, S.A. (2009). The principles of effective correctional treatment also apply to sexual offenders: A meta-analysis. *Criminal Justice and Behavior*, 37, 477-481.

Hanson, R.K., Harris, A.J.R., & Morton, K.E. (2003). Sexual offender recidivism risk: What we know and what we need to know. *Sexually Coercive Behavior: Annals of the New York Academy of Sciences*, 989, 154-166.

Harkins, L., & Beech, A.R. (2011). Paraphilias and sexual offending. In Sturmey, M., & M. Hersen, (eds.), *Handbook of Evidence-based Practice in Clinical Psychology, Volume 2*. Hoboken, NJ: Wiley.

Hart, S. D., Laws, D. R., Kropp, P. R., Klaver, J., Logan, C., & Watt, K. A. (2003). *Structured Professional Guidelines for Assessing Risk of Sexual Violence: the Risk of Sexual Violence Protocol*. Burnaby, BC Canada: Simon Fraser University, Mental Health, Law and Policy Institute.

Harwin, N., & Barron, J. (2000). Domestic violence and social policy perspectives from Women's Aid. In Hanmer, J., *Home Truths about Domestic Violence: Feminist Influences on Policy and Practice – A Reader*. Oxford: Routledge.

Hawkins, K. (2003). *Law as Last Resort*. Oxford: Oxford University Press.

Heise, L. L. (1998). Violence against women: An integrated ecological framework. *Violence Against Women*, 4, 262-290.

Henry, S., & Milovanovic, D. (1999). Constitutive Criminology: Origins, core concepts, and evaluation. *Social Justice*, 27, 268-290.

Hillyard, P. (1993). *Suspect Community: People's Experiences of the Prevention of Terrorism Acts in Britain*. London: Pluto Press.

(2005) *The "War on Terror": Lessons From Ireland, Essays for Civil Liberties and Democracy in Europe*. European Civil Liberties Network in Europe. www.ecln.org/essays/essay-1.pdf

HM Government, (2007). *PSA Delivery Agreement 21: Build More Cohesive, Empowered and Active Communities*. London: TSO.

(2009) *PSA Delivery Agreement 23: Make Communities Safer*. London: TSO.

(2010) *The Coalition: Our Programme for Government*. London: TSO.

Hobsbawm, E. (1994). *Age of Extremes: The Short Twentieth Century, 1914-1991*. London: Abacus.

Hoffman, S., & Macdonald, S. (2010). Should the ASBO be civilized? *Criminal Law Review*, 6, 457-473.

Home Office, (2002). *Respect and Responsibility*. London: Home Office.

(2002) *The Safer Communities Initiative. Circular 14/200*. London: Home Office.

(2003) *Building Safer Communities Together*. London: TSO.

(2003) *Respect and Responsibility – Taking a Stand Against Anti-Social Behaviour*. White Paper, Cm 5778. London: TSO.

(2003) *Safety and Justice – The Government's Proposals on Domestic Violence*, London: TSO.

(2004) *Building Communities, Beating Crime*. White Paper, Cm 6360. London. TSO.

(2004) *Defining and Measuring Anti-Social Behaviour*. Development and Practice Report 26. London: TSO.

(2005) *National Report on Domestic Violence*. London: TSO.

(2006) *A Guide to Anti-Social Behaviour Orders*. London: Home Office.

(2007) *National Community Safety Plan 2008-11*. London: Home Office.

(2008) *The Way Ahead for Safer Communities: Government Response to Casey Review*. London: Home Office.

(2008) *From the Neighbourhood to the National: Policing our Communities Together*. Green Paper, Cm 7448. London: Home Office.

(2009) *Delivering the Prevent Strategy: An Updated Guide for Local Partners 2009*. Office of Security and Counter-Terrorism. London: Home Office.

Hood, C. (1991). A Public Management for all Seasons? *Public Administration*, 69, 3-19.

Hopkins Burke, R., & Morrill, R. (2002). Anti-social behaviour orders: An infringement of the Human Rights Act 1998? *Nottingham Law Journal,* 11, 2, 1-16.

Hornqvist, M. (2007). *The Organised Nature of Power: On Productive and Repressive Based Consideration of Risk.* Stockholm: Stockholm University.

House of Commons Justice Committee (2009). *The Case for Justice Reinvestment,* First Report, 'Cutting Crime', London: TSO.

(2010) *Time for a Fresh Start,* Report of the Independent Commission on Youth Crime and Antisocial Behaviour. London: TSO.

Howell, J. (2006). The global war on terror. *Development and Civil Society,* 18, 121-135.

Hudson, B. (2003). *Justice in the Risk Society.* London: Sage.

Huebner, B., Schafer, J., & Bynum, T. (2004). African-American and White Perceptions of Police Services: Within and between group variation. *Journal of Criminal Justice,* 32, 123-155.

Hughes, G. (2007). *The Politics of Crime and Community.* Basingstoke: Palgrave Macmillan.

Hughes, G., & Rowe, M. (2007). Neighborhood policing and community safety: Researching the instabilities of the local governance of crime, disorder and security in contemporary UK. *Criminology and Criminal Justice,* 7, 317-346.

Husak, (1995). The nature and justifiability of non-consummate offenses. *Arizona Law Review,* 37, 151-158.

Inamdar, R. (1970). *Functioning of Village Panchayat.* Bombay: Popular Prakashan.

Innes, M. (2004). Reinventing tradition? Reassurance, neighbourhood policing and security. *Criminal Justice,* 4, 151-171.

(2006) Policing uncertainty: Countering terror through community intelligence and democratic policing. *Annals of the American Academy of Political and Social Science,* 605, 1-20.

Innes, M., Abbotts, L., Loew, T., & Roberts, C. (2007). *Hearts and Minds and Eyes and Ears: Reducing Radicalisation Risks Through Reassurance-Oriented Policing.* Cardiff University: Universities Police Science Institute.

Ipsos MORI, (2006). *Attitudes Towards Teenagers and Crime.* London: Ipsos MORI.

Ireland, S. (2005). Anti-social behaviour orders: A nail in the coffin of due process? *Justice Journal,* 94-102.

Jaccoud, M. (1998). Restoring justice in native communities in Canada. In Walgrave, L. (ed.), *Restorative Justice for Juveniles: Potentialities, Risks and Problems for Research.* Leuven: Leuven University Press.

Jackson, J., Bradford, B., Hohl, K., & Farrell, S. (2009). Does fear of crime erode public confidence in policing? *Policing*, 3, 100-111.

Jacobson, J., & Gibbs, P. (2009). *Making Amends: Restorative Youth Justice in Northern Ireland*. London: Prison Reform Trust.

James, A., & Raine, J. (1998). *The New Politics of Criminal Justice*. Harlow: Addison Wesley Longman.

Johnson, N. (2009). *Identity, Ethnic Diversity and Community Cohesion*. London: Sage.

Johnston, L. (2006). Diversifying police recruitment? The deployment of police community support officers in London. *Howard Journal of Criminal Justice*, 45, 388-402.

Johnstone, G. (2002). *Restorative Justice: Ideas, Values, Debates*. Cullompton: Willan.

Jones, T., & Newburn, T. (2001). *Widening access: improving police relations with hard to reach groups. Police Research Series, 138*. London: Home Office. www.homeoffice.gov.uk/rds/prgpdfs/prs138.pdf

Judicial Studies Board (2007) *Anti-Social Behaviour Orders: A Guide for the Judiciary*, 3rd Edn. London: Judicial Studies Board.

Karp, D. (ed.) (1998). *Community Justice: An Emerging Field*. Lanham, MD: Rowman and Littlefield Publishers.

Keasey, P. (2010). *Do Police Community Support Officers Reduce the Fear of Crime in Local Communities?* Unpublished MSc Dissertation, Institute of Local Government Studies, University of Birmingham.

Kemshall, H. (1998). Defensible decisions for risk: Or it's the doers wot get the blame. *Probation Journal*, 45, 67-72.

(2001) *Risk assessment and management of known sexual and violent offenders: A review of current issues. Home Office: Police Series Research Paper, 140*. www.homeoffice.gov.uk/rds/prgpdfs/prs140.pdf

(2008) *Understanding the Community Management of High Risk Offenders*. Milton Keynes: Open University Press.

(2010) Risk rationalities in contemporary social work policy and practice. *British Journal of Social Work*, 40, 1247-1262.

Kemshall, H., & Wood, J. (2009). Community strategies for managing high-risk offenders: The contribution of multi-agency public protection arrangements. In Beech, A., Craig, L., & Browne, K. D., *Assessment and Treatment of Sex Offenders: A Handbook*. Chichester: Wiley.

Kemshall, H., Wood, J., Mackenzie, G., Bailey, R., & Yates, J. (2005). *Strengthening Multi-Agency Public Protection Arrangements (MAPPA)*. London: Home Office.

Kemshall, H., Wood, J., Westwood, S., Stout, B., Wilkinson, B., Kelly, G., & Mackenzie, G. (2010). *Child Sex Offender Review (CSOR) Public Disclosure Pilots: A process evaluation.* Research Report, 32. London: Home Office. www.homeoffice.gov.uk/rds/pdfs10/horr32c.pdf

Kiralfy, A. (1992). Taking the will for the deed: The medieval criminal attempt. *The Journal of Legal History*, 13, 95-100.

Klausen, J. (2009). British counter-terrorism after 7/7: Adapting community policing to the fight against domestic terrorism. *Journal of Ethnic and Migration Studies*, 35, 403-420.

Koss, M. (2000). Blame, shame, and community: Justice responses to violence against women. *American Psychologist*, 55, 1332-1343.

Labour Party, (1995). *A Quiet Life: Tough Action on Criminal Neighbours.* London: Labour Party.

Lacey, N., & Zedner, L. (1995). Discourses on community in criminal justice. *Journal of Law and Society*, 22, 301-325.

Lambert, R. (2008). Empowering Salafis and Islamists Against al-Qaida: A London counter-terrorism case study. *Political Science and Politics*, 41, 31-35.

(2010) *London Police and Muslim Londoners: Countering al-Qaida in Partnership.* Unpublished PhD. University of Exeter.

Levitas, R. (2005). *The Inclusive Society?* 2nd Edition. Basingstoke: Palgrave Macmillan.

Lockton, D., & Ward, R. (1997). *Domestic Violence.* London: Cavendish.

Lowe, T., & Innes, M. (2008). Countering terror: Violent radicalisation and situational intelligence. *Prison Service Journal*, 179, 3-10.

Lyons, J. (2009). 'Hoodie hell on streets every 8 secs', *Daily Mirror*, 4th February.

Macdonald, S., & Telford, M. (2007). The use of ASBOs against young people in England and Wales: Lessons from Scotland. *Legal Studies*, 27, 604-629.

Macdonald, S. (2003). The nature of the anti-social behaviour order- 'R (McCann & Others) v Crown Court at Manchester'. *Modern Law Review*, 66, 630-639.

(2006) A suicidal woman, roaming pigs and a noisy trampolinist: Refining the ASBOs definition of anti-social behaviour. *Modern Law Review*, 69, 183-213.

Maguire, M. (2004). The Crime Reduction Programme in England and Wales: reflections on the vision and the reality. *Criminology and Criminal Justice*, 4, 213-237.

(2006) Crime Data and Statistics. In Maguire, M., Morgan, R.P., & Rainer, P. (eds.). *The Oxford Handbook of Criminology*. 4th Edition, Oxford: Oxford University Press.

Mama, A. (1989). *The Hidden Struggle: Statutory and Voluntary Responses to Violence Against Black Women in the Home*, London Race and Housing Research Unit. London: Runnymede Trust.

Margo, J., & Dixon, M. (2006). *Freedom's Orphans: Raising Youth in a Changing World*. London: Institute for Public Policy Research.

Marshall, T. (1999). *Restorative Justice: An Overview*. London: Home Office.

Maruna, S., & Immarigeon, R. (2004). *After Crime and Punishment: Pathways to Offender Reintegration*. Cullompton: Willan.

Mayer, C. (2008). Britain's Mean Streets. *Time Magazine*, March 26th.

Mazher, I., & Abbas, T. (eds.) (2011). *Honour, Violence, Women and Islam*. Oxford: Routledge.

McAlinden, A. (2008). Restorative justice as a response to sexual offending – Addressing the failings of current punitive approaches. *Sexual Offender Treatment*, 3, 1-12.

McCold, P. (1996). Restorative justice and the role of community. In Galaway, B., & Hudson. J. (eds.), *Restorative Justice: International Perspectives*. Monsey, New York: Criminal Justice Press.

(2004) What is the role of community in restorative justice theory and practice? In Zehr, H., & Toews, B. (eds.), *Critical Issues in Restorative Justice*. Monsey, New York: Criminal Justice Press.

(2008) The recent history of restorative justice: mediation, circles, and conferencing. In Sullivan, D., & Tifft, L. (eds.), *Handbook of Restorative Justice*. Oxford: Routledge.

McCold, P., & Wachtel, B. (1998). Community is not a place: A new look at community justice initiatives. *Contemporary Justice Review*, 1, 71-85.

(2002) Restorative justice theory validation. In Weitekamp, E., & H-J Kerner. (eds.), *Restorative Justice: Theoretical Foundations*, Cullompton: Willan.

McCulloch, T., & McNeill, F. (2007). Commodification and offender management. *Criminology and Criminal Justice*, 7, 223-242.

McCulloch, J., & Pickering, S. (2009). Pre-Crime & Counter terrorism: Imagining future crime in the war on terror. *British Journal of Criminology*, 18, 121-135.

McEvoy, K., & Ellison, G. (2003). Criminological discourses in Northern Ireland: Conflict & conflict resolution. In McEvoy, K., & Newburn, T. (eds.), *Criminology, Conflict Resolution, and Restorative Justice*. Basingstoke: Palgrave Macmillan.

McEvoy, K., & Mika, H. (2002). Restorative Justice and the critique of informalism in Northern Ireland. *British Journal of Criminology*, 42, 534-562.

McNeil, F. (2009). What works and what's just? *European Journal of Probation*, 1, 221-420.

(2009) *Towards Effective Practice in Offender Supervision*. Glasgow: Scottish Centre for Crime and Justice Research.

McSherry, B., Norrie, A., & Bronitt, S. (eds.). (2009). Expanding the boundaries of inchoate crimes: The growing reliance on preparatory offences. In McSherrry, B., Norrie, A., & Bronitt, S. (eds.), *Regulating Deviance: The Redirection of Criminalisation and the Futures of Criminal Law*. Oxford: Hart.

Merritt, J., & Dingwall, G. (2010). Does plural suit rural? Reflections on quasi-policing in the countryside. *International Journal of Police Science and Management*, 12, 388-400.

Millie, A. (2008). Anti-social behaviour, behavioural expectations and an urban aesthetic. *British Journal of Criminology*, 48, 379-394.

Millie, A., Jacobson, J., McDonald, E., & Hough, M. (2005). *Anti-Social Behaviour Strategies: Finding a Balance*. Bristol: Policy Press.

Ministry of Justice, (2007). *Evaluation of the North Liverpool Community Justice Centre*, Ministry of Justice Research Series 12/07. London: TSO.

Morgan, R. (2009). Children, young people; criminalisation and punishment. In Barry, M., & McNeill, F. (eds.), *Youth Offending and Youth Justice*. London: Jessica Kingsley Publishers.

Morley, R. (2000). *Domestic Violence and Housing Home Truths about Domestic Violence: Feminist Influences on Policy and Practice – A Reader*. Oxford: Routledge.

Morris, A. (2002). Critiquing the critics: A brief response to critics of restorative justice. *British Journal of Criminology*, 42, 596-604.

Morris, A., & Maxwell, G. (2000). The practice of family group conferences in New Zealand: assessing the place, potential and pitfalls of restorative justice. In Crawford, A., & Goodey, J. (eds.), *Integrating a Victim Perspective within Criminal Justice: International debates*. Aldershot: Ashgate/Dartmouth.

Morris, A., & Young, W. (2000). Reforming criminal justice: The potential of restorative justice. In Strang, H., & Braithwaite, J. (eds.), *Restorative Justice: Philosophy to Practice*. Aldershot: Ashgate/Dartmouth.

Mullende, A., & Burton, S. (2000). *Reducing Domestic Violence What Works? Perpetrator Programmes*, Policing and Reducing Crime Unit, Crime Reduction Research Series. London: Home Office. www.rds.homeoffice.gov.uk/rds/prgp-dfs/perpet.pdf

Musgrove, A., & Groves, N. (2007). The Domestic Violence, Crime and Victims Act 2004; Relevant or removed legislation. *Journal of Social Welfare and Family Law*, 29, 233-244.

Myhill, A. (2004). *Engagement in Policing: Lessons from the literature*. London: Home Office.

Mythen, G., & Walklate, S. (2006). Criminology and terrorism. *British Journal of Criminology*, 46, 379-398.

(2008) Terrorism, risk and international security: The perils of asking what if? *Security Dialogue*, 39, 2, 221-242.

NACRO, (2008). *Some facts about children and young people who offend – 2006*. Youth Crime Briefing, London: NACRO.

(2009) *Some facts about children and young people who offend – 2007*. Youth Crime Briefing, London: NACRO.

Newburn, T., Crawford, A., & Earle, R. (2002). *The Introduction of Referral Orders into the Youth Justice System: Final Report*. London: Home Office.

Newbury, A. (2008). Youth Crime: Whose Responsibility? *Journal of Law and Society*, 35, 131-149.

Newman, J. (2001). *Modernizing Governance: New Labour, Policy and Society*. London: Sage.

Nichols, C. M., Callanan, M., Legard, R., Tomaszewski, T., Purdon, S., & Webster, S. (2010). *Examining implementation of the Stable and Acute dynamic risk assessment tool pilot in England and Wales*. London: Ministry of Justice. www.justice.gov.uk/about/docs/sexual-offenders-risk.pdf

Nutley, S., Walter, I., & Davies, H. (2007). *Using Evidence: How Research Can Inform Public Service*. Bristol: Policy Press.

Office for Criminal Justice Reform, (2009). *Engaging Communities in Criminal Justice*, Green Paper Cm 7583. London: Home Office.

Olsen, T., Maxwell, G., & Morris, A. (1995). Maori and Youth Justice in New Zealand. In Hazlehurst, K. (ed.), *Popular Justice and Community Regeneration: Pathways of Indigenous Reform*. Westport, CT: Praeger.

Outshoorn, J. (2005). The political debates on prostitution and trafficking of women. *Social Politics: International Studies in Gender, State and Society*, 12, 141-155.

Owen, J. R., & Owen, S. (2006). Domestic violence and rough music: A case of community-based intervention. *British Journal of Community Justice*, 4, 9-22.

Packer, H. (1968). *Limits of the Criminal Sanction*. Stanford, CA: Stanford University Press.

Pahl, J. (1985). *Private Violence and Public Policy*. London: Routledge.

Pantazis, C., & Pemberton, C. (2009). From the old to the new suspect community: Examining the impacts of recent UK counter-terrorist legislation. *British Journal of Criminology*, 49, 646-666.

Pearson, G. (2006). Hybrid law and human rights–banning and behaviour orders in the appeal courts. *Liverpool Law Review*, 27, 125-145.

Pence, E., & McMahon, M. (1999). Duluth: A co-ordinated community response to domestic violence. In N. Harwin et al., *The Multi-Agency Approach to Domestic Violence: New Opportunities, Old Challenges?* London: Whiting and Birch.

Petrunik, M. (2002). Managing unacceptable risk: Sex offenders, community response and social policy in the United States and Canada. *International Journal of Offender Therapy and Comparative Criminology*, 46, 483-511.

Phoenix, J. (2009). Beyond risk assessment: The return of repressive welfarism. In Barry, M., & McNeil, F. (eds.), *Youth Offending and Youth Justice*. London: Jessica Kingsley Publishers.

Power, M. (2004). *The Risk Management of Everything* (2004). London: DEMOS.

Powis, B. (2002). *Offenders' Risk of Serious Harm: A Literature Review*. Home Office RDS Occasional Paper 81. London: Home Office.

Poynting, S., & Mason, V. (2006). The new integrationism, the state and Islamophobia: Retreat from multiculturalism in Australia. *International Journal of Law, Crime and Justice*, 36, 230-246.

Pranis, K. (2002). Restorative values and confronting family violence. In Strang, H., & Braithwaite, J. (eds.), *Restorative Justice and Family Violence*. Cambridge: Cambridge University Press.

Prior, D. (2009). The "problem" of anti-social behaviour and the policy knowledge base: Analyzing the power/knowledge relationship. *Critical Social Policy*, 29, 5-23.

Prior, D., Stewart, J., & Walsh, K. (1995). *Citizenship: Rights, Community and Participation*. London: Pitman.

Raine, J. (2009). Engaging Communities in Criminal Justice: An Appraisal. *EuroVista*, 1, 26-31.

Raine, J., & Willson, M. (1993). *Managing Criminal Justice*. Hemel Hempstead: Harvester Wheatsheaf.

Reisig, M. D., & Parks, R. (2000). Experience, quality of life and neighbourhood context: A hierarchical analysis of satisfaction with the police. *Justice Quarterly*, 17, 607-629.

Respect Task Force, (2006). *Respect Action Plan*. London: Home Office.

Ringen, S. (1997). Family change and family policies: Great Britain. In Kamerman, S., & Kahn. A. (eds.), *Family Change and Family Polices in the West, Vol. 1*. Oxford: Clarendon Press.

Roberts, C. (2004). Offending behaviour programmes: Emerging evidence and implications for practice. In Burnett, R., & Roberts, C. (eds.), *What Works in Probation and Youth Justice, Developing evidence based practice*. Cullompton: Willan.

Roberts, J., & Hough, M. (2005). *Understanding Public Attitudes to Criminal Justice*. Maidenhead: McGraw-Hill Education.

Robinson, A., & Cook, D. (2006). Understanding victim retraction in cases of domestic violence: specialist courts, government policy and victim-centred justice. *Contemporary Justice Review*, 9, 189–213.

Robinson, D., (2008). Community cohesion and the politics of communitarianism. In Flint, J., & Robinson, D. (eds.), *Community Cohesion in Crisis?* Bristol: Policy Press.

Rohit, M., & Neelam, R. (2007). Panchayats turn into kangaroo courts. *The Times of India–Special Report*, 9 September.

Rose, N. (1999). *Powers of Freedom*. Cambridge: Cambridge University Press.

Rutherford, A. (2000). An elephant on the doorstep: Criminal policy without crime in New Labour's Britain. In Green, P., & Rutherford, A. (eds.) *Criminal Policy in Transition*. Oxford: Hart Publishing.

Sadasivam, B. (2000). *Community Justice: West Bengal's Women Draw on Village Tradition to Stop Domestic Violence*. London: Ford Foundation.

Sadurski, W. (1985). *Giving Desert its Due: Social Justice and Legal Theory*. Dordrecht: D Reidal Publishing Company.

Sanders, A. (2008). Can coercive powers be effectively controlled or regulated? The Case for Anchored Pluralism. In Cape, E., & Young, R. (eds.), *Regulating Policing*. Oxford: Hart Publishing.

Sanders, A. (2010). Reconciling the apparently different goals of criminal justice & regulation: the freedom perspective. In Quirk, H., Seddon, T., & Smith, G. (eds.), *Regulation and Criminal Justice*. Cambridge: Cambridge University Press.

Sanders, A., Young, R., & Burton, M. (2010). *Criminal Justice*, 4th Edition. Oxford: Oxford University Press.

Sarat, A. (1997). Vengeance, victims and the identities of law. *Social and Legal Studies*, 6, 163-189.

Savage, S. (2010). More accountability – Less regulation? Coalition plans for policing. *British Society of Criminology Newsletter*, 66, 10-12.

Schwalbe, C. (2004). Re-visioning risk assessment for human service decision-making. *Children and Youth Services Review*, 26, 561-576.

Sharp, D., & Atherton, S. (2007). To serve and protect? The experiences of policing in the community of young people from black and other ethnic minority groups. *British Journal of Criminology*, 47, 746-763.

Sheridan, L. (2006). Islamophobia pre and post September 11th, 2001. *Journal of Interpersonal Violence*, 21, 317-336.

Simester, A. P., & Smith, A.T.H. (eds.). (1996). *Harm and Culpability*, Oxford: Clarendon Press.

Simester, A. P., & von Hirsch, A. (2006). Regulating offensive conduct through two-step prohibitions. In von Hirsch, A., & Simester, A. P. (eds.), *Incivilities: Regulating Offensive Behaviour*. Oxford: Hart Publishing.

Sivanandan, A. (1981). From resistance to rebellion. *Race and Class*, 23, 111-152.

Skoga, W. (2006). Asymmetry in the impact of encounters with the police. *Policing and Society*, 16, 99-126.

Smith, D. J. (2006). Social inclusion and early desistance from crime. *Edinburgh Study of Youth Transitions and Crime Research Digest*, 12. Edinburgh: University of Edinburgh.

Smith, D.J., & Gray, J. (1985). *Police and People in London: The PSI Report*. Aldershot: Gower.

Smith, D. J., & McVie, S. (2003). Theory and method in the Edinburgh Study of youth transitions and crime. *British Journal of Criminology*, 43, 169-195.

Smith, J. C. (1971). The element of chance in criminal liability. *Criminal Law Review*, 63-75.

Social Exclusion Unit. (2002). *Reducing re-offending by ex-prisoners*. Cabinet Office, London: HMSO.

Souhami, A. (2008). Multi-agency practice: Experiences in the youth justice system. In Green, S., Lancaster, E., & Feasey, S. (eds.), *Addressing Offending Behaviour: Context, Practice and Values*. Cullompton: Willan..

Spalek, B., El-Awa, S., & McDonald, L. (2009) *Police-Muslim Engagement and Partnerships for the Purposes of Counter-Terrorism: An examination*. Birmingham: University of Birmingham.

Spalek B., & Lambert, R. (2008). Muslim communities, counter-terrorism and de-radicalisation: A reflective approach to engagement. *International Journal of Law, Crime and Justice*, 36, 257-270.

Spalek, B., & McDonald, L. (2010). Anti-social behaviour powers and the policing of security. *Social Policy and Society*, 9, 123-133.

Squires, P., & Stephen, D. (2005). *Rougher Justice: Anti-social Behaviour and Young People*. Cullompton: Willan.

Stohl, M. (2008). Networks, terrorists and criminals: The implications for community policing. *Crime, Law and Social Change*, 50, 59-72.

Stubbs, J. (1997). Shame, defiance, & violence against women: A critical analysis of "communitarian conferencing". In Cook, S., & Bessant, J. (eds.), *Women's Encounters with Violence: Australian Experiences*. London: Sage.

Stuntz, W.L. (1997). The uneasy relationship between criminal procedure and criminal justice. *Yale Law Journal* 107, 65-74.

Sutherland, A., Merrington, S., Jones, S., Baker, K., & Roberts, C. (2005). *Role of Risk and Protective Factors*. London: Youth Justice Board.

Tadros, V. (2007). Rethinking the presumption of innocence. *Criminal Law and Philosophy*, 1, 139-231.

Tan, C., Basta, J., Sullivan, C. M., & Davidson, W. S. (1995). The role of social support in the lives of women exiting domestic violence shelters: An experimental study. *Journal of Interpersonal Violence*, 10, 437-451.

Tauri, J., & Morris, A. (1997). Re-forming justice: The potential of Maori processes. *Australian and New Zealand Journal of Criminology,* 30, 149-167.

Thornton, D., Mann, R., Webster, S., Blud, L., Travers, R, Friendship, C., & Erikson, M. (2004). Distinguishing and Combining Risks for Sexual and Violent Recidivism. In Prentky, R., Janus, E., Seto, M., and Burgess, A. W. (eds.), *Understanding and managing sexually coercive behavior. Annals of the New York Academy of Sciences,* 989, 225-235.

Titterton, M. (2004). *Risk and Risk Taking In Health and Social Welfare.* London: Jessica Kingsley Publishers.

Tonry, M., & Farrington, D. (eds.) (1995). *Community Crime Prevention: Building a Safer Society.* Chicago, IL: University of Chicago Press.

Trechsel, S., & Summers, S. (2005). *Human Rights in Criminal Proceedings.* Oxford: Oxford University Press.

Truss, L. (2005). *Talk to the Hand: The Utter Bloody Rudeness of Everyday Life.* London: Profile Books.

Turam, B. (2004). The politics of engagement between Islam and the secular state: ambivalences of civil society. *The British Journal of Sociology,* 55, 258-281.

Umbreit, M. (1994). *Victim Meets Offender: The Impact of Restorative Justice and Mediation.* Monsey, New York: Criminal Justice Press.

Van Ness, D. (2002). The shape of things to come: a framework for thinking about a restorative justice system. In Weitekamp, E., & Kerner, H-J. (eds.), *Restorative Justice: Theoretical Foundations.* Cullompton: Willan.

Virta, S. (2006). Community policing. In McLaughlin, E. & Muncie, J. (eds.), *The Sage Dictionary of Criminology,* 2nd edition. London: Sage.

(2008) Community policing meets new challenges. In Virta, S. (ed.), *Policing Meets New Challenges: Preventing Radicalization and Recruitment.* Department of Management Studies, CEPOL, Finland: University of Tampere.

von Hirsch A. (1996). Extending the harm principle: Remote harms and fair imputation. In Simester P & Smith, A. T. H. (eds.), *Harm and Culpability.* Oxford: Clarenden Press.

von Hirsch, V., Roberts, V., Bottoms, A., Roach, K., & Schiff, M. (eds.). (2003). *Restorative Justice and Criminal Justice: Competing or Reconcilable Paradigms.* Oxford: Hart Publishing.

Waiton, S. (2008) Asocial not anti-social: The Respect Agenda and the therapeutic me. In Squires, P. (ed.), *ASBO Nation: The Criminalisation of Nuisance*. Bristol: Policy Press.

(2009) Policing after the crisis: Crime, safety and the vulnerable public. *Punishment and Society*, 11, 359-376.

Walgrave, L. (2002). Restorative justice and the law: The case for an integrated, systemic approach. In Walgrave, L. (ed.), *Restorative Justice and the Law*. Cullompton: Willan.

(2008) *Restorative Justice, Self-Interest and Responsible Citizenship*. Cullompton: Willan.

Walker, A., Flately, J., Kershaw, C., & Moon, D. (eds.). (2009). *Crime in England and Wales, 2008/09. Findings from the British Crime Survey, and Police Recorded Crime. Home Office Statistical Bulletin 11/09*. London: Home Office. www.homeoffice.gov.uk/rds/pdfs09/hosb1109vol1.pdf

Walker, C. (2009). *Blackstone's Guide to the Anti-Terrorism Legislation*. 2nd edition. Oxford: Oxford University Press.

Walklate, S., & Mythen, G. (2008). How scared are we? *British Journal of Criminology*, 48, 209-225.

Walklate, S. (2001). *Gender, Crime and Criminal Justice*. Cullompton: Willan.

(2003) *Understanding Criminology: Current Theoretical Debates*. Milton Keynes: Open University Press.

Ward, T., & Brown, M. (2004). The Good Lives Model and conceptual issues in offender rehabilitation. *Psychology, Crime and Law*, 10, 243-257.

Wellar, P., Feldman, A., & Purdam, K. (2001). *Religious Discrimination in England and Wales*, Home Office Research Development and Statistics Directorate. London: Home Office.

Whitehead, C., Stockdale, J., & Razzu, G. (2003). *The Economic and Social Costs of Anti-Social Behaviour*. London: London School of Economics.

Whitehead, P. (2007). Target practice in probation: Take aim for a reappraisal. *British Journal of Community Justice*, 5, 83-95.

Whyte, D., (2007). Victims of corporate crime. In Walklate, S. (ed.), *Handbook of Victims and Victimology*. Cullompton: Willan.

Wikström, P., & Treiber, K. (2008). *Offending Behaviour Programmes: Source Document*. London: Youth Justice Board.

Williams, A., & Thompson, B. (2004). Vigilance or vigilantes: The Paulsgrove riots and policing paedophiles in the community: Part 1: The Long Slow Fuse, and Part 2: The Lessons of Paulsgrove. *Police Journal*, 77, 99-119 and 193-206.

Wilson, D. (2004). Quality time with paedophiles, *The Guardian*, 18th November.

Wilson, R. J., Picheca, J. E., & Prinzo, M. (2005). *An Evaluation of the Pilot Project in South-Central Ontario, Circles of Support & Accountability*. Ottawa: Correctional Services of Canada. www.csc-scc.gc.ca/text/rsrch/reports/r168/r168_e.pdf

Young, J. (1998). From inclusive to exclusive society: Nightmares in the European dream. In Ruggerio, V., South, N., & Taylor, I. (eds.), *The New European Criminology: Crime and Social Order in Europe*. London: Routledge.

Young, R. (2008). Street Policing after PACE: The drift to summary justice. In Cape, E., & Young, R. (eds.), *Regulating Policing*. Oxford: Hart Publishing.

Youth Justice Board, (2008). *Youth Justice Annual Workload Data 2006/7*. London: Youth Justice Board.

Zedner, L. (2007). Seeking security by eroding rights: The side-stepping of due process. In Goold, B. J., & Lazarus, L. (eds.). *Security and Human Rights*. Oxford: Hart Publishing.

(2007) Pre-crime and post criminology? *Theoretical Criminology*, 11, 1362-1386.

Zehr, H. (1990). *Changing Lenses: A New Focus for Crime and Justice*. Scottdale, PA: Herald Press.

(2002) *The Little Book of Restorative Justice*. Intercourse, PA: Good Books.

Zehr, H., & Mika, H. (1998). Fundamental concepts of restorative justice. *Contemporary Justice Review*, 1, 47-53.

INDEX

Symbols

9/11 *125, 132, 134, 138*

A

abuse
  police by *57*
  sexual abuse *206*
  sexual abuse of children *234*
  wife abuse *224*
alcohol *55, 180*
al-Qaeda *125, 132, 138*
Anti-Social Behaviour Act 2003 *198*
anti-social behaviour (ASB) *16, 22, 25, 26, 27, 29, 34, 38, 162, 168, 169, 176, 178, 179, 183, 187, 194, 195, 196, 197, 198, 201, 202, 203, 243, 244, 245, 248, 251, 252*
  anti-social behaviour order (ASBO) *28, 33, 39, 43, 45, 88, 90, 91, 92, 93, 95, 97, 103, 105, 170, 199, 247, 250*
    fair trial *94, 104*
    legal status *94, 104*
    manipulation of the law *87*
    original proposals for *88, 101*
    proceeding for *95*
  anti-social environments *109*

Anti Terrorism, Crime and Security Act 2001 *128*
Association of Chief Officers of Police (ACPO) *211*

B

Big Society *17, 49, 87, 141, 146, 157, 171, 184, 250*
British Crime Survey (BCS) *18, 226*
burglary *38*

C

CCTV *175*
Circles of Support *217, 220*
Circles of Support and Accountability *215*
Circles UK *215, 217*
citizenship *123, 160, 161*
civil law *46*
civil order *209*
civil-penal orders *34*
Clarke, Kenneth MP *25*
Coalition *15, 17, 28, 87, 145, 157, 171, 184, 249, 250*
Code of Practice for Victims of Crime *40*
communitarianism *161*
community-based policing *132*
community-based sentencing *251, 252*
community-based strategies *159*

277

community engagement *130, 185*
Community Impact Statement *183*
community integration *214*
community justice *173, 188, 201, 244*
community justice centre *177*
community order *181*
Community Payback *183*
community-police relations *131*
community policing *124, 131*
Community Prosecutor *183*
Community Reference Group *180, 181*
community safety *160*
community service order (former) *175*
confidence *19, 179*
   public confidence *20*
CONTEST *129, 134*
Court of Appeal *93, 98, 210*
covert action *34*
covert policing *46*
crime
   crime control *36*
crime and disorder *145, 146, 157, 159, 160, 170, 244*
Crime and Disorder Act 1998 *89, 94, 96, 98, 102, 103, 104, 159, 162, 163, 168, 195, 198, 207*
   CDA *101*
crime control *37, 41, 44, 45, 159, 161, 162*
crime-fighting *87*
crime prevention *109, 174, 175, 178*
crime reduction *16, 108, 160*
criminal

criminal liability *53, 56, 59, 65, 66*
   strict liability *70, 82*
criminal offence *52*
   must be defined *51*
criminal sanction *53*
criminalisation *51, 52, 53, 224*
   risk of inappropriate criminalisation *64*
criminal justice
   criminal justice agencies *16, 21, 24, 107, 120, 122*
   criminal justice system *19, 23*
   Office for Criminal Justice Reform *27*
Criminal Justice Act 2003 *98, 117, 181, 208*
Criminal Justice and Court Services Act 2000 *207*
Criminal Justice and Immigration Act 2008 *117*
Criminal Justice Board
   Local Criminal Justice Board *23*
   National Criminal Justice Board *23*
criminal justice system
   as a 'tool kit' *84*
Crown Court *230*
Crown Prosecution Service (CPS) *40, 183*
curfew *93*
   child curfew order *162*
custody
   custodial net-widening *92*

D

dangerousness *60*
decentralisation *185*
deterrence
    lack of *78*
dispersal order *200*
DNA
    DNA databanks *48*
domestic extremism *203*
domestic violence *25, 29, 33, 168, 223, 227, 228, 233, 234, 236, 239, 240, 244, 249*
    community responses, etc. *229, 237*
    crimes *223*
    definition *225*
    hidden nature, etc. *226*
    in the USA *235*
    offender treatment programmes, etc. *231*
Domestic Violence and Victims Act 2004 *224, 228*
Domestic Violence Intervention Project (DVIP) *235*
drugs *180*
    drug abuse *38*
due process *36, 41, 44, 45*

E

electronic monitoring *238*
empowerment *249*
Engel criteria *100*
environment
    Environment Agency *34, 92*
European Convention on Human Rights (ECHR) *37, 38, 88, 93, 94, 97, 98, 105*
European Court of Human Rights (ECtHR) *41, 98*
evidence-based influences *118*
exclusion zones *93*
ex offenders *142*
extremism *123, 203*

F

Family Law Act 1996 *228*
fear
    fear of crime *19, 20, 21, 179*
Finland
    Penal Code *71*
fixed penalty *39*
Forest Gate *133*
Fraud Act 2006 *55*
freedom *33*
    erosion of freedom *33*
    'freedom' approach *28*
    Freedom Perspective *246*

G

Good Lives Model *116*
graffiti *91*
guns *168*

H

harm 37, 51, 53, 54, 56, 58, 59, 60, 62, 63, 66, 68, 147, 148, 149, 152, 155, 156, 247, 251
    exceptions to the harm paradigm 58
    future harm 61, 64
hate crime 168
health and safety 34, 36, 40
    Health and Safety Executive 34
healthcare 205
Her Majesty's Court Service 24, 25
High Court 210
HM Inspectorate of Probation 120
HM Revenue and Customs 34
Home Affairs Select Committee 137
Home Office 93, 169, 174, 195, 197, 207
Home Secretary 79, 178, 216
honour-related violence 225
House of Commons Select Committee 26
House of Lords 94, 96, 97, 98, 99, 100, 102, 105
human rights 38, 41, 44, 45, 47, 127, 191, 210

I

Iceland 71
immigration
    illegal immigration 34
inchoate liability 55, 56, 61, 62, 64, 67

inchoate offence 56, 57, 58, 60, 61, 64, 67, 68
India 223
information technology 118
insecurity 123
Institute for Public Policy Research 191
Institute of Race Relations 137
intimate partner violence 224, 225, 226, 234, 237
Irish Republican Army (IRA) 127
Islam 126, 134
    war against Islam 135
Islamophobia 124

J

judicial process 176
Judicial Studies Board 93
jury
    jury trial 37, 44
Justice Secretary 25, 37, 251

K

knives 168
Korea 71

L

Law Commission 56, 57, 58
Law Lords 96

liberty *95*
  civil liberties *36*
Local Area Agreement *164, 165, 166, 167*
localism
  new localism *17, 27, 244, 245*
London bombings *128, 138*
Lord Chief Justice *178*

M

magistrate *246*
mediation *175*
Megan's Law *216*
mental health *178*
mentoring *246*
Ministry of Justice *15, 119, 174, 199, 210*
MORI *190*
multi-agency approach *208*
multi-agency dimension *210*
Multi Agency Public Protection Arrangements (MAPPA) *111, 207, 216, 219*
multi-agency working *25, 179, 183*
Muslim aspects *123, 136, 138*
  Muslim communities and police *125*
  Muslim communities' experiences, etc. *134*
  Muslim Contact Unit (MCU) *124, 132*
  Muslim minorities *124, 128, 132, 134*
  Muslim minorities' feelings of (un)safety *126*

N

Nacro *189*
naming and shamiing *93*
National Community Safety Plan *165, 167, 168*
National Health Service *38, 208*
National Offender Management Service (NOMS) *24, 25, 108, 121*
Neighbourhood Justice Panels *145*
neighbourhood policing *16, 22, 169, 182, 203, 220, 249*
neighbourhood renewal *16*
neighbourhood support *237*
Neighbourhood Watch *174, 176, 237*
net-widening *92*
New Deal for Communities *27*
New Labour *15, 16, 17, 21, 22, 23, 25, 26, 27, 160, 248, 249, 250*
New Public Management *23*
new terrorism *139*
North Liverpool Community Justice Centre *177, 179, 180, 181, 182*
Norway *71*

O

offence
  inchoate offence *55*

preparatory offence *55*
sexual offences *64*
Offender Assessment System (OASys) *24, 214*
offender management *32, 244*
offender rehabilitation *232*

P

Pakistan *223*
pimping *71, 247*
police authority *184*
police community support officer (PCSO) *21, 22, 169, 176, 182*
Police Reform Act 2002 *198*
policing *123*
Policing and Crime Act 2009 *70, 72, 73, 74, 75, 76, 77, 79, 83, 84, 85*
pollution *34, 36*
preventative justice *101*
Prevention of Terrorism Act 2005 *128*
Prevention of Terrorism (Temporary Provisions) Act 1974 *128*
Prevention of Terrorism (Temporary Provisions) Act 1989 *127*
Prevention of Violence Act 1939 *127*
prison officer *245*
prison population *16*
prison service *24, 210*
Privy Council *98*
probation *40, 110, 176*
Probation Board/Trust *184*
probation officer *245*

probation service *24, 206, 207, 210*
problem-solving *177, 180, 181, 182, 183, 184, 246*
prolific offender *39*
prosecutor *61*
prostitution *38, 44, 69, 72, 80, 81, 91, 247*
Wolfenden Committee *74*
Protection from Harassment Act 1997 *96, 228*
protection of the public *108, 110, 204*
publicity campaigns *93*
public order *38*
Public Service Agreement *164, 165, 166, 167, 168, 169, 171*
public spending *157, 204*

R

racism *124*
Institute of Race Relations *137*
racially motivated violence *168*
rape *38, 41, 65, 73, 75*
Red Hook *177, 178*
referral order *144, 145, 205*
regulation *33*
rehabilitation *232*
relational justice *232*
reparation *175*
restoration *147*
restorative justice (RJ) *39, 141, 143, 145, 146, 147, 149, 150, 152, 154, 161, 178, 183, 204, 232, 246, 248, 250, 251, 252*

restorative justice processes *144, 154, 155, 156*
strengthening, etc. communities *150*
risk *31, 51, 54, 55, 59, 60, 64, 68, 82, 107, 109, 110, 112, 115, 119, 122, 123, 127, 131, 134, 136, 203, 204, 205, 206, 208, 212, 215, 218, 219, 244, 246, 248, 249, 251*
    heightened risk from terrorism *125*
    high risk offenders *110*
    management *117*
    managing risk *243*
    prediction and factors *116*
    risk assessment *211, 212, 247*
        tools *114*
    risk factors *252*
        effectiveness approaches *119*
        sexual offenders *213*
    risk-led approaches *117, 118*
    risk management *207, 209, 215*
        framework *206*
    Risk Matrix 2000 *213*
    Risk, Need and Responsivity (RNR) *111*
    risk of harm *247*
    risk reducing central state *243*
    unprecedented threat and risk to the world *126*
Royal Ulster Constabulary *127*

S

Safer Cities *174*
safer communities *165, 167, 244*
Safer Communities *141, 160, 163, 164, 170, 171*
safety *139*
sanction *53*
Sarah's Law *216*
scrutiny *57*
security *123*
Self-Regulation Model *215*
sentencing
    community-based sentencing *251, 252*
sex offenders *29, 34, 203, 204, 205, 206, 207, 209, 210, 211, 212, 213, 214, 216, 217, 218, 220*
    Sex Offender Register *207, 210*
    Sex Offenders Act 1997 *207, 213*
sex slaves *80*
sexually transmitted disease (STD) *73*
sexual offences *64, 65, 66, 168*
    sexual abuse of children *234*
    sexual assault *66*
    Sexual Offences Act 2003 *65, 71, 209, 210*
    sexual violence *227*
sex workers *45, 69, 72, 73, 74, 75, 76, 78, 79, 82, 84*
shoot-to-kill *127*
social cohesion *244, 248*
South Africa *71*
special constable *176, 184, 246*

stakeholders *146, 147, 150, 151, 153, 155, 156*
  empowerment of *149*
state
  state power *33, 42, 45, 48*
Steyn, Lord *97*
stop and search *34, 35, 43, 46*
strict liability *82*
Stronger Communities *164*
suicide bomber *126, 139*
Supreme Court *211*
Sure Start *27*
surveillance *34*
Sweden *71, 84*

T

targetting *73*
tax evasion *36*
tax laws *34*
terrorism *64, 203*
  counter-terrorism *134*
    preventive framework *135*
  counter-terrorism context *129, 131, 132*
  counter-terrorism legislation *123, 124, 129*
  global terrorism *125*
  legislation *127*
  'new terrorism' *123, 124, 126, 127, 129, 132, 134*
    terminology of *125*
Terrorism Act 2000 *64*
theft *38*

Theft Act 1968 *63*
The Youth Justice Board (YJB) *190*
torture *38*
Total Place *172*
trafficking *71*
  anti-trafficking legislation *71*
  controlled women *31*
  Council of Europe Convention on Action against Trafficking in Human Beings *71*
  human trafficking *69*
trust *19, 20*

U

United Nations Convention against Transnational Organised Crime, *71*

V

victims *18, 35, 53, 143, 144, 145, 147, 148, 149, 151, 152, 155, 156, 176, 224, 228, 230, 232, 236, 237, 239*
  Code of Practice for Victims of Crime *40*
  human rights *38*
  support for *230*
  victimisation *150, 175*
  victimisation of Muslims *123*
  Victim Support *174, 176, 181*
village councils *223, 233*
violence *82, 123*

gang-based violence *168*
honour-related violence *225*
intimate partner violence *224, 225, 226, 234, 237*
sexual violence *227*
violent crime *16*
violent extremism *205*
violent offenders *42*

W

war on terror *123, 125, 128, 132, 134, 136, 137, 138, 244, 248*
What Works/What Works? *17, 112*
witnesses *35*

Y

young offender *204*
Youth Crime Commission *26*
Youth Justice Board (YJB) *24, 108*
Youth Justice Service *117*
youth justice system *145*
Youth Offender Panel *184, 205*
youth offending services *210*

Z

zero tolerance *228*

Fifty Year Stretch
Prisons and Imprisonment 1980-2030
by Stephen Shaw, Foreword by Martin Narey

By one of the UK's leading experts on prisons and penal reform, this book charts developments across a fifty year time frame beginning in 1980 at the start of a growth in the prison population of England and Wales (and other parts of the world) and ending with a prospective view taking events up to 2030.

Shaw deals with key events, issues and developments and the book will be invaluable to anyone wishing to cut through the mass of fine detail and data which can be found in other works in favour of a direct, authoritative and well-informed short history.

'A masterly account of prison, drawing from his own wealth of experience and reflections, which provides a challenging read for the layman and prison practitioners alike': *Internet Law Book Reviews*

ISBN 9781904380573 (Hardback) 9781906534844 (Ebook)
June 2010 | 134 pages

WatersidePress.co.uk

Crime, State and Citizen
A Field Full of Folk
by David Faulkner, Foreword by Rod Morgan

Comprises an unrivalled overview of criminal justice and penal affairs, including at its core an analysis of fundamental questions about how the actions of the state, police and other public services are to be balanced with the democratic rights and legitimate expectations of ordinary citizens.

'The best book I have ever read on Criminal Justice': *Justice Of The Peace*

'A measured analysis that will command respect and recognition whatever the ideological predisposition of the reader': *Vista*

ISBN 9781904380238 (Paperback) 9781906534073 (Ebook)
February 2006 | 384 pages

WatersidePress.co.uk

'Every student entering law school should have a copy and read it':
Criminal Law and Justice Weekly

A History of Criminal Justice in England and Wales
by John Hostettler

An ideal introduction, charting all the main developments of criminal justice, from Anglo-Saxon dooms to the Common Law, struggles for political, legislative and judicial ascendency and the formation of the modern-day Criminal Justice System.

Among a wealth of topics the book looks at the Rule of Law, the development of the criminal courts, police forces, jury, justices of the peace and individual crimes and punishments. It locates all the iconic events of criminal justice history and law reform within a wider background and context - demonstrating a wealth and depth of knowledge.

'A captivating book that will have readers, who are interested in the subject matter and/or students studying any element of criminal justice absorbed ... a thoroughly enjoyable read': *Internet Law Book Reviews*

'Highly recommended': *Choice*

'This is a good book from a well-respected publishing house. [It] could helpfully form part of the required reading on the programmes which develop the criminal justice system's senior managers, as well as occupying a place on the bookshelves of many other people': *Prison Service Journal*

ISBN 9781904380511 (Paperback) 9781906534790 (Ebook) January 2009 | 352 pages